# THE ALL-IN-ONE
# PREGNANCY
# CALENDAR

## *daily countdown, planner & journal*

### BY NANCY J. PRICE

FOUNDING EDITOR OF EPREGNANCY & PREGNANCY MAGAZINES
CO-FOUNDER OF SHEKNOWS.COM & MYRIA.COM

# The All-in-One Pregnancy Calendar, Daily Countdown, Planner & Journal

Copyright © 2016 by Nancy J. Price

**Find out more about pregnancy, birth, babies & beyond at Myria.com**

Excerpts from this calendar are also available in three shorter books. Look for...
*The All-in-One Pregnancy Calendar, Daily Countdown, Planner & Journal: First Trimester*
*The All-in-One Pregnancy Calendar, Daily Countdown, Planner & Journal: Second Trimester*
*The All-in-One Pregnancy Calendar, Daily Countdown, Planner & Journal: Third Trimester*

**Published by Synchronista LLC — Gilbert, Arizona, USA**
Synchronista® is a registered trademark of Synchronista LLC
**www.Synchronista.com**

synchronista

# contents

This book is dedicated to
the four amazing people
who made me
a mom.

# *from the author*

**By my best estimate, I've spent more than 1,100 days pregnant.** It took me more than a thousand days to bring four babies — 41 pounds of newborn sweetness — into this world.

This is how I know that pregnancy can feel like a permanent condition when you're in the midst of it all... but compared to all the amazing things you have ahead of you, these 280 or so days will seem to have passed in the blink of an eye. Your life will soon be full of first smiles, first steps, first birthdays... and before you know it, first grade. All the weeks spent growing your baby (or babies) can end up as just a hazy memory.

To that end, this book was created for both your present self *and* your future self. While you're expecting, the ideas and questions and countdowns can remind you to find a few moments to reflect upon each day. Then, in the years to come, everything between these covers will serve as a record of your symptoms, progress and mindset during this pregnancy.

**Why a countdown?** To me, there are at least three reasons:

1. As moms-to-be (whether for the first time, or when expecting a second or later baby), we're excited, curious, impatient and sometimes a little bit nervous about meeting this new person we're making. Each day, we get one day closer to that goal!

2. At times, pregnancy can be tough. Whether you're dealing with endless morning sickness or heartburn or sleeplessness or achy ribs from where your babe keeps kicking you from the inside, it's not always rainbows and butterflies. Every 24 hours, that's one day less we have to deal with the not-so-fun stuff.

3. There may be no better way to appreciate the little moments than to really experience every day of the journey.

**The idea for this book was planted years ago, when I was expecting my first child.** Instead of getting it published, I put my energy into website development, and created one of the first online day-by-day pregnancy calendars. While I was fortunate enough to have that interactive calendar syndicated to numerous sites — ultimately reaching millions of women worldwide — I never stopped thinking about my print concept.

*(Continued on the next page)*

*(Continued)*

I wanted to create a day-by-day calendar for pregnancy in which you could track time counting down and counting up, plus see the time passed in charts and percentages. Every page would feature timely tidbits, ideas to consider, information you need to know, and space to record your own thoughts. Plus, there needed to be extras — like charts, checklists and planners — to help you prepare for the next stage, and to make it easy to remember everything you need.

And now you have in your hands the book I wish I'd had during my own pregnancies — and I hope you will enjoy making it your own! Write down your thoughts about your pregnancy as the days pass, and fill in the spaces with your own details and answers to the questions. Take pictures every month of you standing sideways against the same door or wall so you can compare photos and see your progress. You can even manage your prenatal appointments, keep track of your pregnancy firsts, and plan what you need for birth and for baby with the checklists and reminder pages in the back of this book.

**For all its ups and downs, pregnancy is measured in days, weeks and months — while the rest of our life is usually counted in years.** So at some point in the future — maybe two babies or two decades from now — I hope you'll be glad to have a keepsake full of memories from this fleeting, amazing, life-changing time.

All the best,

*Nancy*

Nancy J. Price
Editor-in-Chief, Myria.com

P.S. Keep track of your place with the bookmark on page 219!

*Photos on previous page: Me with my newborns, each on the day he or she joined the world. From top to bottom — and oldest to youngest: Charlotte (9 pounds, 9 ounces), McKenna (9 pounds), Kieran (11 pounds, 8 ounces), and Quinn (11 pounds).*

# THE ALL-IN-ONE
# PREGNANCY CALENDAR

*daily countdown, planner & journal*

# START HERE

*Some things you should know about using this book*

## THE BASICS OF "CROWN TO RUMP"

The crown-rump length (CRL) is one important way that the baby is measured via ultrasound during early pregnancy: from the top of the head (crown) to the bottom of the buttocks (rump).

This measurement method is used until around week 14 of pregnancy. At this stage of development, the embryo/young fetus is curled into a C shape, so head to foot measurements are not practical. The baby's size is instead determined by direct line measurements from one end of the C to the other (as shown below)

The precise CRL helps to precisely figure out age since conception, which means you can have a more accurate estimated due date!

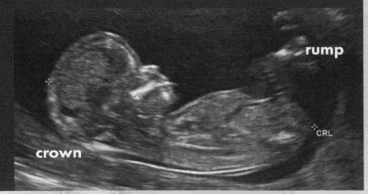
crown · rump · CRL

## [ helpful tips & notes ]

| | TRIMESTER 1 | |
|---|---|---|
| | MONTH | WEEKS |
| | ONE | 1 - 4 |
| | TWO | 5 - 8 |
| | THREE | 9 - 13 |

| | TRIMESTER 2 | |
|---|---|---|
| | MONTH | WEEKS |
| | FOUR | 14 - 18 |
| | FIVE | 19 - 22 |
| | SIX | 23 - 27 |

| | TRIMESTER 3 | |
|---|---|---|
| | MONTH | WEEKS |
| | SEVEN | 28 - 31 |
| | EIGHT | 32 - 36 |
| | NINE+TEN | 37 - 42 |

**1** This calendar starts at Week 1, and week numbers change when each week is completed. (This is much the same way that baby celebrates a first birthday 12 months after birth.)

**2** Keep track of your pregnancy and your place in this book by cutting out the bookmark on page 219. That's also the section where you will find checklists and other bonus goodies!

# HOW TO BE PREGNANT WITHOUT BEING PREGNANT

Most healthcare providers consider a typical pregnancy to last 280 days, when counting from the first day of your last menstrual period (LMP) until your due date. (The LMP was apparently chosen as a starting point because most women remember that date, while the date of conception is often much less obvious.)

It all means that during the first two weeks of pregnancy — when counting by typical dating standards — you're not actually pregnant at all! For example, when you're 12 weeks along, the baby's age — time since conception — is really 10 weeks. (Yes, it can be confusing.)

## The LMP dating method

The 280-day default pregnancy length is based on an average 28-day cycle... but menstrual cycles aren't all the same, and can range from 21 to 45 days.

Therefore, if you have more or less time in between periods (usually the variability is in the time before you ovulate), it might influence your due date. That's because ovulation typically occurs approximately 14 days before the next menstrual period, not simply at midpoint of any length of cycle.

For instance, if you had a 28-day cycle:
LMP: January 1
Ovulation: January 14
Next period due: January 28
Due date: October 7

Whereas if you had a 31-day cycle:
LMP: January 1
Ovulation: January 17
Next period due: January 31
Due date: October 10

Your due date may be calculated differently if you have had assisted reproductive technology (ART), or it may be reassessed based on measurements of the embryo/fetus taken during an ultrasound exam.

When are you due? Calculate your due date with the chart on page 234!

## Due date do's

Although you probably won't be able to resist marking it on the calendar and speaking the name of that magical month to everyone, it's important to remember that your estimated due date (EDD) is really just an educated guess based on averages.

In truth, only about five percent of babies arrive on their due date. And that's okay! Your baby may arrive a week before or after your EDD and will still be perfectly "on time."

To allow for a range of delivery dates, this book goes up to day 294, which is 42 weeks. After this point is considered "post-term," and most medical professionals will not let a pregnancy extend beyond.)

So, you may want to keep that variability in mind when telling people your due date... and unless you want to spend your last couple weeks of pregnancy dodging texts and social media messages from everyone asking, "Is your baby here yet?" you might want to consider keeping your actual date vague ("late this summer" or simply "September"), or take a tip from paparazzi-plagued celebs and add a few weeks to your due date.

In reality, a baby almost always develops at a perfect pace for him or her, and doesn't care about calendars or due dates. As long as your little one is growing well and is healthy, and you're healthy, everything should happen right when it should.

## Month madness

How many months pregnant will you be at given point in pregnancy? Believe it or not, that answer depends on how you're counting.

In day-to-day life, we use a typical calendar month to measure time. But in this book, we're following the lead of many healthcare professionals in the US who use a 28-day "lunar calendar" — every 4 weeks, you're one more month pregnant. These four-week "months" approximate lunar months.

This dating method has the benefit of consistency — making every month the same length — rather than the calendar months that may have 28, 29, 30 or 31 days.

The bottom line? An average 280 day pregnancy (dating from LMP to your estimated due date, or EDD) translates to 40 weeks, or ten 28-day lunar months.

Months offer a general idea of our place in pregnancy — and certainly milestones we can easily conceptualize! But it's worth knowing that a more accurate way of keeping track of far along you are — and the way most medical providers will probably date your pregnancy — is to use the number of weeks.

# ONE MORE THING

## The margin space on the daily pages shows at a glance how far along you are

**Day ranges run down the left**
**Weeks run down the right**
The days/weeks completed are shaded, and the first dates without shading show you where you are now.

**Months run along the top**
The months completed are shaded (in this example, 1-7), and the first month shown without shading (8) is the current month.

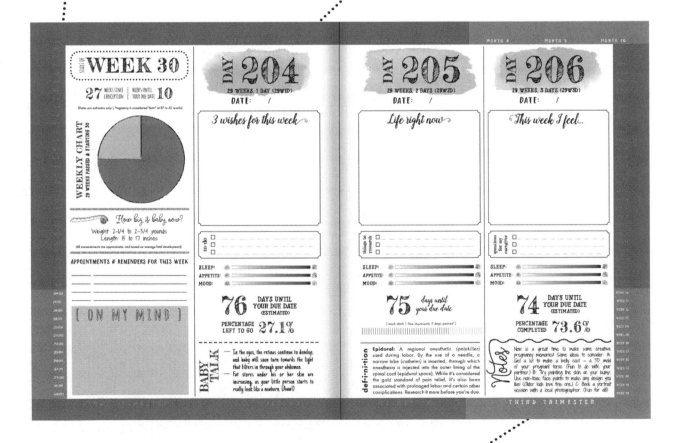

**Trimester numbers run along the bottom**
The trimesters completed are shaded (in this example, second), and the first one shown without shading (third) is the current trimester.

let's go!

# PRE-CONCEPTION

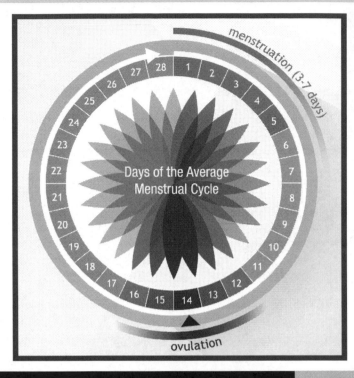

Days of the Average Menstrual Cycle

menstruation (3-7 days)

ovulation

27 28 1 2 3 4 5 6 7 8 9 10 11 12 13 14 15 16 17 18 19 20 21 22 23 24 25 26

## MOMS BY AGE

Who are going to be the moms with kids the same age as yours? Here is a look at pregnancy rates for seven different age groups, ranked from highest fertility rates to the lowest.

1. **25-29 years** (157.1 pregnancies per 1000 women)

2. **20-24 years** (144.6 pregnancies per 1000 women)

3. **30-34 years** (136.5 pregnancies per 1000 women)

4. **18-19 years** (96.8 pregnancies per 1000 women)

5. **35-39 years** (76.5 pregnancies per 1000 women)

6. **15-17 years** (32.2 pregnancies per 1000 women)

7. **40-44 years** (19.4 pregnancies per 1000 women)

*Source: US National Survey of Family Growth (NSFG) for 2010*

## PREGNANCY TRACKER?

**If your wearable fitness tracker starts to consistently show that your heart rate is higher than it was before, that may be a sign of pregnancy. (Take a test!)**

### A quick reminder

Alcohol can harm your developing baby before you even know you're pregnant. The CDC notes that <u>any</u> amount of alcohol (including wine and beer) could harm an embryo or fetus. That damage can last a lifetime because the baby's brain, body, and organs can be affected by alcohol at any time. Drinking while pregnant can also increase the risk of miscarriage, stillbirth, prematurity and sudden infant death syndrome (SIDS).

## positive thinking

If it's too early to test but you're still wondering if you're pregnant, what symptoms might you notice?

Here are just a few of the most common early signs of pregnancy:

- Nausea, vomiting and/or food aversions that can hit you at any time of day (not just mornings!)
- Unusual new food cravings
- Frequent urination
- New or unusual pelvic heaviness or other sensations
- Tender, swollen or tingly breasts
- Darkening of the areolas (area around the nipples)
- Fatigue and/or sleepiness

Complicating the picture is the simple fact that not all women experience pregnancy in the same way. One expectant mom may have every symptom in the book to the maximum degree, while another might not even realize she's pregnant because she doesn't feel one thing out of the ordinary. Most of us, though, will fall somewhere in between, with a few weeks of feeling *bleh* until the second trimester starts.

While you may not know what to expect, soon enough there will be a positive pregnancy test — and before you know it, you'll be feeling kicks and wiggles from the inside out!

# Why take a pregnancy test first thing in the morning?

**If you pick up a pregnancy test on your lunch break, waiting the rest of the day and all of the night to test the next morning can seem unnecessary — and frustrating. So what's the deal?**

Although many modern pregnancy tests say you *can* use pee from any time of day, they do agree that first morning urine usually contains the highest levels of the hormone it's looking for — and the earlier in your cycle that you test, the more important it is to use a.m. urine.

That's because pee-on-a-stick pregnancy tests attempt to identify human chorionic gonadotropin (hCG), a hormone only present during pregnancy. The more concentrated your urine, the more hCG there will be in the sample. And the more hCG in the sample, the better chance of you getting a positive result if you're actually pregnant... and less of a chance of a negative result due to dilution.

First thing in the morning, after a good night's sleep, you probably haven't been drinking anything and have not used the bathroom for several hours, so your urine will be concentrated. (A simple way to tell if your pee is potent: Concentrated urine will be lemon yellow, versus the pale yellow/clear urine you usually have when you're well-hydrated. Note that some vitamin supplements can make your pee look extra yellow.)

Always be certain to wet the test area completely for exactly as long as the directions say (usually 5 seconds). Most pregnancy tests also offer directions about how to test pee in a cup if a mid-stream catch is too tricky.

For the most accurate result, don't test too early. Though some tests *can* work earlier, there just may not be enough hCG present... so that stick will be wasted, and you'll probably stress yourself out by wondering non-stop as you wait to test again. *Patience you must have, my young padawan.*

# STAYIN' ALIVE
**How long can an egg and sperm survive?**

**Egg lifespan:** About 24 hours after ovulation
**Sperm lifespan:** 3 to 5 days after intercourse

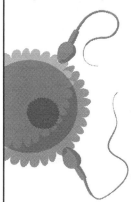

Bottom line: You can get pregnant if you have sex anywhere from five days before ovulation until one day after the ovum is released. Also know that your chance of achieving pregnancy is highest when live sperm are present in the fallopian tubes when you ovulate. (Source: ACOG)

# CHART SMART

If pregnancy has been elusive, you might want to start keeping a fertility chart each month! (A full-size version of the chart shown below is included on page 234.)

The basics: Each morning, use a special basal body thermometer to take your temperature before getting out of bed. Graph it on your chart, recording to the closest tenth of a degree, then connect the dots from day to day to figure out when you're ovulating. After ovulation, you'll see a spike in your temperature (between 0.5 and 1.6 degrees). You are most fertile two to three days before ovulation, and for approximately 12 to 24 hours afterward.

Your fertility pattern may vary from cycle to cycle, but over time you will begin to see when you typically ovulate.

In the cervical mucus blanks along the bottom, note the kind of fluid you observe. You can also record when an ovulation prediction kit (OPK) shows a surge in luteinizing hormone (LH), and when you feel some ovulation pain.

Check out a site like TCOYF.com or FertilityFriend.com for many more details and advice about how to chart the smart way to achieve your pregnancy goals.

## FERTILITY CHART

CYCLE DATES:     CYCLE NUMBER:

| Cycle day | Day of week | Date | Temp time |
|---|---|---|---|

Basal body temperatures (degrees F.)

99.0
98.9
98.8
98.7
98.6
98.5
98.4
98.3
98.2
98.1
98.0
97.9
97.8
97.7
97.6
97.5
97.4
97.3
97.2
97.1
97.0

CM type
OPK LH surge
Ovulation pain
Intercourse

Abbreviation key: P=Period! — Cervical mucus (CM) types: D=Dry | S=Sticky | C=Creamy | W=Watery | E=Egg white

# TRIMESTER 1

## YOUR DUE DATE: __ __ __

| THE FIRST TRIMESTER | MONTH | WEEKS |
|---|---|---|
| | ONE | 1 - 4 |
| | TWO | 5 - 8 |
| | THREE | 9 - 13 |

### PREGNANCY NO-NOS: THINGS TO AVOID

| | |
|---|---|
| SOFT CHEESES + DELI MEATS | ALCOHOL + CAFFEINE |
| RAW/UNDERCOOKED MEAT | SOME ARTIFICIAL SWEETENERS |
| RAW EGGS (DOUGH/BATTER) | MEDICATIONS/DRUGS/HERBS |
| UNPASTEURIZED JUICE + MILK | BUG SPRAY, CLEANERS, SOLVENTS |
| RAW/UNDERCOOKED SPROUTS | CAT LITTER BOXES |
| SHARK, SWORDFISH, TILEFISH | CIGARETTES, SMOKE + E-CIGS |

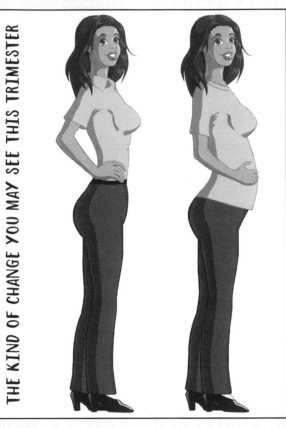

THE KIND OF CHANGE YOU MAY SEE THIS TRIMESTER

### A quick reminder

Whenever you consult with any health professional for non-prenatal care (including dentists, optometrists, opticians, dermatologists, chiropractors, acupuncturists, physical therapists, massage therapists or others), be sure she or he knows that you are pregnant. Even if you wrote it on a form, it can't hurt to offer them a reminder before any treatment.

Attach an ultrasound picture here!
(Don't have one? Add a pre-pregnancy photo of yourself instead.)

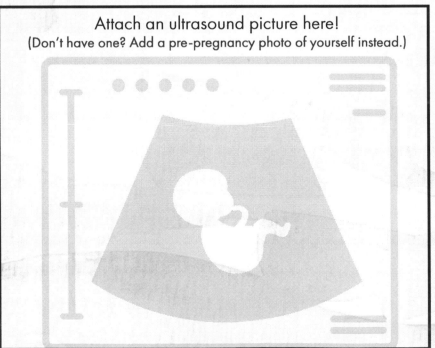

# Your period until the end of week 13

## HEALTH & MEDICAL TESTS IN TRIMESTER ONE

*This is a basic overview some of typical prenatal care offered in the US*

**6-8 WEEKS:** You may have a transvaginal ultrasound to confirm pregnancy and estimate a due date.

**AFTER 6-8 WEEKS:** The baby's heartbeat may be heard with a fetal doppler audio ultrasound device.

**10 WEEKS:** Some women will have chorionic villus sampling (CVS), an invasive prenatal test that can detect Down syndrome and certain other genetic disorders. (See more about CVS on day 44.)

**11-14 WEEKS:** Nuchal translucency screening ultrasound. NT screening looks for extra fluid at the base of the baby's neck (at the nuchal fold), which could be a sign of Down syndrome, certain heart defects, and some other genetic disorders. This screening is often combined with a blood test.

**8-12 WEEKS:** First prenatal checkup, where your caregivers will check your weight, height, blood pressure, pulse/blood oxygen, and do a physical examination (including a pelvic exam and pap smear/other cultures). Most women will have one prenatal appointment each month until about week 28.

**LAB WORK:** You may have blood and urine screening/tests including: Blood type (including Rh factor), CBC (complete blood count), rubella viral antigen screen, cystic fibrosis screen, hepatitis panel, HIV test, genetic diseases, infections and certain other disorders.

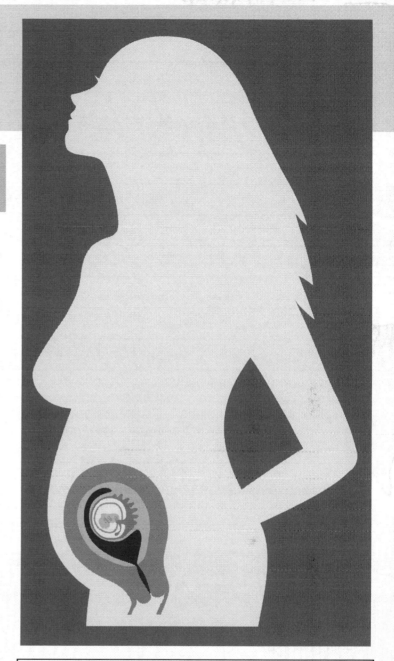

### 4 questions for your first prenatal visit

1. Does your estimated due date seem to be accurate (based upon baby's size, blood hCG testing, size of uterus, ability to hear the heartbeat)?
2. Is your pregnancy considered high risk, or is there anything particular you need to consider?
3. What prenatal tests does she or he recommend?
4. If you're not already taking prenatal vitamins, which ones should you take?

## TRIMESTER 1 PARALLELS

My theme song:

Sitcom title:

Superhero identity:

Actress in my life story:

Product I could endorse:

The animal I would be:

# Notes from the first trimester

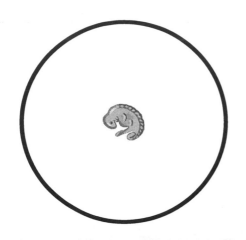

**By the end of this month (week 4, or two weeks after conception), your baby will be about as big as a poppy seed!**

The tiny ball of cells with your little one and the gestational sac is no more than a millimeter long. That's roughly the size of a poppy seed, the tip of a fine-point pen, or the period at the end of this sentence.

# MONTH 1

## WEEK 1, WEEK 2 WEEK 3 & WEEK 4

## How do you feel?

At the beginning of this month, rate how you're feeling with a line, X or circle

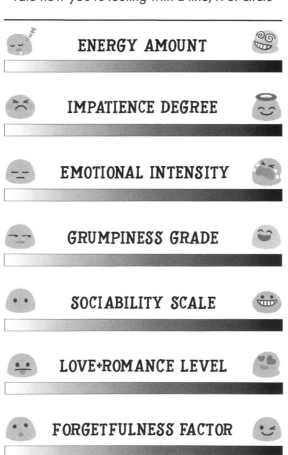

ENERGY AMOUNT

IMPATIENCE DEGREE

EMOTIONAL INTENSITY

GRUMPINESS GRADE

SOCIABILITY SCALE

LOVE+ROMANCE LEVEL

FORGETFULNESS FACTOR

9 MO GROWTH GUESSTIMATE

Add a picture of yourself at 1 month here
Photos not your thing? Estimate your pre-pregnancy size and shape by drawing over the shadowed image below

## One year from now
(assuming you give birth around 40 weeks)

*Your baby will be about 4 months old!*

### YOU & BABY

Starting weight:

Belly circumference:

Pregnancy test dates/results:

### 3 WORDS FOR WHAT'S ON YOUR MIND RIGHT NOW

### 4 things to know this month

1. Consider starting your prenatal vitamins even before you get pregnant.
2. When it's time to take a pregnancy test, be sure to completely read the directions before you open the package.
3. Pregnancy test results – positive or negative – aren't always 100% correct. When in doubt, test again a day or two later.
4. When you find out you're pregnant, you may feel shocked (or panicked). The stress should soon pass, but hopefully the amazement will remain with you!

### notes

DAYS 1-7
8-14
15-21
22-28
29-35
36-42
43-49
50-56
57-63
64-70
71-77
78-84
85-91
92-98
99-105
106-112
113-119
120-126
127-133
134-140
141-147
148-154
155-161
162-168
169-175
176-182
183-189
190-196
197-203
204-210
211-217
218-224
225-231
232-238
239-245
246-252
253-259
260-266
267-273
274-280
281-287
288-294

START OF

# WEEK 1

**02** WEEKS UNTIL OVULATION    WEEKS UNTIL YOUR DUE DATE **39**

(Dates are estimates only | Pregnancy is considered "term" at 37 to 42 weeks)

(An illustration of a human ovum before fertilization — not actual size!)

## How big is baby now?

The human egg (ovum) is about 0.12 millimeters in diameter.

(All measurements are approximate, and based on average fetal development)

## APPOINTMENTS & REMINDERS FOR THIS WEEK

_____  _____
_____  _____
_____  _____
_____  _____

{ ON MY MIND }

DAY **1**

**14 DAYS UNTIL OVULATION**

DATE:        /

*And so it begins!*

to-do
☐ ..............................................
☐ ..............................................
☐ ..............................................

SLEEP:
APPETITE:
MOOD:

**279** DAYS UNTIL YOUR DUE DATE (ESTIMATED)

When determining a due date, caregivers often assume an average 28-day cycle, meaning you get your period once every four weeks.

In reality, menstrual cycles often last anywhere from around 23 to 34 days (or more), and may even vary from month to month.

Ovulation is typically considered to occur about 14 days before your next period is due. A urine-based ovulation test can help you get the conception timing just right.

DAY  **2**

**13 DAYS UNTIL OVULATION**

DATE:        /

## How long we've been trying

things to research
- ☐ ....................................................
- ☐ ....................................................
- ☐ ....................................................

SLEEP: ▮▮▮▮▮▮▮▮▮▮▮▮▮▮

APPETITE: ▮▮▮▮▮▮▮▮▮▮▮▮▮▮

MOOD: ▮▮▮▮▮▮▮▮▮▮▮▮▮▮

**278** *days until your due date*

**def·i·ni·tions**

**Ovum:** A female reproductive cell, also called an egg or oocyte.

**Ovary:** One of the two female reproductive organs in which eggs are formed.

**Ovulation:** The release of the ovum/egg from the ovary.

**Follicle:** A fluid-filled sac in the ovary that sustains the developing ovum, and from which the mature ovum is released during ovulation.

---

 DAY  **3**

**12 DAYS UNTIL OVULATION**

DATE:        /

## This time next year...

questions for my caregiver
- ☐ ....................................................
- ☐ ....................................................
- ☐ ....................................................

SLEEP: ▮▮▮▮▮▮▮▮▮▮▮▮▮▮

APPETITE: ▮▮▮▮▮▮▮▮▮▮▮▮▮▮

MOOD: ▮▮▮▮▮▮▮▮▮▮▮▮▮▮

**277** **DAYS UNTIL YOUR DUE DATE** (ESTIMATED)

**BABY TALK**

Sperm usually meet the egg in the outer third of the fallopian tube. According to researchers from the University of Missouri School of Medicine, "A sperm 'recognizes' an egg when proteins on the head of the sperm meet and match a series of specific sugars in the egg's outer coat...The outside surfaces of the sperm and egg bind together before they merge."

WEEK 1
WEEK 2
WEEK 3
WEEK 4
WEEK 5
WEEK 6
WEEK 7
WEEK 8
WEEK 9
WEEK 10
WEEK 11
WEEK 12
WEEK 13
WEEK 14
WEEK 15
WEEK 16
WEEK 17
WEEK 18
WEEK 19
WEEK 20
WEEK 21
WEEK 22
WEEK 23
WEEK 24
WEEK 25
WEEK 26
WEEK 27
WEEK 28
WEEK 29
WEEK 30
WEEK 31
WEEK 32
WEEK 33
WEEK 34
WEEK 35
WEEK 36
WEEK 37
WEEK 38
WEEK 39
WEEK 40
WEEK 41
WEEK 42

DAYS 1-7
8-14
15-21
22-28
29-35
36-42
43-49
50-56
57-63
64-70
71-77
78-84
85-91
92-98
99-105
106-112
113-119
120-126
127-133
134-140
141-147
148-154
155-161
162-168
169-175
176-182
183-189
190-196
197-203
204-210
211-217
218-224
225-231
232-238
239-245
246-252
253-259
260-266
267-273
274-280
281-287
288-294

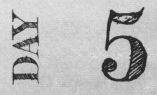

## DAY 4

### 11 DAYS UNTIL OVULATION

DATE:        /

*Getting my body ready*

grateful for...
☐ .............................................
☐ .............................................
☐ .............................................

SLEEP:
APPETITE:
MOOD:

## 276 DAYS UNTIL YOUR DUE DATE (ESTIMATED)

> " The longer you wait for something, the more you'll appreciate it when you get it. Because anything worth having is definitely worth waiting for. "
>
> - Anonymous

## DAY 5

### 10 DAYS UNTIL OVULATION

DATE:        /

*I love to imagine...*

to tell my partner
☐ .............................................
☐ .............................................
☐ .............................................

SLEEP:
APPETITE:
MOOD:

## 275 *days until your due date (approximately)*

ABOUT YOU

Even as you read this, several eggs (ova) are beginning to ripen within your ovaries. Usually only one of these (an ovum) will reach maturity this month, bursting out of a ovarian follicle and making a journey down the fallopian tube toward the uterus so it can be fertilized. (If two reach maturity, you might end up with fraternal twins.)

You were born with a million or two immature eggs, most of which will never make a sperm's acquaintance.

DAY  **6**

**9 DAYS UNTIL OVULATION**

DATE: /

## How I'm tracking fertility

to-do
- [ ] .................................
- [ ] .................................
- [ ] .................................

SLEEP: ▢▬▬▬▬▬▬▬▬▬▬ 
APPETITE: ▢▬▬▬▬▬▬▬▬▬▬ 
MOOD: ▢▬▬▬▬▬▬▬▬▬▬ 

**274** days until
your due date
(estimated)

*Notes*

Couples trying to get pregnant should have intercourse two to three times a week, say Dr Zev Rosenwaks and Dr Marc Goldstein, fertility specialists at NewYork-Presbyterian Hospital/ Weill Cornell Medical Center. "They can also time sex for her most fertile period. As a rule of thumb, if she counts the first day of her period as day one, and she has regular periods every 28 to 30 days, the couple should try every other day starting on day 12 to 16 or so."

---

DAY  **7**

**8 DAYS UNTIL OVULATION**

DATE: /

## What my partner thinks

shopping wish list
- [ ] .................................
- [ ] .................................
- [ ] .................................

SLEEP: ▢▬▬▬▬▬▬▬▬▬▬ 
APPETITE: ▢▬▬▬▬▬▬▬▬▬▬ 
MOOD: ▢▬▬▬▬▬▬▬▬▬▬ 

**273** days until
your due date
(thereabouts)

~ A LITTLE NOTE TO THE FUTURE ~

☐ WISH ☐ PREDICTION ☐ PRAYER ☐ HOPE ☐ REMINDER

WEEK 1
WEEK 2
WEEK 3
WEEK 4
WEEK 5
WEEK 6
WEEK 7
WEEK 8
WEEK 9
WEEK 10
WEEK 11
WEEK 12
WEEK 13
WEEK 14
WEEK 15
WEEK 16
WEEK 17
WEEK 18
WEEK 19
WEEK 20
WEEK 21
WEEK 22
WEEK 23
WEEK 24
WEEK 25
WEEK 26
WEEK 27
WEEK 28
WEEK 29
WEEK 30
WEEK 31
WEEK 32
WEEK 33
WEEK 34
WEEK 35
WEEK 36
WEEK 37
WEEK 38
WEEK 39
WEEK 40
WEEK 41
WEEK 42

## START OF WEEK 2

**01** WEEK UNTIL OVULATION     WEEKS UNTIL YOUR DUE DATE **38**

(Dates are estimates only | Pregnancy is considered "term" at 37 to 42 weeks)

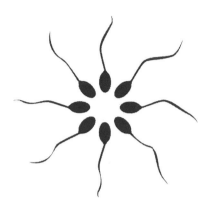

 *How big is baby now?*

Each sperm cell is about 55 micrometers long, and about 3 micrometers wide

(All measurements are approximate, and based on average fetal development)

### APPOINTMENTS & REMINDERS FOR THIS WEEK

_____  _____
_____  _____
_____  _____

{ ON MY MIND }

---

 **DAY**  **8**

**7 DAYS UNTIL OVULATION**

**DATE:**     /

### Why now is the time

**to-do**
☐ ...................................
☐ ...................................
☐ ...................................

SLEEP:
APPETITE:
MOOD:

## 272 DAYS UNTIL YOUR DUE DATE (ESTIMATED)

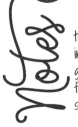 **Notes**

"It's a common recommendation that partners trying to have a baby should engage in regular intercourse to increase the woman's changes of getting pregnant — even during so-called 'non-fertile' periods," says Kinsey Institute research scientist Tierney Lorenz in a Myria.com article.

The bottom line, according to science: Frequent sex seems to cause some immune system changes that boost the chance of conception.

So go on. You know what to do.

DAY **9**

6 DAYS UNTIL OVULATION

DATE: /

## Health & nutrition changes

things to research
- ☐ .........................................
- ☐ .........................................
- ☐ .........................................

SLEEP:
APPETITE:
MOOD:

**271** *days until your due date*

---

WEEK 1
WEEK 2
WEEK 3
WEEK 4
WEEK 5
WEEK 6
WEEK 7
WEEK 8
WEEK 9
WEEK 10
WEEK 11
WEEK 12
WEEK 13
WEEK 14
WEEK 15
WEEK 16
WEEK 17
WEEK 18
WEEK 19
WEEK 20
WEEK 21
WEEK 22
WEEK 23
WEEK 24
WEEK 25
WEEK 26
WEEK 27
WEEK 28
WEEK 29
WEEK 30
WEEK 31
WEEK 32
WEEK 33
WEEK 34
WEEK 35
WEEK 36
WEEK 37
WEEK 38
WEEK 39
WEEK 40
WEEK 41
WEEK 42

DAY **10**

5 DAYS UNTIL OVULATION

DATE: /

## How I'm staying fit

questions for my caregiver
- ☐ .........................................
- ☐ .........................................
- ☐ .........................................

SLEEP:
APPETITE:
MOOD:

**270** DAYS UNTIL YOUR DUE DATE (ESTIMATED)

---

**def·i·ni·tions**

**Fallopian tube:** One of the two narrow tubes leading from the two ovaries on either side of the uterus. Ovaries usually trade off releasing eggs each month. After an egg is released from one of the ovaries, it travels down the fallopian tube, where it can be fertilized.

**Implantation:** When the embryo embeds itself in the thick uterine lining (endometrium) and begins to receive nourishment and grow. This occurs approximately 7 days after conception.

**BABY TALK**

Polycystic Ovarian Syndrome (PCOS) impairs fertility and is closely related to insulin levels. In 2013, researchers found that women with PCOS who increased calorie intake at breakfast (including high protein and carbohydrate content), and reduced calorie intake through the rest of the day, saw a reduction in insulin resistance. This led to lower levels of testosterone and a dramatic increase in the ovulation frequency — meaning a direct impact on fertility, noted Prof. Daniela Jakubowicz of Tel Aviv University's Sackler Faculty of Medicine.

DAYS 1-7
8-14
15-21
22-28
29-35
36-42
43-49
50-56
57-63
64-70
71-77
78-84
85-91
92-98
99-105
106-112
113-119
120-126
127-133
134-140
141-147
148-154
155-161
162-168
169-175
176-182
183-189
190-196
197-203
204-210
211-217
218-224
225-231
232-238
239-245
246-252
253-259
260-266
267-273
274-280
281-287
288-294

## DAY 11

**4 DAYS UNTIL OVULATION**

DATE:          /

### Who inspires me

grateful for...
- ☐ ........................................
- ☐ ........................................
- ☐ ........................................

SLEEP:
APPETITE:
MOOD:

# 269
**DAYS UNTIL
YOUR DUE DATE**
(ESTIMATED)

❝
What isn't today,
might be tomorrow.
❞

— Anonymous

## DAY 12

**3 DAYS UNTIL OVULATION**

DATE:          /

### This made me laugh

to tell my partner
- ☐ ........................................
- ☐ ........................................
- ☐ ........................................

SLEEP:
APPETITE:
MOOD:

# 268
*days until
your due date*
(approximately)

**ABOUT YOU**

The uterus is a hollow, muscular organ positioned right between your bladder and your rectum. Inside the uterus (or womb) the fertilized egg can implant — nestling into the rich lining of the endometrium — and the baby and placenta can then develop.

Considered one of the strongest muscles in the human body, in the pre-pregnant state, it's roughly the shape and size of a small upside-down pear. The top of the uterus is called the fundus, and the cervix is the opening at the bottom.

DAY **13**

2 DAYS UNTIL OVULATION

DATE:        /

*Who I will tell first (& how)*

to-do
- ☐ .................................
- ☐ .................................
- ☐ .................................
- ☐ .................................

SLEEP:
APPETITE:
MOOD:

**267** days until your due date *(estimated)*

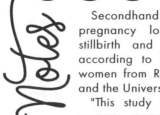 Notes

Secondhand smoking is linked with pregnancy loss, including miscarriage, stillbirth and tubal ectopic pregnancy, according to 2014 research on 80,762 women from Roswell Park Cancer Institute and the University at Buffalo.

"This study offers new information for women regarding the lifetime impact secondhand smoke can have on reproductive outcomes and their ability to successfully bring a pregnancy to full term," says lead investigator Andrew Hyland., PhD.

TRIMESTER

DAY **14**

1 DAY UNTIL OVULATION

DATE:        /

*I can't believe...*

shopping wish list
- ☐ .................................
- ☐ .................................
- ☐ .................................

SLEEP:
APPETITE:
MOOD:

**266** days until your due date *(thereabouts)*

~A LITTLE NOTE TO THE FUTURE~

☐ WISH  ☐ PREDICTION  ☐ PRAYER  ☐ HOPE  ☐ REMINDER

THIRD TRIMESTER

WEEK 1
WEEK 2
WEEK 3
WEEK 4
WEEK 5
WEEK 6
WEEK 7
WEEK 8
WEEK 9
WEEK 10
WEEK 11
WEEK 12
WEEK 13
WEEK 14
WEEK 15
WEEK 16
WEEK 17
WEEK 18
WEEK 19
WEEK 20
WEEK 21
WEEK 22
WEEK 23
WEEK 24
WEEK 25
WEEK 26
WEEK 27
WEEK 28
WEEK 29
WEEK 30
WEEK 31
WEEK 32
WEEK 33
WEEK 34
WEEK 35
WEEK 36
WEEK 37
WEEK 38
WEEK 39
WEEK 40
WEEK 41
WEEK 42

DAYS 1-7
8-14
15-21
22-28
29-35
36-42
43-49
50-56
57-63
64-70
71-77
78-84
85-91
92-98
99-105
106-112
113-119
120-126
127-133
134-140
141-147
148-154
155-161
162-168
169-175
176-182
183-189
190-196
197-203
204-210
211-217
218-224
225-231
232-238
239-245
246-252
253-259
260-266
267-273
274-280
281-287
288-294

## START OF WEEK 3

**0** WEEKS UNTIL OVULATION ⋮ WEEKS UNTIL YOUR DUE DATE **37**

(Dates are estimates only | Pregnancy is considered "term" at 37 to 42 weeks)

### WEEKLY CHART
### 2 WEEKS PASSED & STARTING 3

### How big is baby now?

4 days after ovulation, a fertilized egg (now a blastocyst) is 0.1 to 0.2 millimeters in diameter.

(All measurements are approximate, and based on average fetal development)

### APPOINTMENTS & REMINDERS FOR THIS WEEK

_____    _____

_____

_____    Estimate your due date with the chart @ end of book

{ ON MY MIND }

---

## DAY 15

### 2 WEEKS, 1 DAY (2W1D)

DATE:        /

*It's ovulation time!*

to-do
☐ .................................................
☐ .................................................
☐ .................................................

SLEEP:
APPETITE:
MOOD:

## 265 DAYS UNTIL YOUR DUE DATE (ESTIMATED)

### OVULATION DAY

**BABY TALK**

— The fertilized egg (zygote) divides quickly, usually landing in the uterus 3 to 5 days after fertilization.

— The fertilized egg soon becomes a blastocyst, a hollow ball of cells with a fluid cavity. The outside layer of cells (trophectoderm) contributes to the placenta, and the inside layer (inner cell mass or ICM) will become the embryo — your baby.

# DAY 16

**2 WEEKS, 2 DAYS (2W2D)**

DATE:        /

### Why this is the month

WEEK 1
WEEK 2
WEEK 3
WEEK 4
WEEK 5
WEEK 6
WEEK 7
WEEK 8
WEEK 9
WEEK 10
WEEK 11
WEEK 12
WEEK 13
WEEK 14
WEEK 15
WEEK 16
WEEK 17
WEEK 18
WEEK 19
WEEK 20
WEEK 21
WEEK 22
WEEK 23
WEEK 24
WEEK 25
WEEK 26
WEEK 27
WEEK 28
WEEK 29
WEEK 30
WEEK 31
WEEK 32
WEEK 33
WEEK 34
WEEK 35
WEEK 36
WEEK 37
WEEK 38
WEEK 39
WEEK 40
WEEK 41
WEEK 42

**things to research**
- ☐ ...................................
- ☐ ...................................
- ☐ ...................................

SLEEP: 😴 ▭▭▭▭▭ 🐾
APPETITE: 😋 ▭▭▭▭▭ 🤢
MOOD: 🙂 ▭▭▭▭▭ 😣

# 264 *days until your due date*

## 1 DAY PAST OVULATION (DPO)

**def·i·ni·tion**

**Menstrual age:** Most caregivers date pregnancy based upon your LMP (last menstrual period). Menstrual age differs from gestational age because conception has not yet occurred during the first two weeks after menstruation. When dating a pregnancy from LMP, a full pregnancy lasts 280 days, or 40 weeks.

---

# DAY 17

**2 WEEKS, 3 DAYS (2W3D)**

DATE:        /

### This week I feel...

**questions for my caregiver**
- ☐ ...................................
- ☐ ...................................
- ☐ ...................................

SLEEP: 😴 ▭▭▭▭▭ 🐾
APPETITE: 😋 ▭▭▭▭▭ 🤢
MOOD: 🙂 ▭▭▭▭▭ 😣

# 263 **DAYS UNTIL YOUR DUE DATE (ESTIMATED)**

## 2 DAYS PAST OVULATION (DPO)

*Notes*

Listeria monocytogenes (Listeria) is a bacteria found in some soft cheese made with unpasteurized milk — like queso fresco, Feta, Brie and Camembert. The US Department of Health & Human Services notes that during pregnancy, you and your baby are both especially vulnerable to this dangerous infection, so minimize your risk and skip the soft cheese. (Other sources of Listeria may include deli meats, hot dogs, pâté and smoked seafood.)

TRIMESTER                    THIRD TRIMESTER

DAYS 1-7
8-14
15-21
22-28
29-35
36-42
43-49
50-56
57-63
64-70
71-77
78-84
85-91
92-98
99-105
106-112
113-119
120-126
127-133
134-140
141-147
148-154
155-161
162-168
169-175
176-182
183-189
190-196
197-203
204-210
211-217
218-224
225-231
232-238
239-245
246-252
253-259
260-266
267-273
274-280
281-287
288-294

## DAY 18
### 2 WEEKS, 4 DAYS (2W4D)

DATE:      /

*Did it work? I think...*

grateful for...
☐ ......................................
☐ ......................................
☐ ......................................

SLEEP:
APPETITE:
MOOD:

# 262
### DAYS UNTIL YOUR DUE DATE
(ESTIMATED)

## 3 DAYS PAST OVULATION (DPO)

❝ Hope is a renewable option:
If you run out of it at the end
of the day, you get to
start over in the morning. ❞
- Anonymous

## DAY 19
### 2 WEEKS, 5 DAYS (2W5D)

DATE:      /

*Food/drink I'm quitting*

to tell my partner
☐ ......................................
☐ ......................................
☐ ......................................

SLEEP:
APPETITE:
MOOD:

# 261
### days until your due date
(approximately)

## 4 DAYS PAST OVULATION (DPO)

ABOUT YOU

If you have been recording your basal body temperatures (BBT), a pattern of 18 or more temperatures above the "coverline" generally means that you're pregnant. So keep charting — and eat well and take great care of your body in the meantime! (See the back of this book for a fertility chart to track your BBT.)

**DAY 20**

2 WEEKS, 6 DAYS (2W6D)

DATE:        /

*What I'm stressed about*

to-do
☐ ......................................
☐ ......................................
☐ ......................................

SLEEP:
APPETITE:
MOOD:

**260** days until your due date (estimated)

5 DAYS PAST OVULATION (DPO)

BABY NAMES

**BOYS IN TAHITI**

*Hiro, Teiki, Moana, Manua, Marama, Teiva, Teva, Maui, Tehei, Tamatoa, Ioane, Tapuarii*

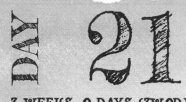

**DAY 21**

3 WEEKS, 0 DAYS (3W0D)

DATE:        /

*Pre-pregnancy stats & sizes*

shopping wish list
☐ ......................................
☐ ......................................
☐ ......................................

SLEEP:
APPETITE:
MOOD:

**259** days until your due date (thereabouts)

6 DAYS PAST OVULATION (DPO)

~ A LITTLE NOTE TO THE FUTURE ~
☐ WISH  ☐ PREDICTION  ☐ PRAYER  ☐ HOPE  ☐ REMINDER

WEEK 1
WEEK 2
WEEK 3
WEEK 4
WEEK 5
WEEK 6
WEEK 7
WEEK 8
WEEK 9
WEEK 10
WEEK 11
WEEK 12
WEEK 13
WEEK 14
WEEK 15
WEEK 16
WEEK 17
WEEK 18
WEEK 19
WEEK 20
WEEK 21
WEEK 22
WEEK 23
WEEK 24
WEEK 25
WEEK 26
WEEK 27
WEEK 28
WEEK 29
WEEK 30
WEEK 31
WEEK 32
WEEK 33
WEEK 34
WEEK 35
WEEK 36
WEEK 37
WEEK 38
WEEK 39
WEEK 40
WEEK 41
WEEK 42

DAYS 1-7
8-14
15-21
22-28
29-35
36-42
43-49
50-56
57-63
64-70
71-77
78-84
85-91
92-98
99-105
106-112
113-119
120-126
127-133
134-140
141-147
148-154
155-161
162-168
169-175
176-182
183-189
190-196
197-203
204-210
211-217
218-224
225-231
232-238
239-245
246-252
253-259
260-266
267-273
274-280
281-287
288-294

## START OF WEEK 4

**01** WEEK SINCE CONCEPTION : WEEKS UNTIL YOUR DUE DATE **36**

(Dates are estimates only | Pregnancy is considered "term" at 37 to 42 weeks)

### WEEKLY CHART
3 WEEKS PASSED & STARTING 4

 *How big is baby now?*

Your baby is tiny – not even as big as the period at the end of this sentence (less than 1 mm).

(All measurements are approximate, and based on average fetal development)

### APPOINTMENTS & REMINDERS FOR THIS WEEK

_____ _____

_____ _____

_____ _____

**{ ON MY MIND }**

---

## DAY 22

3 WEEKS, 1 DAY (3W1D)

DATE:    /

*3 wishes for this week*

to-do
☐ ...................................................
☐ ...................................................
☐ ...................................................

SLEEP:
APPETITE:
MOOD:

## 258 DAYS UNTIL YOUR DUE DATE (ESTIMATED)

7 DAYS PAST OVULATION (DPO)

- - - - - - - - - - - - - - - -

### BABY TALK

— Once the blastocyst arrives in the uterus, it implants in the uterine wall, where it will become comfortably embedded.
— About ten days after fertilization, the embryo becomes visible within the blastocyst. That's your baby!

MONTH 6          MONTH 7          MONTH 8          MONTH 9          MONTH 10

WEEK 1
WEEK 2
WEEK 3
WEEK 4
WEEK 5
WEEK 6
WEEK 7
WEEK 8
WEEK 9
WEEK 10
WEEK 11
WEEK 12
WEEK 13
WEEK 14
WEEK 15
WEEK 16
WEEK 17
WEEK 18
WEEK 19
WEEK 20
WEEK 21
WEEK 22
WEEK 23
WEEK 24
WEEK 25
WEEK 26
WEEK 27
WEEK 28
WEEK 29
WEEK 30
WEEK 31
WEEK 32
WEEK 33
WEEK 34
WEEK 35
WEEK 36
WEEK 37
WEEK 38
WEEK 39
WEEK 40
WEEK 41
WEEK 42

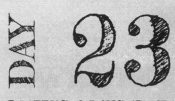

## DAY 23

**3 WEEKS, 2 DAYS (3W2D)**

DATE:          /

### Health, vitamins & diet

things to research
- [ ] ........................
- [ ] ........................
- [ ] ........................

SLEEP: 
APPETITE: 
MOOD: 

**257** *days until your due date*

8 DAYS PAST OVULATION (DPO)

**def·i·ni·tion**

**Cervix:** The neck/opening of the uterus at the top of the vagina. Sperm need to enter through the cervix into the uterus to penetrate the egg. the cervix secretes cervical mucus, which, near ovulation, is thin and stretchy and actually helps the sperm reach the egg. Though pregnancy, the cervix is firm and closed, but during labor, it eventually enlarges enough for baby to emerge.

## DAY 24

**3 WEEKS, 3 DAYS (3W3D)**

DATE:          /

### This week I feel...

questions for my caregiver
- [ ] ........................
- [ ] ........................
- [ ] ........................

SLEEP: 
APPETITE: 
MOOD: 

**256** **DAYS UNTIL YOUR DUE DATE (ESTIMATED)**

9 DAYS PAST OVULATION (DPO)

*Notes*

Decades ago, pregnancy was confirmed by injecting a urine sample into a female rabbit. Five days later, the rabbit was killed and its ovaries were checked. If the woman was pregnant, her hCG (human chorionic gonadotropin) levels would cause the rabbit's ovaries to enlarge and redden. Now you can appreciate today's pee stick tests a bit more.

**TRIMESTER          THIRD TRIMESTER**

DAYS 1-7
8-14
15-21
22-28
29-35
36-42
43-49
50-56
57-63
64-70
71-77
78-84
85-91
92-98
99-105
106-112
113-119
120-126
127-133
134-140
141-147
148-154
155-161
162-168
169-175
176-182
183-189
190-196
197-203
204-210
211-217
218-224
225-231
232-238
239-245
246-252
253-259
260-266
267-273
274-280
281-287
288-294

## DAY 25

### 3 WEEKS, 4 DAYS (3W4D)

DATE:      /

### Impatient? Nervous? Both?

grateful for...
☐ ............................
☐ ............................
☐ ............................

SLEEP: ▭
APPETITE: ▭
MOOD: ▭

## 255 DAYS UNTIL YOUR DUE DATE (ESTIMATED)

## 10 DAYS PAST OVULATION (DPO)

66

Everything comes
gradually and
at its appointed hour.

99

- Ovid

## DAY 26

### 3 WEEKS, 5 DAYS (3W5D)

DATE:      /

### Wouldn't it be nice if...

to tell my partner
☐ ............................
☐ ............................
☐ ............................

SLEEP: ▭
APPETITE: ▭
MOOD: ▭

## 254 days until your due date (approximately)

## 11 DAYS PAST OVULATION (DPO)

ABOUT YOU

Apart from a positive pregnancy test, there are several things that might indicate that you're pregnant, including: a missed menstrual period, nausea and/or vomiting (morning sickness); frequent urination, breast tenderness and changes, excessive salivation and fatigue. You might also notice an increased heart rate, although for some women, it's as simple as "just feeling pregnant."

### DAY 27

3 WEEKS, 6 DAYS (3W6D)

DATE:        /

*How I am getting ready*

to-do
- [ ] ............................
- [ ] ............................
- [ ] ............................

SLEEP:
APPETITE:
MOOD:

## 253 days until your due date (estimated)

# 12 DAYS PAST OVULATION (DPO)

**BABY NAMES**

**BOYS IN RUSSIA**

*Alexander, Sergei, Dmitry,
Andrei Alexey Maxim, Evgeny,
Ivan, Mikhail, Artem, Daniil,
Dmitry, Ivan, Kirill, Ilya*

---

### DAY 28

4 WEEKS, 0 DAYS (4W0D)

DATE:        /

*This made me laugh*

shopping wish list
- [ ] ............................
- [ ] ............................
- [ ] ............................

SLEEP:
APPETITE:
MOOD:

## 252 days until your due date (thereabouts)

# 13 DAYS PAST OVULATION (DPO)

**~ A LITTLE NOTE TO THE FUTURE ~**

☐ WISH  ☐ PREDICTION  ☐ PRAYER  ☐ HOPE  ☐ REMINDER

WEEK 1
WEEK 2
WEEK 3
WEEK 4
WEEK 5
WEEK 6
WEEK 7
WEEK 8
WEEK 9
WEEK 10
WEEK 11
WEEK 12
WEEK 13
WEEK 14
WEEK 15
WEEK 16
WEEK 17
WEEK 18
WEEK 19
WEEK 20
WEEK 21
WEEK 22
WEEK 23
WEEK 24
WEEK 25
WEEK 26
WEEK 27
WEEK 28
WEEK 29
WEEK 30
WEEK 31
WEEK 32
WEEK 33
WEEK 34
WEEK 35
WEEK 36
WEEK 37
WEEK 38
WEEK 39
WEEK 40
WEEK 41
WEEK 42

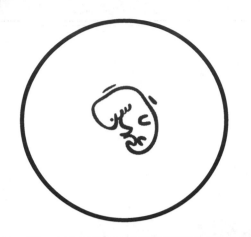

**By the end of this month (the end of week 8), your baby will be about 1/3 the width of a quarter!**

That little embryo is around 8 millimeters long (about 1/3 of an inch) from crown to rump (or, right now, from his neck to his bottom) — and about half of that length is the head.

# MONTH 2

## WEEK 5, WEEK 6
## WEEK 7 & WEEK 8

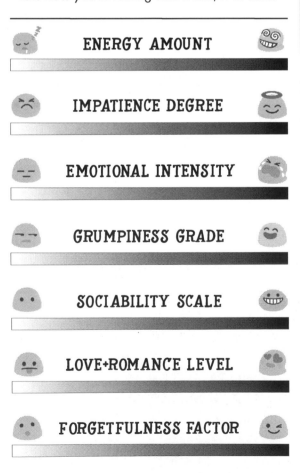

## How do you feel?

At the beginning of this month, rate how you're feeling with a line, X or circle

**ENERGY AMOUNT**

**IMPATIENCE DEGREE**

**EMOTIONAL INTENSITY**

**GRUMPINESS GRADE**

**SOCIABILITY SCALE**

**LOVE+ROMANCE LEVEL**

**FORGETFULNESS FACTOR**

**GROWTH GAUGE**

Add a picture of yourself at 2 months here
Photos not your thing? Estimate your pregnancy size and shape by drawing over the shadowed image below

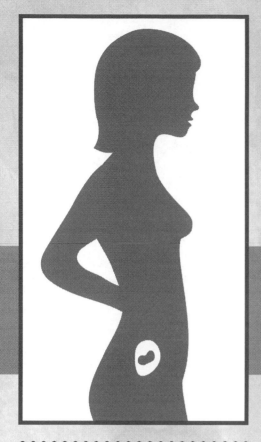

## One year from now
(assuming you give birth around 40 weeks)

### Your baby will be about 5 months old!

**This bites:** Food aversions are typical throughout pregnancy, particularly toward fatty and/or strong-smelling foods. You may even get queasy at the very thought of visiting certain restaurants. In fact, when you're in the thick of morning sickness, you might want to avoid certain foods and restaurants you really enjoy, because some little part of your brain may forever associate them with repeated bouts of vomiting.

### 3 WORDS FOR WHAT'S ON YOUR MIND RIGHT NOW

## 4 things to know this month

1. Your first prenatal health appointment probably won't be until around week 12.
2. What you eat and drink (and breathe) can have a huge impact on your baby's development right now. Play it super safe and avoid medications, cigarettes and alcohol.
3. About 25% of women have some bleeding during early pregnancy. Light spotting is most common, usually between 7 and 10 weeks after LMP.
4. The uterus grows from two ounces to about two pounds during pregnancy. Postpartum, it will get almost as compact.

### notes

START OF
# WEEK 5

**02** WEEKS SINCE CONCEPTION : WEEKS UNTIL YOUR DUE DATE **35**

(Dates are estimates only | Pregnancy is considered "term" at 37 to 42 weeks)

## WEEKLY CHART
### 4 WEEKS PASSED & STARTING 5

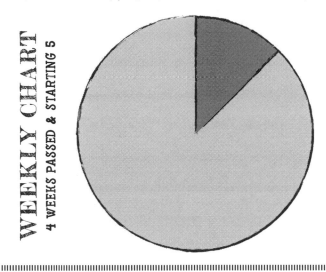

### How big is baby now?

Your baby is developing, but not growing much in size, and is about a millimeter long.

(All measurements are approximate, and based on average fetal development)

## APPOINTMENTS & REMINDERS FOR THIS WEEK

_____ _____
_____ _____
_____ _____
_____ _____

{ ON MY MIND }

## DAY 29

### 4 WEEKS, 1 DAY (4W1D)

DATE:        /

### Ready to find out?

to-do
☐ .................................
☐ .................................
☐ .................................
☐ .................................

SLEEP:
APPETITE:
MOOD:

**251** DAYS UNTIL YOUR DUE DATE (ESTIMATED)

PERCENTAGE COMPLETED **10.4%**

## BABY TALK

— This week, the head, heart, spinal cord, and some of the larger blood vessels begin to form.
— Shortly after the heart begins to start pumping fluid through the blood vessels, the first red blood cells are created.
— The embryo would now just be barely visible to the naked eye.

DAYS 1-7
8-14
15-21
22-28
29-35
36-42
43-49
50-56
57-63
64-70
71-77
78-84
85-91
92-98
99-105
106-112
113-119
120-126
127-133
134-140
141-147
148-154
155-161
162-168
169-175
176-182
183-189
190-196
197-203
204-210
211-217
218-224
225-231
232-238
239-245
246-252
253-259
260-266
267-273
274-280
281-287
288-294

## DAY 30

4 WEEKS, 2 DAYS (4W2D)

DATE: /

### How many pregnancy tests?

WEEK 1
WEEK 2
WEEK 3
WEEK 4
WEEK 5
WEEK 6
WEEK 7
WEEK 8
WEEK 9
WEEK 10
WEEK 11
WEEK 12
WEEK 13
WEEK 14
WEEK 15
WEEK 16
WEEK 17
WEEK 18
WEEK 19
WEEK 20
WEEK 21
WEEK 22
WEEK 23
WEEK 24
WEEK 25
WEEK 26
WEEK 27
WEEK 28
WEEK 29
WEEK 30
WEEK 31
WEEK 32
WEEK 33
WEEK 34
WEEK 35
WEEK 36
WEEK 37
WEEK 38
WEEK 39
WEEK 40
WEEK 41
WEEK 42

**things to research**
- ☐ ......................
- ☐ ......................
- ☐ ......................

SLEEP:
APPETITE:
MOOD:

**250** *days until your due date*

*fraction completed* **3/28**

**def·i·ni·tion**

**Umbilical cord:** The lifeline for your baby, this is the connection between the fetus at its abdomen and the placenta. The cord transports oxygen and nutrients from you (via the placenta) to the baby. There are normally three vessels in the umbilical cord: two arteries and one vein. You might see your baby holding the cord on an ultrasound — but don't worry: he or she can't squeeze too tight!

TRIMESTER

---

## DAY 31

4 WEEKS, 3 DAYS (4W3D)

DATE: /

### This week I feel...

**questions for my caregiver**
- ☐ ......................
- ☐ ......................
- ☐ ......................

SLEEP:
APPETITE:
MOOD:

**249** **DAYS UNTIL YOUR DUE DATE** (ESTIMATED)

**PERCENTAGE REMAINING 88.9%**

**Notes**

The first prenatal checkup is often around 11 to 12 weeks of pregnancy. Make sure you know the date of your LMP before scheduling your appointment. Also, some insurance plans require you to get pre-approval for or a referral to an obstetric caregiver, so take care of this before you go to your appointment to make the process as smooth as possible.

THIRD TRIMESTER

MONTH 1          MONTH 2          MONTH 3          MONTH 4          MONTH 5

DAYS 1-7
8-14
15-21
22-28
29-35
36-42
43-49
50-56
57-63
64-70
71-77
78-84
85-91
92-98
99-105
106-112
113-119
120-126
127-133
134-140
141-147
148-154
155-161
162-168
169-175
176-182
183-189
190-196
197-203
204-210
211-217
218-224
225-231
232-238
239-245
246-252
253-259
260-266
267-273
274-280
281-287
288-294

## DAY 32

### 4 WEEKS, 4 DAYS (4W4D)

DATE:          /

### How I reacted to the news

grateful for...
☐ .........................................
☐ .........................................
☐ .........................................

SLEEP: ▭▭▭▭▭▭

APPETITE: ▭▭▭▭▭▭

MOOD: ▭▭▭▭▭▭

# 248   DAYS UNTIL YOUR DUE DATE (ESTIMATED)

### PERCENTAGE REMAINING 88.6%

66 I knew I had to wait to tell him in person.
I wanted to look into his eyes when I said
'I'm pregnant.' I wanted to feel his hug
when he grabbed me with excitement. 99
   - Vanessa Lachey on Nick Lachey

## DAY 33

### 4 WEEKS, 5 DAYS (4W5D)

DATE:          /

### How I told my partner

to tell my partner
☐ .........................................
☐ .........................................
☐ .........................................

SLEEP: ▭▭▭▭▭▭

APPETITE: ▭▭▭▭▭▭

MOOD: ▭▭▭▭▭▭

# 247   days until your due date

### how far you have come 11.8%

**ABOUT YOU**

In some cases, instead of missing your monthly
visitor, you may have what seems like a very light
or very short period... and could still be pregnant.
   The cause of this little show of blood may
be implantation bleeding (or spotting), which some
medical experts think is caused by the fertilized
egg embedding itself in the uterine lining.
   When in doubt, it's probably best to assume
you're pregnant and play it safe.

## DAY 34

**4 WEEKS, 6 DAYS (4W6D)**

DATE:        /

### Ways I'm staying healthy

to-do
- [ ] .............................................
- [ ] .............................................
- [ ] .............................................

SLEEP: [ ]
APPETITE: [ ]
MOOD: [ ]

## 246 days until your due date (estimated)

percentage remaining **87.8%**

**BABY NAMES**

### GIRLS IN ENGLAND

Amelia, Olivia, Emily, Isla, Poppy, Ava, Isabella, Jessica, Lily, Sophie

## DAY 35

**5 WEEKS, 0 DAYS (5W0D)**

DATE:        /

### My mind is racing

shopping wish list
- [ ] .............................................
- [ ] .............................................
- [ ] .............................................

SLEEP: [ ]
APPETITE: [ ]
MOOD: [ ]

## 245 days until your due date (thereabouts)

fraction completed **1/8**

### ~A LITTLE NOTE TO THE FUTURE~

☐ WISH  ☐ PREDICTION  ☐ PRAYER  ☐ HOPE  ☐ REMINDER

WEEK 1
WEEK 2
WEEK 3
WEEK 4
WEEK 5
WEEK 6
WEEK 7
WEEK 8
WEEK 9
WEEK 10
WEEK 11
WEEK 12
WEEK 13
WEEK 14
WEEK 15
WEEK 16
WEEK 17
WEEK 18
WEEK 19
WEEK 20
WEEK 21
WEEK 22
WEEK 23
WEEK 24
WEEK 25
WEEK 26
WEEK 27
WEEK 28
WEEK 29
WEEK 30
WEEK 31
WEEK 32
WEEK 33
WEEK 34
WEEK 35
WEEK 36
WEEK 37
WEEK 38
WEEK 39
WEEK 40
WEEK 41
WEEK 42

## START OF WEEK 6

**03** WEEKS SINCE CONCEPTION  :  WEEKS UNTIL YOUR DUE DATE **34**

(Dates are estimates only | Pregnancy is considered "term" at 37 to 42 weeks)

**WEEKLY CHART**
5 WEEKS PASSED & STARTING 6

### How big is baby now?

Your baby is developing, but not growing much in size, and is still just about a millimeter long.

(All measurements are approximate, and based on average fetal development)

## APPOINTMENTS & REMINDERS FOR THIS WEEK

_____ _____

_____ _____

_____ _____

{ ON MY MIND }

**DAY 36**

5 WEEKS, 1 DAY (5W1D)

DATE:        /

### 3 wishes for this week

**to-do**
☐ ..............................................
☐ ..............................................
☐ ..............................................

SLEEP: ◁━━━━━━━━━━━▷
APPETITE: ◁━━━━━━━━━━━▷
MOOD: ◁━━━━━━━━━━━▷

**244** DAYS UNTIL YOUR DUE DATE (ESTIMATED)

PERCENTAGE COMPLETED **12.9%**

**BABY TALK**

— The neural tube, which extends from the top of your baby's head to the base of the spine, is now under construction. The important tube, which will soon become the baby's brain and spine, should be completely formed five weeks after conception.

— Your nutrition matters a lot now, so eat well and get enough folic acid and vitamin B12.

DAY **37**

**5 WEEKS, 2 DAYS (5W2D)**

DATE:    /

### Recent changes

things to research
- ☐ ....................................
- ☐ ....................................
- ☐ ....................................

SLEEP:
APPETITE:
MOOD:

**243** *days until your due date*

*percentage completed* **13.2%**

**def·i·ni·tion**

**Ultrasound:** A tool that uses high frequency sound waves to visualize the fetus. A hand-held transducer may be moved against the outside of your abdomen so that the baby, placenta, amniotic sac and uterus can be seen. The gestational sac may be visible as early as 5 weeks menstrual age (3 weeks after conception); and the embryo may be seen at 6-7 weeks after LMP.

DAY **38**

**5 WEEKS, 3 DAYS (5W3D)**

DATE:    /

### This week I feel...

questions for my caregiver
- ☐ ....................................
- ☐ ....................................
- ☐ ....................................

SLEEP:
APPETITE:
MOOD:

**242** **DAYS UNTIL YOUR DUE DATE** (ESTIMATED)

**PERCENTAGE REMAINING** **86.4%**

*Notes*

One kind of Non-Invasive Prenatal Testing (NIPT) is cell-free DNA (cfDNA) testing, which maps and counts DNA fragments in mom's blood sample (taken after week 10), then compares the measurements to normal reference samples. Says Diana W. Bianchi, MD, of Tufts Medical Center, "Prenatal testing using cell-free DNA as a primary screen could eliminate the need for many of the invasive diagnostic procedures (such as amniocentesis) that are performed to confirm a positive screen."

WEEK 1
WEEK 2
WEEK 3
WEEK 4
WEEK 5
WEEK 6
WEEK 7
WEEK 8
WEEK 9
WEEK 10
WEEK 11
WEEK 12
WEEK 13
WEEK 14
WEEK 15
WEEK 16
WEEK 17
WEEK 18
WEEK 19
WEEK 20
WEEK 21
WEEK 22
WEEK 23
WEEK 24
WEEK 25
WEEK 26
WEEK 27
WEEK 28
WEEK 29
WEEK 30
WEEK 31
WEEK 32
WEEK 33
WEEK 34
WEEK 35
WEEK 36
WEEK 37
WEEK 38
WEEK 39
WEEK 40
WEEK 41
WEEK 42

DAYS 1-7
8-14
15-21
22-28
29-35
36-42
43-49
50-56
57-63
64-70
71-77
78-84
85-91
92-98
99-105
106-112
113-119
120-126
127-133
134-140
141-147
148-154
155-161
162-168
169-175
176-182
183-189
190-196
197-203
204-210
211-217
218-224
225-231
232-238
239-245
246-252
253-259
260-266
267-273
274-280
281-287
288-294

## DAY 39
### 5 WEEKS, 4 DAYS (5W4D)
DATE:        /

*New & unusual*

grateful for...
☐ .......................................
☐ .......................................
☐ .......................................

SLEEP:
APPETITE:
MOOD:

## 241 DAYS UNTIL YOUR DUE DATE (ESTIMATED)

### PERCENTAGE COMPLETED 13.9%

 In the pregnancy process, I have come to realize how much of the burden is on the female partner. She's got a construction zone going on in her belly. - Al Roker

## DAY 40
### 5 WEEKS, 5 DAYS (5W5D)
DATE:        /

*I love to imagine...*

to tell my partner
☐ .......................................
☐ .......................................
☐ .......................................

SLEEP:
APPETITE:
MOOD:

## 240 days until your due date

how far you have come 1/7

**ABOUT YOU**

Your healthcare provider (and you!) may want to confirm your pregnancy via transvaginal ultrasound. The scanner for this is long and narrow, and often covered with a gel-filled condom. It is entered into your vagina, up to the cervix.

With this kind of ultrasound, you can see the embryo — and, at about week six, a tiny fluttering heartbeat! Precise measurements can help determine exactly how far along you are.

## DAY 41

**5 WEEKS, 6 DAYS (5W6D)**

DATE:          /

### Food aversions & cravings

to-do
- ☐ ..............................................
- ☐ ..............................................
- ☐ ..............................................

SLEEP:
APPETITE:
MOOD:

## 239 days until your due date
(estimated)

percentage remaining **85.4%**

**BABY NAMES**

### ASTRONOMY NAMES FOR BOYS

Archer, Orion, Janus, Cosmo, Nash, Galileo, Rigel, Hamal, Deimos, Leo, Phoenix

## DAY 42

**6 WEEKS, 0 DAYS (6W0D)**

DATE:          /

### What if it's twins?

shopping wish list
- ☐ ..............................................
- ☐ ..............................................
- ☐ ..............................................

SLEEP:
APPETITE:
MOOD:

## 238 days until your due date
(thereabouts)

percentage completed **15%**

### ~A LITTLE NOTE TO THE FUTURE~
☐ WISH  ☐ PREDICTION  ☐ PRAYER  ☐ HOPE  ☐ REMINDER

WEEK 1
WEEK 2
WEEK 3
WEEK 4
WEEK 5
WEEK 6
WEEK 7
WEEK 8
WEEK 9
WEEK 10
WEEK 11
WEEK 12
WEEK 13
WEEK 14
WEEK 15
WEEK 16
WEEK 17
WEEK 18
WEEK 19
WEEK 20
WEEK 21
WEEK 22
WEEK 23
WEEK 24
WEEK 25
WEEK 26
WEEK 27
WEEK 28
WEEK 29
WEEK 30
WEEK 31
WEEK 32
WEEK 33
WEEK 34
WEEK 35
WEEK 36
WEEK 37
WEEK 38
WEEK 39
WEEK 40
WEEK 41
WEEK 42

MONTH 1     MONTH 2     MONTH 3     MONTH 4     MONTH 5

DAYS 1-7
1-14
15-21
22-28
29-35
36-42
43-49
50-56
57-63
64-70
71-77
78-84
85-91
92-98
99-105
106-112
113-119
120-126
127-133
134-140
141-147
148-154
155-161
162-168
169-175
176-182
183-189
190-196
197-203
204-210
211-217
218-224
225-231
232-238
239-245
246-252
253-259
260-266
267-273
274-280
281-287
288-294

## START OF WEEK 7

**04** WEEKS SINCE CONCEPTION : WEEKS UNTIL YOUR DUE DATE **33**

(Dates are estimates only | Pregnancy is considered "term" at 37 to 42 weeks)

### WEEKLY CHART
6 WEEKS PASSED & STARTING 7

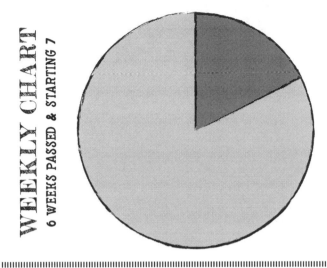

*How big is baby now?*

From crown to rump, baby is probably just over a millimeter long.

(All measurements are approximate, and based on average fetal development)

## APPOINTMENTS & REMINDERS FOR THIS WEEK

_____ _____

_____ _____

_____ _____

### { ON MY MIND }

## DAY 43

**6 WEEKS, 1 DAY (6W1D)**

DATE:    /

*3 ideas for this week*

to-do
- ☐ .........................................
- ☐ .........................................
- ☐ .........................................

SLEEP:

APPETITE:

MOOD:

## 237 DAYS UNTIL YOUR DUE DATE (ESTIMATED)

PERCENTAGE LEFT TO GO **84.6%**

**BABY TALK**

— Leg and arm buds appear this week, and the embryo continues to grow at an amazingly fast rate.

— The heart chambers are starting to being built while the brain and nervous system continue to develop.

DAY 44

6 WEEKS, 2 DAYS (6W2D)

DATE:        /

## What I'm doing differently

things to research
- ☐ ....................
- ☐ ....................
- ☐ ....................

SLEEP: ▱▱▱▱▱▱▱▱▱▱
APPETITE: ▱▱▱▱▱▱▱▱▱▱
MOOD: ▱▱▱▱▱▱▱▱▱▱

# 236 days until your due date

percentage completed **15.7%**

**def·i·ni·tion**

**CVS:** Short for Chorionic Villus Sampling, this is a prenatal test done between 10 and 13 weeks of pregnancy. Guided by ultrasound, a small piece of the placenta is removed for testing, either via the vagina and cervix, or through the abdomen and uterine wall. The biopsied tissue is then analyzed for genetic diseases like Down syndrome, cystic fibrosis, Tay-Sachs and sickle cell disease.

TRIMESTER

---

DAY 45

6 WEEKS, 3 DAYS (6W3D)

DATE:        /

## This week I feel...

questions for my caregiver
- ☐ ....................
- ☐ ....................
- ☐ ....................

SLEEP: ▱▱▱▱▱▱▱▱▱▱
APPETITE: ▱▱▱▱▱▱▱▱▱▱
MOOD: ▱▱▱▱▱▱▱▱▱▱

# 235 DAYS UNTIL YOUR DUE DATE (ESTIMATED)

[ each dark | line represents 5 days passed ]

 Notes

According to research from the University of Missouri published on Myria.com, "Store and fast food receipts, airline tickets, ATM receipts and other thermal papers all use massive amounts of BPA (Bisphenol A) on the surface of the paper as a print developer." Worse yet, hand sanitizers, creams, soaps and sunscreens on our hands drastically increase the BPA absorption rate.

THIRD TRIMESTER

WEEK 1
WEEK 2
WEEK 3
WEEK 4
WEEK 5
WEEK 6
WEEK 7
WEEK 8
WEEK 9
WEEK 10
WEEK 11
WEEK 12
WEEK 13
WEEK 14
WEEK 15
WEEK 16
WEEK 17
WEEK 18
WEEK 19
WEEK 20
WEEK 21
WEEK 22
WEEK 23
WEEK 24
WEEK 25
WEEK 26
WEEK 27
WEEK 28
WEEK 29
WEEK 30
WEEK 31
WEEK 32
WEEK 33
WEEK 34
WEEK 35
WEEK 36
WEEK 37
WEEK 38
WEEK 39
WEEK 40
WEEK 41
WEEK 42

DAYS 1-7
8-14
15-21
22-28
29-35
36-42
43-49
50-56
57-63
64-70
71-77
78-84
85-91
92-98
99-105
106-112
113-119
120-126
127-133
134-140
141-147
148-154
155-161
162-168
169-175
176-182
183-189
190-196
197-203
204-210
211-217
218-224
225-231
232-238
239-245
246-252
253-259
260-266
267-273
274-280
281-287
288-294

# DAY 46

6 WEEKS, 4 DAYS (6W4D)

DATE:        /

## I cannot believe...

grateful for...
- ☐ .................................................
- ☐ .................................................
- ☐ .................................................

SLEEP: 😴 ▭▭▭▭▭ 🐾

APPETITE: 😋 ▭▭▭▭▭ 🤢

MOOD: 😊 ▭▭▭▭▭ 😟

## 234  DAYS UNTIL YOUR DUE DATE (ESTIMATED)

PERCENTAGE COMPLETED 16.4%

66  Whether your pregnancy was
meticulously planned, medically coaxed,  99
or happened by surprise, one thing is
certain — your life will never be the same.
- Catherine Jones

# DAY 47

6 WEEKS, 5 DAYS (6W5D)

DATE:        /

## My personal support system

to tell my partner
- ☐ .................................................
- ☐ .................................................
- ☐ .................................................

SLEEP: 😴 ▭▭▭▭▭ 🐾

APPETITE: 😋 ▭▭▭▭▭ 🤢

MOOD: 😊 ▭▭▭▭▭ 😟

## 233  days until your due date

percentage remaining 83.2%

**ABOUT YOU**

You might want to be careful where you keep your phone right now. Patti Wood, a visiting scholar at Adelphi University School of Nursing and Public Health, says, "We're just recommending avoiding carrying your cell phone directly on your body, not in a pocket, not in a bra, not in a bag that you carry on you all the time." Likewise, don't prop up your phone, tablet or laptop on your baby bump.

MONTH 6　　　MONTH 7　　　MONTH 8　　　MONTH 9　　　MONTH 10

WEEK 1
WEEK 2
WEEK 3
WEEK 4
WEEK 5
WEEK 6

DAY **48**

6 WEEKS, 6 DAYS (6W6D)

DATE: /

## How I am getting ready

to-do
- ☐ ........................................
- ☐ ........................................
- ☐ ........................................

SLEEP: 
APPETITE: 
MOOD: 

**232** days until
your due date
(estimated)

fraction
completed **6/35**

### BOYS IN ICELAND

BABY NAMES

Aron, Alexander, Viktor, Kristján,
Jón, Guðmundur, Kristófer, Gunnar,
Ólafur/Olav, Benedikt, Dagur, Emil

DAY **49**

7 WEEKS, 0 DAYS (7W0D)

DATE: /

## It's hard to keep a secret

shopping wish list
- ☐ ........................................
- ☐ ........................................
- ☐ ........................................

SLEEP: 
APPETITE: 
MOOD: 

**231** days until
your due date
(thereabouts)

percentage
completed **17.5%**

~A LITTLE NOTE TO THE FUTURE~

☐ WISH　☐ PREDICTION　☐ PRAYER　☐ HOPE　☐ REMINDER

WEEK 7
WEEK 8
WEEK 9
WEEK 10
WEEK 11
WEEK 12
WEEK 13
WEEK 14
WEEK 15
WEEK 16
WEEK 17
WEEK 18
WEEK 19
WEEK 20
WEEK 21
WEEK 22
WEEK 23
WEEK 24
WEEK 25
WEEK 26
WEEK 27
WEEK 28
WEEK 29
WEEK 30
WEEK 31
WEEK 32
WEEK 33
WEEK 34
WEEK 35
WEEK 36
WEEK 37
WEEK 38
WEEK 39
WEEK 40
WEEK 41
WEEK 42

## START OF WEEK 8

**05** WEEKS SINCE CONCEPTION ⋮ WEEKS UNTIL YOUR DUE DATE **32**

(Dates are estimates only | Pregnancy is considered "term" at 37 to 42 weeks)

**WEEKLY CHART**
7 WEEKS PASSED & STARTING 8

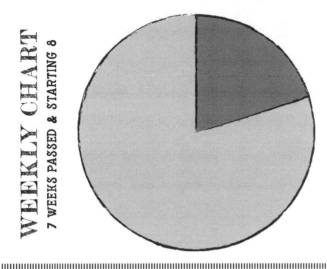

||||||||||||||||||||||||||||||||||||||||||||||||||||||||

*How big is baby now?*

From crown to rump,
baby is just about 2 millimeters long

(All measurements are approximate, and based on average fetal development)

||||||||||||||||||||||||||||||||||||||||||||||||||||||||

## APPOINTMENTS & REMINDERS FOR THIS WEEK

———————  ————————————————
———————  ————————————————
———————  ————————————————
———————  ————————————————

### { ON MY MIND }

**DAY 50**

7 WEEKS, 1 DAY (7W1D)

DATE:          /

*3 wishes for this week*

to-do
☐ ..................................................
☐ ..................................................
☐ ..................................................

SLEEP:
APPETITE:
MOOD:

**230** DAYS UNTIL YOUR DUE DATE (ESTIMATED)

FRACTION COMPLETED **5/28**

**BABY TALK**

— Amazingly, your little one is starting to look like a tiny human now!
— Elbows and knees can be seen as your baby's tail (yes, a real tail) is reabsorbed by the body.
— Heart valves are developed, eyelids & retinas are forming, and a speck of a nose is visible.

DAY 51

7 WEEKS, 2 DAYS (7W2D)

DATE:        /

### Recent changes

things to research
- [ ] ..........................................
- [ ] ..........................................
- [ ] ..........................................

SLEEP:

APPETITE:

MOOD:

## 229 days until your due date

percentage remaining **81.8%**

**def·i·ni·tion**

**Placenta:** A temporary organ that acts as baby's life support system. It attaches to the uterine wall on one side, and from the other side, the umbilical cord emerges and connects to the baby. (The amniotic sac also grows from the placenta around the embryo.) It's often referred to as the "afterbirth" because it's delivered after the baby.

DAY 52

7 WEEKS, 3 DAYS (7W3D)

DATE:        /

### This week I feel...

questions for my caregiver
- [ ] ..........................................
- [ ] ..........................................
- [ ] ..........................................

SLEEP:

APPETITE:

MOOD:

## 228 DAYS UNTIL YOUR DUE DATE (ESTIMATED)

PERCENTAGE COMPLETED **18.6%**

*Notes*

Be sure you're getting enough liquids! Dehydration isn't good for you or the baby. If you are having a hard time keeping anything down, try chilled water infused with lemon, cucumber, ginger or peppermint leaves; water mixed with fruit juice; tea (ginger tea can ease nausea) or suck on crushed ice or frozen juice/lemonade cubes.

WEEK 1
WEEK 2
WEEK 3
WEEK 4
WEEK 5
WEEK 6
WEEK 7
WEEK 8
WEEK 9
WEEK 10
WEEK 11
WEEK 12
WEEK 13
WEEK 14
WEEK 15
WEEK 16
WEEK 17
WEEK 18
WEEK 19
WEEK 20
WEEK 21
WEEK 22
WEEK 23
WEEK 24
WEEK 25
WEEK 26
WEEK 27
WEEK 28
WEEK 29
WEEK 30
WEEK 31
WEEK 32
WEEK 33
WEEK 34
WEEK 35
WEEK 36
WEEK 37
WEEK 38
WEEK 39
WEEK 40
WEEK 41
WEEK 42

# DAY 53

### 7 WEEKS, 4 DAYS (7W4D)

DATE:      /

## This never happened before

grateful for...
☐ ......................................
☐ ......................................
☐ ......................................

SLEEP:
APPETITE:
MOOD:

# 227 DAYS UNTIL YOUR DUE DATE (ESTIMATED)

## PERCENTAGE COMPLETED 18.9%

66  First, I took like 12 tests to confirm it. Then I took all the socks out of his drawer and filled it with diapers and a bib that said, 'I love Daddy.'  99

- Danielle Jonas on telling husband Kevin Jonas about her pregnancy

# DAY 54

### 7 WEEKS, 5 DAYS (7W5D)

DATE:      /

## Thoughts on childbirth

to tell my partner
☐ ......................................
☐ ......................................
☐ ......................................

SLEEP:
APPETITE:
MOOD:

# 226 days until your due date

## percentage remaining 80.7%

**ABOUT YOU**

If you have a dog, how about going for a walk? Researchers found that, through brisk walking, pregnant women who owned dogs were approximately 50% more likely to achieve a recommended 30 minutes of activity per day. "As a low-risk exercise, dog walking can help women — who may otherwise find it hard to meet exercise targets — keep active and fit during pregnancy," notes Dr Sandra McCune.

DAY **55**

7 WEEKS, 6 DAYS (7W6D)

DATE:        /

## Any 'morning' sickness?

to-do
- ☐ ........................................
- ☐ ........................................
- ☐ ........................................

SLEEP:
APPETITE:
MOOD:

**225** days until your due date
(estimated)

[ each dark | line represents 5 days passed ]

||||||||||||||||||||||||||||||||||||||||||

### GIRLS IN MOROCCO

**BABY NAMES**

Fatima, Khadija, Aicha, Malika, Naima, Rachida, Nadia, Karima, Amina, Saida

---

DAY **56**

8 WEEKS, 0 DAYS (8W0D)

DATE:        /

## The best thing this week

shopping wish list
- ☐ ........................................
- ☐ ........................................
- ☐ ........................................

SLEEP:
APPETITE:
MOOD:

**224** days until your due date
(thereabouts)

fraction completed **1/5**

~ A LITTLE NOTE TO THE FUTURE ~
☐ WISH  ☐ PREDICTION  ☐ PRAYER  ☐ HOPE  ☐ REMINDER

WEEK 1
WEEK 2
WEEK 3
WEEK 4
WEEK 5
WEEK 6
WEEK 7
WEEK 8
WEEK 9
WEEK 10
WEEK 11
WEEK 12
WEEK 13
WEEK 14
WEEK 15
WEEK 16
WEEK 17
WEEK 18
WEEK 19
WEEK 20
WEEK 21
WEEK 22
WEEK 23
WEEK 24
WEEK 25
WEEK 26
WEEK 27
WEEK 28
WEEK 29
WEEK 30
WEEK 31
WEEK 32
WEEK 33
WEEK 34
WEEK 35
WEEK 36
WEEK 37
WEEK 38
WEEK 39
WEEK 40
WEEK 41
WEEK 42

By the end of this month (the end of week 12, or about 10 weeks after conception), your baby will be about the size of a big strawberry!

That little embryo is about an inch and a half from head to bottom. What else is half an inch long? A small lime, or the width of a large egg.

# MONTH 3

## How do you feel?

At the beginning of this month,
rate how you're feeling with a line, X or circle

 **ENERGY AMOUNT**

 **IMPATIENCE DEGREE**

 **EMOTIONAL INTENSITY**

**GRUMPINESS GRADE**

**SOCIABILITY SCALE**

 **LOVE+ROMANCE LEVEL**

 **FORGETFULNESS FACTOR**

 **GROWTH GAUGE**

Add a picture of yourself at 3 months here
Photos not your thing? Estimate your pregnancy size and
shape by drawing over the shadowed image below

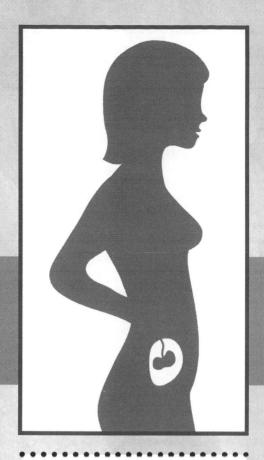

## One year from now

(assuming you give birth around 40 weeks)

Your baby will be
about 6 months old!

### YOU & BABY

Weight change:

Blood pressure:

Belly circumference:

Fundal height:

Baby's heart rate:

### 3 WORDS FOR WHAT'S ON YOUR MIND RIGHT NOW

## 4 things to know this month

1. You will probably have your first prenatal appointment!
2. Do whatever you can to keep your partner involved in your pregnancy. If at all possible, schedule your medical appointments so you can both attend.
3. We're all for playing it safe, so during pregnancy, try not to pump your own gas. Either get full-serve or have someone else fill up your tank.
4. Be sure to drink lots of water! Dehydration can lead to a build-up of toxins in the bloodstream (many of which can reach the baby).

### notes

DAYS 1-7
8-14
15-21
22-28
29-35
36-42
43-49
50-56
57-63
64-70
71-77
78-84
85-91
92-98
99-105
106-112
113-119
120-126
127-133
134-140
141-147
148-154
155-161
162-168
169-175
176-182
183-189
190-196
197-203
204-210
211-217
218-224
225-231
232-238
239-245
246-252
253-259
260-266
267-273
274-280
281-287
288-294

START OF

# WEEK 9

**06** WEEKS SINCE CONCEPTION : WEEKS UNTIL YOUR DUE DATE **31**

(Dates are estimates only | Pregnancy is considered "term" at 37 to 42 weeks)

## WEEKLY CHART
### 8 WEEKS PASSED & STARTING 9

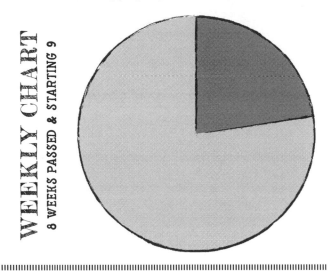

*How big is baby now?*

From crown to rump, baby is between 2 and 4.5 millimeters long.

(All measurements are approximate, and based on average fetal development)

## APPOINTMENTS & REMINDERS FOR THIS WEEK

_____   _____

_____   _____

_____   _____

*See the caregiver interview checklist @ end of book*

{ ON MY MIND }

**DAY 57**

8 WEEKS, 1 DAY (8W1D)

DATE:        /

*3 goals for this week*

to-do
☐ ...........................................
☐ ...........................................
☐ ...........................................

SLEEP: 
APPETITE: 
MOOD: 

**223** DAYS UNTIL YOUR DUE DATE (ESTIMATED)

PERCENTAGE REMAINING **79.6%**

**BABY TALK**

Would a glass or wine or bottle of beer really hurt anything? Well, in 2016, researchers in Toronto identified more than 400 distinct disease conditions that may occur along with Fetal Alcohol Syndrome (FASD). These affect nearly the entire body, including the central nervous system, vision, hearing, heart, circulation, digestion, along with musculoskeletal and respiratory systems. Visit FASDCENTER.SAMHSA.GOV for details.

## DAY 58

**8 WEEKS, 2 DAYS (8W2D)**

DATE:     /

### What I'm doing differently

**things to research**
- ☐ ...........................
- ☐ ...........................
- ☐ ...........................

SLEEP: 😴 ▬▬▬▬▬▬▬▬▬ 🌀

APPETITE: 😋 ▬▬▬▬▬▬▬▬▬ 🤢

MOOD: 🙂 ▬▬▬▬▬▬▬▬▬ 😣

## 222 days until your due date

*percentage completed* **20.7%**

**def·i·ni·tion**

**Fundus:** The top of the uterus. At 12 weeks of pregnancy, the fundus can be felt at the top of the pubic bone (*symphysis pubis*). At approximately 20 weeks, the fundus will have reached your belly button. After the 20th week, fundal height in centimeters (measured from just above the pubic bone) is equal to the number of weeks of gestation. (For example, when you're 25 weeks along, the fundus will be about 25cm above the pubic bone.)

---

## DAY 59

**8 WEEKS, 3 DAYS (8W3D)**

DATE:     /

### This week I feel...

**questions for my caregiver**
- ☐ ...........................
- ☐ ...........................
- ☐ ...........................

SLEEP: 😴 ▬▬▬▬▬▬▬▬▬ 🌀

APPETITE: 😋 ▬▬▬▬▬▬▬▬▬ 🤢

MOOD: 🙂 ▬▬▬▬▬▬▬▬▬ 😣

## 221 DAYS UNTIL YOUR DUE DATE (ESTIMATED)

**PERCENTAGE REMAINING** **78.9%**

*Notes*

Do you have to color your hair? If you can't wait, don't dye it during the first trimester, leave the color on for less time, and try to keep it off your skin and scalp. Motherisk (UK) reviewed 25 studies in 2008, and concluded, "For the average pregnant woman, receiving hair treatments 3 to 4 times during pregnancy does not appear to increase risk of adverse effects on the fetus."

WEEK 1
WEEK 2
WEEK 3
WEEK 4
WEEK 5
WEEK 6
WEEK 7
WEEK 8
WEEK 9
WEEK 10
WEEK 11
WEEK 12
WEEK 13
WEEK 14
WEEK 15
WEEK 16
WEEK 17
WEEK 18
WEEK 19
WEEK 20
WEEK 21
WEEK 22
WEEK 23
WEEK 24
WEEK 25
WEEK 26
WEEK 27
WEEK 28
WEEK 29
WEEK 30
WEEK 31
WEEK 32
WEEK 33
WEEK 34
WEEK 35
WEEK 36
WEEK 37
WEEK 38
WEEK 39
WEEK 40
WEEK 41
WEEK 42

DAYS 1-7
8-14
15-21
22-28
29-35
36-42
43-49
50-56
57-63
64-70
71-77
78-84
85-91
92-98
99-105
106-112
113-119
120-126
127-133
134-140
141-147
148-154
155-161
162-168
169-175
176-182
183-189
190-196
197-203
204-210
211-217
218-224
225-231
232-238
239-245
246-252
253-259
260-266
267-273
274-280
281-287
288-294

## DAY 60
### 8 WEEKS, 4 DAYS (8W4D)

DATE:        /

*New & different*

_____

grateful for...
☐ ......................................
☐ ......................................
☐ ......................................

SLEEP:
APPETITE:
MOOD:

### 220 DAYS UNTIL YOUR DUE DATE
(ESTIMATED)

FRACTION COMPLETED 3/14

66 *Many months went by with negative pregnancy tests and a lot of shared frustration... Then it happened.* 99 *I woke up one morning in June and there it was, a positive pregnancy test. I was in shock. Happy shock, but shock.*
- Cassie McConnell Kelley

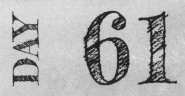

## DAY 61
### 8 WEEKS, 5 DAYS (8W5D)

DATE:        /

*I cannot believe...*

_____

to tell my partner
☐ ......................................
☐ ......................................
☐ ......................................

SLEEP:
APPETITE:
MOOD:

### 219 *days until your due date*

*how far you have come* 21.8%

**ABOUT YOU**

Have morning sickness? While it may be the last thing on your mind right now, try to give your teeth a little extra TLC. To neutralize acid after vomiting, Patricia Meredith, DDS, FAGD, spokesperson for the Academy of General Dentistry, says to rinse your mouth with a mixture of a teaspoon of baking soda dissolved in a cup of water. "The teeth should be brushed only after the mouth has been rinsed and the acid has been neutralized to prevent further damage to the enamel."

FIRST TRIMESTER                    SECOND

DAY **62**

8 WEEKS, 6 DAYS (8W6D)

DATE:        /

## How I imagine baby now

to-do
- ☐ ......................................
- ☐ ......................................
- ☐ ......................................

SLEEP: 😣 �█▓▒░ 😴
APPETITE: 😋 ░▒▓█ 🤢
MOOD: 😊 ░▒▓█ 😣

**218** days until your due date (estimated)

percentage remaining **77.9%**

### BOYS IN ITALY

**BABY NAMES**

*Francesco, Alessandro, Lorenzo, Andrea, Leonardo, Mattia, Matteo, Gabriele, Riccardo, Tommaso*

DAY **63**

9 WEEKS, 0 DAYS (9W0D)

DATE:        /

## The best thing this week

shopping wish list
- ☐ ......................................
- ☐ ......................................
- ☐ ......................................

SLEEP: 😣 �█▓▒░ 😴
APPETITE: 😋 ░▒▓█ 🤢
MOOD: 😊 ░▒▓█ 😣

**217** days until your due date (thereabouts)

percentage completed **22.5%**

### ~ A LITTLE NOTE TO THE FUTURE ~

☐ WISH  ☐ PREDICTION  ☐ PRAYER  ☐ HOPE  ☐ REMINDER

WEEK 1
WEEK 2
WEEK 3
WEEK 4
WEEK 5
WEEK 6
WEEK 7
WEEK 8
WEEK 9
WEEK 10
WEEK 11
WEEK 12
WEEK 13
WEEK 14
WEEK 15
WEEK 16
WEEK 17
WEEK 18
WEEK 19
WEEK 20
WEEK 21
WEEK 22
WEEK 23
WEEK 24
WEEK 25
WEEK 26
WEEK 27
WEEK 28
WEEK 29
WEEK 30
WEEK 31
WEEK 32
WEEK 33
WEEK 34
WEEK 35
WEEK 36
WEEK 37
WEEK 38
WEEK 39
WEEK 40
WEEK 41
WEEK 42

MONTH 1    MONTH 2    MONTH 3    MONTH 4    MONTH 5

DAYS 1-7
8-14
15-21
22-28
29-35
36-42
43-49
50-56
57-63
64-70
71-77
78-84
85-91
92-98
99-105
106-112
113-119
120-126
127-133
134-140
141-147
148-154
155-161
162-168
169-175
176-182
183-189
190-196
197-203
204-210
211-217
218-224
225-231
232-238
239-245
246-252
253-259
260-266
267-273
274-280
281-287
288-294

START OF

# WEEK 10

**07** WEEKS SINCE CONCEPTION  :  WEEKS UNTIL YOUR DUE DATE **30**

(Dates are estimates only | Pregnancy is considered "term" at 37 to 42 weeks)

## WEEKLY CHART
### 9 WEEKS PASSED & STARTING 10

 *How big is baby now?*

From crown to rump, baby is between 5 and 11.5 millimeters long (average 8 mm)

(All measurements are approximate, and based on average fetal development)

## APPOINTMENTS & REMINDERS FOR THIS WEEK

_____ _____
_____ _____
_____ _____
_____ _____

{ ON MY MIND }

DAY **64**

9 WEEKS, 1 DAY (9W1D)

DATE:        /

*3 wishes for this week*

to-do
☐ .........................................
☐ .........................................
☐ .........................................

SLEEP: ▭
APPETITE: ▭
MOOD: ▭

**216** DAYS UNTIL YOUR DUE DATE (ESTIMATED)

PERCENTAGE COMPLETED **22.9%**

BABY TALK

— Floating in a tiny ocean, your son or daughter is starting to move around a lot now.
— Most of the joints have formed, and, although you still can't feel it yet, baby can now wiggle his or her brand-new shoulders, knees and toes... as well as ankles, elbows and wrists.

## DAY 65

**9 WEEKS, 2 DAYS (9W2D)**

DATE:     /

### Recent changes

things to research
- ☐ ...........................................................
- ☐ ...........................................................
- ☐ ...........................................................

SLEEP: 😴 ▓▓▓▓▓▓▓▓▓ 😫

APPETITE: 😋 ▓▓▓▓▓▓▓▓▓ 😖

MOOD: 🙂 ▓▓▓▓▓▓▓▓▓ 😣

## 215 days until your due date

[ each dark | line represents 5 days passed ]

||||||||||||||||||||||||||||||||||||||||||||||||||||||

**def·i·ni·tion**

**Midwife:** A professional caregiver trained to give prenatal and postpartum care to women with low-risk/uncomplicated pregnancies. A CNM (certified nurse midwife) is both a registered nurse and a midwife. According to the Midwives Alliance of North America (MANA), midwives attend approximately 10% of births in the US across all settings, including those in hospitals, birth centers and at home.

## DAY 66

**9 WEEKS, 3 DAYS (9W3D)**

DATE:     /

### This week I feel...

questions for my caregiver
- ☐ ...........................................................
- ☐ ...........................................................
- ☐ ...........................................................

SLEEP: 😴 ▓▓▓▓▓▓▓▓▓ 😫

APPETITE: 😋 ▓▓▓▓▓▓▓▓▓ 😖

MOOD: 🙂 ▓▓▓▓▓▓▓▓▓ 😣

## 214 DAYS UNTIL YOUR DUE DATE (ESTIMATED)

**PERCENTAGE REMAINING 76.4%**

**Notes**

Your blood doesn't flow directly into the baby through the umbilical cord, because the placenta works as a filter. Oxygen, nutrients and water enter; while waste and carbon dioxide exit back into your body. But not only the good stuff gets through — some other things can pass from mom to baby, so be super aware of what you eat, drink, touch, breathe and put on your skin.

WEEK 1
WEEK 2
WEEK 3
WEEK 4
WEEK 5
WEEK 6
WEEK 7
WEEK 8
WEEK 9
WEEK 10
WEEK 11
WEEK 12
WEEK 13
WEEK 14
WEEK 15
WEEK 16
WEEK 17
WEEK 18
WEEK 19
WEEK 20
WEEK 21
WEEK 22
WEEK 23
WEEK 24
WEEK 25
WEEK 26
WEEK 27
WEEK 28
WEEK 29
WEEK 30
WEEK 31
WEEK 32
WEEK 33
WEEK 34
WEEK 35
WEEK 36
WEEK 37
WEEK 38
WEEK 39
WEEK 40
WEEK 41
WEEK 42

DAY **67**

9 WEEKS, 4 DAYS (9W4D)

DATE:        /

## New & different

grateful for...
☐ ...................................................
☐ ...................................................
☐ ...................................................

SLEEP:
APPETITE:
MOOD:

**213** DAYS UNTIL YOUR DUE DATE (ESTIMATED)

PERCENTAGE COMPLETED **23.9%**

" A baby is God's opinion that the world should go on. "

- Carl Sandburg

DAY **68**

9 WEEKS, 5 DAYS (9W5D)

DATE:        /

## What makes me nervous

to tell my partner
☐ ...................................................
☐ ...................................................
☐ ...................................................

SLEEP:
APPETITE:
MOOD:

**212** days until your due date

percentage remaining **75.7%**

ABOUT YOU

For baby's sake (and yours!) Always be honest and forthcoming with your caregiver about any medications or herbal remedies or supplements you're taking (including those to bring on labor), if you have been smoking or drinking, or if you have been involved in any high-risk activity. Doctor-patient confidentiality and the HIPAA Privacy Rule protect what you disclose to licensed medical providers.

# DAY 69

### 9 WEEKS, 6 DAYS (9W6D)

DATE:        /

## How I am getting ready

to-do
- [ ] ..............................
- [ ] ..............................
- [ ] ..............................

SLEEP: 
APPETITE: 
MOOD: 

## 211 days until your due date
(estimated)

percentage completed **24.6%**

## BABY NAMES

### GIRLS IN SWEDEN

Elsa, Alice, Maja,
Agnes, Lily, Olivia, Julia,
Ebba, Linnea, Molly

# DAY 70

### 10 WEEKS, 0 DAYS (10W0D)

DATE:        /

## I am thankful to...

shopping wish list
- [ ] ..............................
- [ ] ..............................
- [ ] ..............................

SLEEP: 
APPETITE: 
MOOD: 

## 210 days until your due date
(thereabouts)

fraction completed **1/4!**

### ~ A LITTLE NOTE TO THE FUTURE ~

- [ ] WISH  - [ ] PREDICTION  - [ ] PRAYER  - [ ] HOPE  - [ ] REMINDER

WEEK 1
WEEK 2
WEEK 3
WEEK 4
WEEK 5
WEEK 6
WEEK 7
WEEK 8
WEEK 9
WEEK 10
WEEK 11
WEEK 12
WEEK 13
WEEK 14
WEEK 15
WEEK 16
WEEK 17
WEEK 18
WEEK 19
WEEK 20
WEEK 21
WEEK 22
WEEK 23
WEEK 24
WEEK 25
WEEK 26
WEEK 27
WEEK 28
WEEK 29
WEEK 30
WEEK 31
WEEK 32
WEEK 33
WEEK 34
WEEK 35
WEEK 36
WEEK 37
WEEK 38
WEEK 39
WEEK 40
WEEK 41
WEEK 42

MONTH 1   MONTH 2   MONTH 3   MONTH 4   MONTH 5

DAYS 1-7
8-14
15-21
22-28
29-35
36-42
43-49
50-56
57-63
64-70
71-77
78-84
85-91
92-98
99-105
106-112
113-119
120-126
127-133
134-140
141-147
148-154
155-161
162-168
169-175
176-182
183-189
190-196
197-203
204-210
211-217
218-224
225-231
232-238
239-245
246-252
253-259
260-266
267-273
274-280
281-287
288-294

## START OF WEEK 11

**08** WEEKS SINCE CONCEPTION : WEEKS UNTIL YOUR DUE DATE **29**

(Dates are estimates only | Pregnancy is considered "term" at 37 to 42 weeks)

**WEEKLY CHART**
10 WEEKS PASSED & STARTING 11

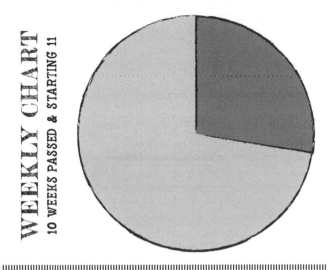

*How big is baby now?*

From crown to rump, baby is between 4/10 inch and 3/4 inch long (average = 15.3mm)

(All measurements are approximate, and based on average fetal development)

### APPOINTMENTS & REMINDERS FOR THIS WEEK

_____  _____
_____  _____
_____  _____
_____  _____

{ ON MY MIND }

**DAY 71**

10 WEEKS, 1 DAY (10W1D)

DATE:        /

*3 goals for this week*

to-do
☐ ......................................
☐ ......................................
☐ ......................................

SLEEP:     😴 �⬛ 🐾
APPETITE:  😋 ▭⬛ 🐣
MOOD:      😊 ▭⬛ 😣

**209** DAYS UNTIL YOUR DUE DATE (ESTIMATED)

PERCENTAGE COMPLETED **25.3%**

**BABY TALK**

— Most of the vital systems are developed now, and baby will begin to put his or her energy into growing a lot.
— The placenta starts to function this week, circulating blood and other fluids between you and your tiny offspring.

## DAY 72

**10 WEEKS, 2 DAYS (10W2D)**

DATE:        /

### My life right now...

things to research
- ☐ ........................................
- ☐ ........................................
- ☐ ........................................

SLEEP:
APPETITE:
MOOD:

**208** *days until your due date*

*fraction completed* **9/35**

**def·i·ni·tion**

**Amniotic fluid:** A colorless or slightly yellow liquid that surrounds and cushions the baby inside the womb, protecting from outside pressure and providing a clean, warm environment. The fluid is made up of about 98% water, and the remainder is composed of nutrients, hormones, antibodies — along with urine and from the baby. You will have 600ml to 1 liter of amniotic fluid at full term.

## DAY 73

**10 WEEKS, 3 DAYS (10W3D)**

DATE:        /

### This week I feel...

questions for my caregiver
- ☐ ........................................
- ☐ ........................................
- ☐ ........................................

SLEEP:
APPETITE:
MOOD:

**207** **DAYS UNTIL YOUR DUE DATE (ESTIMATED)**

**PERCENTAGE REMAINING 73.9%**

*Notes*

How will you know if you're pregnant with twins, triplets or more? Signs include having a uterus that measures large for dates, extra weight gain, and amplified pregnancy symptoms (such as severe morning sickness, lots of breast tenderness or excessive fatigue). Still, a woman carrying twins or more may not experience any particularly unusual symptoms.

TRIMESTER        THIRD TRIMESTER

WEEK 1
WEEK 2
WEEK 3
WEEK 4
WEEK 5
WEEK 6
WEEK 7
WEEK 8
WEEK 9
WEEK 10
WEEK 11
WEEK 12
WEEK 13
WEEK 14
WEEK 15
WEEK 16
WEEK 17
WEEK 18
WEEK 19
WEEK 20
WEEK 21
WEEK 22
WEEK 23
WEEK 24
WEEK 25
WEEK 26
WEEK 27
WEEK 28
WEEK 29
WEEK 30
WEEK 31
WEEK 32
WEEK 33
WEEK 34
WEEK 35
WEEK 36
WEEK 37
WEEK 38
WEEK 39
WEEK 40
WEEK 41
WEEK 42

MONTH 1    MONTH 2    MONTH 3    MONTH 4    MONTH 5

DAYS 1-7
8-14
15-21
22-28
29-35
36-42
43-49
50-56
57-63
64-70
71-77
78-84
85-91
92-98
99-105
106-112
113-119
120-126
127-133
134-140
141-147
148-154
155-161
162-168
169-175
176-182
183-189
190-196
197-203
204-210
211-217
218-224
225-231
232-238
239-245
246-252
253-259
260-266
267-273
274-280
281-287
288-294

# DAY 74

10 WEEKS, 4 DAYS (10W4D)

DATE:        /

## Plans to spread the news

grateful for...
- ☐ .................................................
- ☐ .................................................
- ☐ .................................................

SLEEP: 😴 ▮▮▮▮▮▮▮▮▮ 🌀
APPETITE: 😋 ▮▮▮▮▮▮▮▮▮ 🤢
MOOD: 🙂 ▮▮▮▮▮▮▮▮▮ 😣

## 206 DAYS UNTIL YOUR DUE DATE (ESTIMATED)

PERCENTAGE COMPLETED 26.4%

66 It is the most powerful creation to have life growing inside of you There is no bigger gift. 99

- Beyoncé

# DAY 75

10 WEEKS, 5 DAYS (10W5D)

DATE:        /

## I can't believe...

to tell my partner
- ☐ .................................................
- ☐ .................................................
- ☐ .................................................

SLEEP: 😴 ▮▮▮▮▮▮▮▮▮ 🌀
APPETITE: 😋 ▮▮▮▮▮▮▮▮▮ 🤢
MOOD: 🙂 ▮▮▮▮▮▮▮▮▮ 😣

## 205 days until your due date

[ each dark | line represents 5 days passed ]

▮▮▮▮▮▮▮▮▮▮▮▮▮▮▮▮▮▮▮▮▮▮▮▮▮▮▮▮▮▮▮▮▮▮▮▮▮▮

ABOUT YOU

Be sure to alert your caregiver if you're vomiting more than once a day. Especially severe morning sickness (hyperemesis gravidium) sometimes requires admission to a hospital for IV therapy to control dehydration, excessive weight loss, and to correct any electrolyte imbalance. Treatments may include hydration, psychological support, dietary alterations, and specific anti-nausea medications.

# DAY 76

**10 WEEKS, 6 DAYS (10W6D)**

DATE:        /

## Getting ready for baby

to-do
- ☐ ................................
- ☐ ................................
- ☐ ................................

SLEEP:
APPETITE:
MOOD:

**204** days until
your due date
(estimated)

percentage remaining **72.9%**

BABY NAMES

### BOYS IN IRELAND

Jack, James, Daniel, Conor,
Adam, Ryan, Harry, Liam,
Luke, Charlie

# DAY 77

**11 WEEKS, 0 DAYS (11W0D)**

DATE:        /

## Mood ups & downs

shopping wish list
- ☐ ................................
- ☐ ................................
- ☐ ................................

SLEEP:
APPETITE:
MOOD:

**203** days until
your due date
(thereabouts)

fraction left to go **29/40**

~ A LITTLE NOTE TO THE FUTURE ~

☐ WISH  ☐ PREDICTION  ☐ PRAYER  ☐ HOPE  ☐ REMINDER

WEEK 1
WEEK 2
WEEK 3
WEEK 4
WEEK 5
WEEK 6
WEEK 7
WEEK 8
WEEK 9
WEEK 10
WEEK 11
WEEK 12
WEEK 13
WEEK 14
WEEK 15
WEEK 16
WEEK 17
WEEK 18
WEEK 19
WEEK 20
WEEK 21
WEEK 22
WEEK 23
WEEK 24
WEEK 25
WEEK 26
WEEK 27
WEEK 28
WEEK 29
WEEK 30
WEEK 31
WEEK 32
WEEK 33
WEEK 34
WEEK 35
WEEK 36
WEEK 37
WEEK 38
WEEK 39
WEEK 40
WEEK 41
WEEK 42

DAYS 1-7
8-14
15-21
22-28
29-35
36-42
43-49
50-56
57-63
64-70
71-77
78-84
85-91
92-98
99-105
106-112
113-119
120-126
127-133
134-140
141-147
148-154
155-161
162-168
169-175
176-182
183-189
190-196
197-203
204-210
211-217
218-224
225-231
232-238
239-245
246-252
253-259
260-266
267-273
274-280
281-287
288-294

## START OF WEEK 12

**09** WEEKS SINCE CONCEPTION : WEEKS UNTIL YOUR DUE DATE **28**

(Dates are estimates only | Pregnancy is considered "term" at 37 to 42 weeks)

### WEEKLY CHART
**11 WEEKS PASSED & STARTING 12**

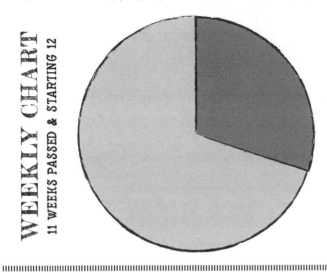

### How big is baby now?

From crown to rump, baby is between 7/10 inch and 1.1 inches long (average=23.8mm)

(All measurements are approximate, and based on average fetal development)

### APPOINTMENTS & REMINDERS FOR THIS WEEK

_____  _____
_____  _____
_____  _____

{ ON MY MIND }

## DAY 78

**11 WEEKS, 1 DAY (11W1D)**

DATE:          /

### 3 wishes for this week

to-do
☐ .................................
☐ .................................
☐ .................................

SLEEP:
APPETITE:
MOOD:

**202** DAYS UNTIL YOUR DUE DATE (ESTIMATED)

PERCENTAGE COMPLETED **27.9%**

### BABY TALK

— Your baby has tiny, soft nails on those fingers and toes, and may even start to suck a thumb.
— Many of his or her body systems are starting to work now. For example, the digestive system practices moving food along the newly-formed intestines.

**DAY 79**

11 WEEKS, 2 DAYS (11W2D)

DATE:     /

### Recent changes

things to research
- ☐ ...........................................
- ☐ ...........................................
- ☐ ...........................................

SLEEP:

APPETITE:

MOOD:

**201** *days until your due date*

*percentage remaining* **71.8%**

**def·i·ni·tion**

**Amniocentesis:** Often shortened to "amnio," this is a prenatal test done between 16 and 20 weeks of pregnancy. A hollow needle is inserted into the abdomen, uterus and amniotic sac to withdraw a tiny sample of amniotic fluid around the baby. The sample is then cultured and analyzed for genetic diseases such as Down syndrome, cystic fibrosis, Tay-Sachs and sickle cell disease.

TRIMESTER

---

**DAY 80**

11 WEEKS, 3 DAYS (11W3D)

DATE:     /

### This week I feel...

questions for my caregiver
- ☐ ...........................................
- ☐ ...........................................
- ☐ ...........................................

SLEEP:

APPETITE:

MOOD:

**200** **DAYS UNTIL YOUR DUE DATE** (ESTIMATED)

**FRACTION COMPLETED** **2/7**

Notes

Let your healthcare provider know if you're suffering from stress or depression. All of these can have an impact on your health and your baby's health. Your caregiver needs to know what is going on in your life in order to make sure he or she is taking the best possible care of you both.

THIRD TRIMESTER

WEEK 1
WEEK 2
WEEK 3
WEEK 4
WEEK 5
WEEK 6
WEEK 7
WEEK 8
WEEK 9
WEEK 10
WEEK 11
WEEK 12
WEEK 13
WEEK 14
WEEK 15
WEEK 16
WEEK 17
WEEK 18
WEEK 19
WEEK 20
WEEK 21
WEEK 22
WEEK 23
WEEK 24
WEEK 25
WEEK 26
WEEK 27
WEEK 28
WEEK 29
WEEK 30
WEEK 31
WEEK 32
WEEK 33
WEEK 34
WEEK 35
WEEK 36
WEEK 37
WEEK 38
WEEK 39
WEEK 40
WEEK 41
WEEK 42

## DAY 81

**11 WEEKS, 4 DAYS (11W4D)**

DATE:   /

### Something unexpected

grateful for...
- ☐ .............................................
- ☐ .............................................
- ☐ .............................................

SLEEP:

APPETITE:

MOOD:

**199** DAYS UNTIL YOUR DUE DATE (ESTIMATED)

PERCENTAGE COMPLETED **28.9%**

66

*Babies are such a nice way to start people.*

99

– Don Herrold

## DAY 82

**11 WEEKS, 5 DAYS (11W5D)**

DATE:   /

### How I'm handling pressure

to tell my partner
- ☐ .............................................
- ☐ .............................................
- ☐ .............................................

SLEEP:

APPETITE:

MOOD:

**198** days until your due date (approximately)

percentage remaining **70.7%**

**ABOUT YOU**

Though it's still early, you might want to sign up for childbirth classes soon. (Check with your caregiver, the local hospital or birthing center for references.) Classes usually begin around the seventh month, and help you prepare for labor and delivery (both vaginal and Cesarean), newborn care, postpartum changes, relaxation methods and breathing techniques.

DAYS 1-7
8-14
15-21
22-28
29-35
36-42
43-49
50-56
57-63
64-70
71-77
78-84
85-91
92-98
99-105
106-112
113-119
120-126
127-133
134-140
141-147
148-154
155-161
162-168
169-175
176-182
183-189
190-196
197-203
204-210
211-217
218-224
225-231
232-238
239-245
246-252
253-259
260-266
267-273
274-280
281-287
288-294

## DAY 83

11 WEEKS, 6 DAYS (11W6D)

DATE:        /

### These next few months...

to-do
- [ ] ..................................
- [ ] ..................................
- [ ] ..................................

SLEEP:
APPETITE:
MOOD:

## 197 days until your due date (estimated)

percentage completed **29.6%**

## BABY NAMES

### GIRLS IN POLAND

Lena, Zuzanna, Julia, Maja, Hanna, Aleksandra, Amelia, Zofia, Natalia, Wiktoria

## DAY 84

12 WEEKS, 0 DAYS (12W0D)

DATE:        /

### Boy or girl?

shopping wish list
- [ ] ..................................
- [ ] ..................................
- [ ] ..................................

SLEEP:
APPETITE:
MOOD:

## 196 days until your due date (thereabouts)

fraction left to go **7/10**

~A LITTLE NOTE TO THE FUTURE~

☐ WISH  ☐ PREDICTION  ☐ PRAYER  ☐ HOPE  ☐ REMINDER

WEEK 1
WEEK 2
WEEK 3
WEEK 4
WEEK 5
WEEK 6
WEEK 7
WEEK 8
WEEK 9
WEEK 10
WEEK 11
WEEK 12
WEEK 13
WEEK 14
WEEK 15
WEEK 16
WEEK 17
WEEK 18
WEEK 19
WEEK 20
WEEK 21
WEEK 22
WEEK 23
WEEK 24
WEEK 25
WEEK 26
WEEK 27
WEEK 28
WEEK 29
WEEK 30
WEEK 31
WEEK 32
WEEK 33
WEEK 34
WEEK 35
WEEK 36
WEEK 37
WEEK 38
WEEK 39
WEEK 40
WEEK 41
WEEK 42

**By the end of this month (week 16), your baby will be about the size of a lemon.**

When measured from the top of his or her (very large) head to his or her bottom, your little boy or girl is about 3½ inches long.

# MONTH 4

## WEEK 13, WEEK 14
## WEEK 15 & WEEK 16

## How do you feel?

At the beginning of this month,
rate how you're feeling with a line, X or circle

 **ENERGY AMOUNT**

**IMPATIENCE DEGREE**

**EMOTIONAL INTENSITY**

**GRUMPINESS GRADE**

**SOCIABILITY SCALE**

**LOVE+ROMANCE LEVEL**

**FORGETFULNESS FACTOR**

**GROWTH GAUGE**

Add a picture of yourself at 4 months here
Photos not your thing? Estimate your pregnancy size and shape by drawing over the shadowed image below

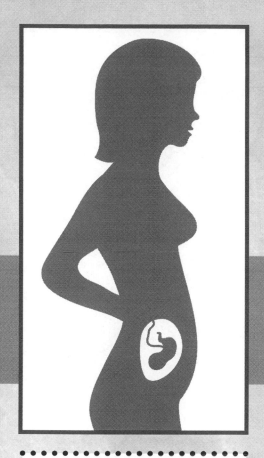

## One year from now

(assuming you give birth around 40 weeks)

Your baby will be about 7 months old!

### YOU & BABY

Weight change:

Belly circumference:

Fundal height:

Baby's heart rate:

Baby's position:

### 4 WORDS FOR WHAT'S ON YOUR MIND RIGHT NOW

## notes

DAYS 1-7
8-14
15-21
22-28
29-35
36-42
43-49
50-56
57-63
64-70
71-77
78-84
85-91
92-98
99-105
106-112
113-119
120-126
127-133
134-140
141-147
148-154
155-161
162-168
169-175
176-182
183-189
190-196
197-203
204-210
211-217
218-224
225-231
232-238
239-245
246-252
253-259
260-266
267-273
274-280
281-287
288-294

## START OF WEEK 13

**10** WEEKS SINCE CONCEPTION : WEEKS UNTIL YOUR DUE DATE **27**

(Dates are estimates only | Pregnancy is considered "term" at 37 to 42 weeks)

### WEEKLY CHART
**12 WEEKS PASSED & STARTING 13**

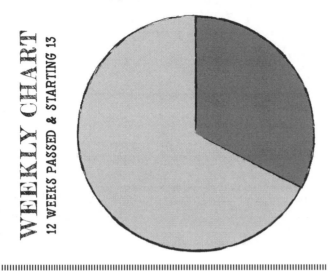

### How big is baby now?

From crown to rump, baby is between 1.1 inches and 1.6 inches long (average=33.5mm)

(All measurements are approximate, and based on average fetal development)

### APPOINTMENTS & REMINDERS FOR THIS WEEK

_____  _____

_____  _____

_____  _____

Reminder: Tell employer / Plan maternity leave

### { ON MY MIND }

## DAY 85

**12 WEEKS, 1 DAY (12W1D)**

DATE:         /

---

### 3 ideas for this week

---

to-do
- ☐ ..........................................
- ☐ ..........................................
- ☐ ..........................................

SLEEP: ▭▭▭▭▭▭▭
APPETITE: ▭▭▭▭▭▭▭
MOOD: ▭▭▭▭▭▭▭

## 195 DAYS UNTIL YOUR DUE DATE (ESTIMATED)

[ each dark | line represents 5 days passed ]

|||||||||||||||||||||||||||||||||||||||||||||||

### BABY TALK

— The placenta has grown and developed so much, it's ready to begin taking over hormone production, required to maintain pregnancy.
— In other news, the baby's eyelids are now firmly shut, and will stay closed until the third trimester.

### DAY 86
**12 WEEKS, 2 DAYS (12W2D)**
DATE:        /

*My life right now...*

things to research
☐ ......................................
☐ ......................................
☐ ......................................

SLEEP:
APPETITE:
MOOD:

## 194 *days until your due date*

*percentage remaining* **69.3%**

WEEK 1
WEEK 2
WEEK 3
WEEK 4
WEEK 5
WEEK 6
WEEK 7
WEEK 8
WEEK 9
WEEK 10
WEEK 11
WEEK 12
WEEK 13
WEEK 14
WEEK 15
WEEK 16
WEEK 17
WEEK 18
WEEK 19
WEEK 20
WEEK 21
WEEK 22
WEEK 23
WEEK 24
WEEK 25
WEEK 26
WEEK 27
WEEK 28
WEEK 29
WEEK 30
WEEK 31
WEEK 32
WEEK 33
WEEK 34
WEEK 35
WEEK 36
WEEK 37
WEEK 38
WEEK 39
WEEK 40
WEEK 41
WEEK 42

**def·i·ni·tion**

**Triple screen/quad screen:** Common prenatal blood tests done between 15 and 20 weeks of pregnancy to screen for Down syndrome, Trisomy 18 and neural tube defects. The tests measure AFP (alpha fetoprotein, a protein made by baby's liver); hCG (human chorionic gonadotropin) and estriol (a type of estrogen). The quad screen also looks for inhibin-A (made by the placenta).

### DAY 87
**12 WEEKS, 3 DAYS (12W3D)**
DATE:        /

*This week I feel...*

questions for my caregiver
☐ ......................................
☐ ......................................
☐ ......................................

SLEEP:
APPETITE:
MOOD:

## 193 DAYS UNTIL YOUR DUE DATE (ESTIMATED)

**PERCENTAGE COMPLETED 31.1%**

*Notes*

Whether the egg (with an X sex chromosome) is fertilized by a sperm with an X or a Y sex chromosome determines if you'll have a boy or a girl. (XX gets you a girl, XY means it's a boy.)

In a nutshell — so to speak — the father determines the baby's biological gender at the moment of conception, and that can't change during pregnancy.

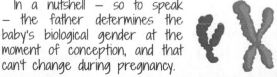

TRIMESTER                    THIRD TRIMESTER

MONTH 1        MONTH 2        MONTH 3        MONTH 4        MONTH 5

DAYS 1-7
8-14
15-21
22-28
29-35
36-42
43-49
50-56
57-63
64-70
71-77
78-84
85-91
92-98
99-105
106-112
113-119
120-126
127-133
134-140
141-147
148-154
155-161
162-168
169-175
176-182
183-189
190-196
197-203
204-210
211-217
218-224
225-231
232-238
239-245
246-252
253-259
260-266
267-273
274-280
281-287
288-294

## DAY 88

### 12 WEEKS, 4 DAYS (12W4D)

DATE:          /

### How I told the family

grateful for...
- ☐ .................................................
- ☐ .................................................
- ☐ .................................................

SLEEP:
APPETITE:
MOOD:

## 192  DAYS UNTIL YOUR DUE DATE (ESTIMATED)

### FRACTION REMAINING  24/35

66

To be pregnant is to be vitally alive,
thoroughly woman, and distressingly inhabited.
Soul and spirit are stretched — along with body —
making pregnancy a time of transition, growth, and
profound beginnings. - Anne Christian Buchanan

99

## DAY 89

### 12 WEEKS, 5 DAYS (12W5D)

DATE:          /

### How I spend my days

to tell my partner
- ☐ .................................................
- ☐ .................................................
- ☐ .................................................

SLEEP:
APPETITE:
MOOD:

## 191  days until your due date

### how far you have come  31.9%

ABOUT YOU

Start practicing your Kegel exercises whenever
you remember! This means tightening the pelvic
floor muscles like you would do when trying to
stop the flow of urine mid-stream.

Start slowly, but work your way up to two
or three sets of ten, holding each one for 10
seconds. These should help you both during labor
and after birth.

## DAY 90
### 12 WEEKS, 6 DAYS (12W6D)
DATE: 　 /

*I can't wait until...*

to-do
- ☐ ....................................
- ☐ ....................................
- ☐ ....................................

SLEEP:
APPETITE:
MOOD:

# 190
days until
your due date
(estimated)

fraction
completed **9/28**

**BABY NAMES**

### GIRL NAMES FROM THE 1960S

*Lisa, Susan, Karen, Kimberly,
Patricia, Linda, Donna, Michelle,
Cynthia, Sandra, Deborah, Pamela,
Lori, Julie, Laura, Brenda*

## DAY 91
### 13 WEEKS, 0 DAYS (13W0D)
DATE: 　 /

*Baby name ideas*

shopping
wish list
- ☐ ....................................
- ☐ ....................................
- ☐ ....................................

SLEEP:
APPETITE:
MOOD:

# 189
days until
your due date
(thereabouts)

percentage
left to go **67.5%**

~ A LITTLE NOTE TO THE FUTURE ~
☐ WISH　☐ PREDICTION　☐ PRAYER　☐ HOPE　☐ REMINDER

TRIMESTER　　　　　THIRD TRIMESTER

WEEK 1
WEEK 2
WEEK 3
WEEK 4
WEEK 5
WEEK 6
WEEK 7
WEEK 8
WEEK 9
WEEK 10
WEEK 11
WEEK 12
WEEK 13
WEEK 14
WEEK 15
WEEK 16
WEEK 17
WEEK 18
WEEK 19
WEEK 20
WEEK 21
WEEK 22
WEEK 23
WEEK 24
WEEK 25
WEEK 26
WEEK 27
WEEK 28
WEEK 29
WEEK 30
WEEK 31
WEEK 32
WEEK 33
WEEK 34
WEEK 35
WEEK 36
WEEK 37
WEEK 38
WEEK 39
WEEK 40
WEEK 41
WEEK 42

# TRIMESTER 2

DATE I FIRST FELT BABY MOVE:          BELLY POPPED OUT ON:

| THE SECOND TRIMESTER | MONTH | WEEKS |
|---|---|---|
| | FOUR | 14 - 18 |
| | FIVE | 19 - 22 |
| | SIX | 23 - 27 |

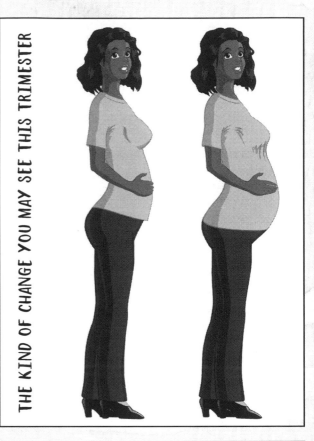

THE KIND OF CHANGE YOU MAY SEE THIS TRIMESTER

## PREGNANCY NO-NOS: THINGS TO AVOID

Soft cheeses + deli meats    Alcohol + caffeine

Raw/undercooked meat    Some artificial sweeteners

Raw eggs (dough/batter)    Medications/drugs/herbs

Unpasteurized juice + milk    Bug spray, cleaners, solvents

Raw/undercooked sprouts    Cat litter boxes

Shark, swordfish, tilefish    Cigarettes, smoke + e-cigs

## A quick reminder

Here are some things to watch for and to report to your caregiver.

- Contractions or strong cramps
- Vaginal bleeding
- Suspected amniotic fluid leak
- Persistent headaches
- Nausea, vomiting, diarrhea
- Inability to eat or drink
- Dizziness/vision problems
- Lower abdomen pain/cramps
- Swelling face, hands, feet
- Reduced or increased urination
- Flu-like symptoms
- Decreased movement from baby

Attach an ultrasound picture here!
(Don't have one? Add a pregnancy photo or draw your baby instead.)

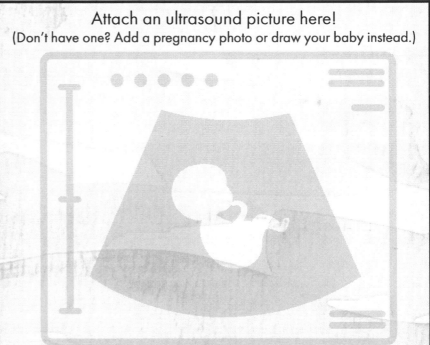

# Week 14 until end of week 27

## HEALTH & MEDICAL TESTS IN TRIMESTER TWO

*This is a basic overview of some typical prenatal care offered in the US*

**16-18 WEEKS:** Amniocentesis, also known as an "amnio," is a prenatal test typically used to check for chromosomal defects, and is most common for women over age 35.

Guided by ultrasound, a doctor inserts a large hollow needle through your abdomen and the uterine wall, then punctures the amniotic sac and withdraws a small amount of amniotic fluid. The fluid draw itself is generally done in about a minute. The fetal cells contained within the amniotic fluid are then sent to a lab for culturing and testing. Results take 2 to 3 weeks.

**18-20 WEEKS:** Ultrasound works by using high frequency sound waves transmitted through the surface of the skin to the uterus, then reflected back in different ways, depending on the density of the various tissues.

For a routine anatomy ultrasound, the baby's heart chambers and lobes of the brain are viewed and counted. Gestational age can be confirmed by measuring the baby's skull in several places and by measuring length of the arm and leg bones.

The exam takes anywhere from 15 to 60 minutes, depending on how cooperative your little one is, the skill of the technician, and the level of detail required. An ultrasound is painless, considered harmless to you and the baby, and can be an excellent diagnostic tool.

If an ultrasound technician (not a doctor) performs the scan, he or she will not be allowed to discuss the anything seen (or not seen) during the exam. Results should be ready in 1-2 days.

**24-28 WEEKS:** Screening for gestational diabetes (GD) by loading you up with sugar (on an empty stomach, usually first thing in the morning) and drawing blood one hour later.

### 4 things you'll know by the end of T2

1. What it feels like to drip hot food or drink onto the sensitive skin on top of your baby bump.
2. How strange it is not to be able to see your privates — or, a lot of the time — your feet.
3. That your belly button actually has an inside, and it can get completely stretched out — or pop!
4. Just how amazingly buoyant swimming pool water (or lake/ocean water) can be.

## TRIMESTER 2 PARALLELS

My theme song:

Sitcom title:

Superhero identity:

Actress in my life story:

Product I could endorse:

The animal I would be:

# Notes from the second trimester

## START OF WEEK 14

**11** WEEKS SINCE CONCEPTION · WEEKS UNTIL YOUR DUE DATE **26**

(Dates are estimates only | Pregnancy is considered "term" at 37 to 42 weeks)

### WEEKLY CHART
**13 WEEKS PASSED & STARTING 14**

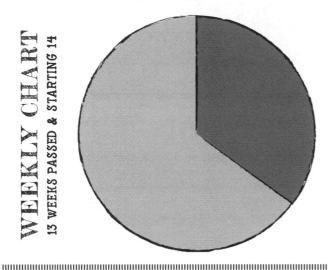

*How big is baby now?*

From crown to rump, baby is between 1.5 inches and 2 inches long (average = 44.5mm)

(All measurements are approximate, and based on average fetal development)

### APPOINTMENTS & REMINDERS FOR THIS WEEK

_____  _____

_____  _____

_____  _____

_____  _____

{ ON MY MIND }

**DAY 92**

**13 WEEKS, 1 DAY (13W1D)**

DATE:        /

---

*3 wishes for this week*

---

to-do
- ☐ ....................................
- ☐ ....................................
- ☐ ....................................

---

SLEEP:
APPETITE:
MOOD:

**188** DAYS UNTIL YOUR DUE DATE (ESTIMATED)

PERCENTAGE COMPLETED **32.8%**

### BABY TALK

— Your baby's head will soon be upright as his neck muscles become stronger, which also means his eyes will begin to face forward.

— Around now, little lungs start to practice breathing in and breathing out.

## DAY 93

### 13 WEEKS, 2 DAYS (13W2D)

DATE:     /

### Recent changes

**things to research**
- ☐ .......................................
- ☐ .......................................
- ☐ .......................................

SLEEP:
APPETITE:
MOOD:

## 187 *days until your due date*

*fraction completed* 1/3

---

**def·i·ni·tion**

**Birth center:** A home-away-from-home place to birth, equipped to care for low risk women in family-centered environment. Certified nurse-midwives (CNMs), nurses, women's health nurse practitioners (WHNP), doulas, lactation consultants and others usually staff a freestanding birth center, and most have an obstetrician on call for emergencies. (Learn more at birthcenters.org)

## DAY 94

### 13 WEEKS, 3 DAYS (13W3D)

DATE:     /

### This week I feel...

**questions for my caregiver**
- ☐ .......................................
- ☐ .......................................
- ☐ .......................................

SLEEP:
APPETITE:
MOOD:

## 186 DAYS UNTIL YOUR DUE DATE (ESTIMATED)

**PERCENTAGE REMAINING** 66.4%

---

*Notes*

Warm baths are generally considered safe to take throughout pregnancy, unless your amniotic sac has ruptured or your healthcare provider has told you otherwise. But before you step (carefully!) into the bathtub, make sure the bath water isn't too hot — excess heat isn't good for you or the baby right now. (Also be careful about using hot tubs.)

WEEK 1
WEEK 2
WEEK 3
WEEK 4
WEEK 5
WEEK 6
WEEK 7
WEEK 8
WEEK 9
WEEK 10
WEEK 11
WEEK 12
WEEK 13
WEEK 14
WEEK 15
WEEK 16
WEEK 17
WEEK 18
WEEK 19
WEEK 20
WEEK 21
WEEK 22
WEEK 23
WEEK 24
WEEK 25
WEEK 26
WEEK 27
WEEK 28
WEEK 29
WEEK 30
WEEK 31
WEEK 32
WEEK 33
WEEK 34
WEEK 35
WEEK 36
WEEK 37
WEEK 38
WEEK 39
WEEK 40
WEEK 41
WEEK 42

# DAY 95

### 13 WEEKS, 4 DAYS (13W4D)

DATE:        /

## Early reactions to the news

grateful for...
- ☐ ......................
- ☐ ......................
- ☐ ......................

SLEEP:
APPETITE:
MOOD:

## 185 DAYS UNTIL YOUR DUE DATE (ESTIMATED)

[ each dark | line represents 5 days passed ]

❝ A baby is a blank cheque made payable to the human race. ❞

— Barbara Christine Seifert

# DAY 96

### 13 WEEKS, 5 DAYS (13W5D)

DATE:        /

## Aversions & cravings

to tell my partner
- ☐ ......................
- ☐ ......................
- ☐ ......................

SLEEP:
APPETITE:
MOOD:

## 184 days until your due date

how far you have come **34.2%**

**ABOUT YOU**

Try to nap when you can, but don't dismiss the idea of exercise. Amazingly, a brisk walk in the afternoon will often wake you up enough so you not only won't fall asleep before dinner, you might even get better rest when you finally do get to snooze.

To get more comfortable in bed at night as your belly grows, experiment with different sleeping positions. You can try gently bending your leg forward at the knee and the hip, and use a pillow under your leg.

DAY  97

13 WEEKS, 6 DAYS (13W6D)

DATE:        /

### I am impatient for...

to-do
☐ .........................................
☐ .........................................
☐ .........................................

SLEEP:
APPETITE:
MOOD:

## 183 days until your due date (estimated)

percentage remaining **65.4%**

**BABY NAMES**

### BOYS IN SWEDEN

Lucas, William, Oscar, Oliver, Liam, Elias, Hugo, Vincent, Charlie, Alexander

---

DAY  98

14 WEEKS, 0 DAYS (14W0D)

DATE:        /

### How my partner's doing

shopping wish list
☐ .........................................
☐ .........................................
☐ .........................................

SLEEP:
APPETITE:
MOOD:

## 182 days until your due date (thereabouts)

fraction left to go **13/20**

~ A LITTLE NOTE TO THE FUTURE ~

☐ WISH  ☐ PREDICTION  ☐ PRAYER  ☐ HOPE  ☐ REMINDER

WEEK 1
WEEK 2
WEEK 3
WEEK 4
WEEK 5
WEEK 6
WEEK 7
WEEK 8
WEEK 9
WEEK 10
WEEK 11
WEEK 12
WEEK 13
WEEK 14
WEEK 15
WEEK 16
WEEK 17
WEEK 18
WEEK 19
WEEK 20
WEEK 21
WEEK 22
WEEK 23
WEEK 24
WEEK 25
WEEK 26
WEEK 27
WEEK 28
WEEK 29
WEEK 30
WEEK 31
WEEK 32
WEEK 33
WEEK 34
WEEK 35
WEEK 36
WEEK 37
WEEK 38
WEEK 39
WEEK 40
WEEK 41
WEEK 42

DAYS 1-7
8-14
15-21
22-28
29-35
36-42
43-49
50-56
57-63
64-70
71-77
78-84
85-91
92-98
99-105
106-112
113-119
120-126
127-133
134-140
141-147
148-154
155-161
162-168
169-175
176-182
183-189
190-196
197-203
204-210
211-217
218-224
225-231
232-238
239-245
246-252
253-259
260-266
267-273
274-280
281-287
288-294

## START OF WEEK 15

**12** WEEKS SINCE CONCEPTION : WEEKS UNTIL YOUR DUE DATE **25**

(Dates are estimates only | Pregnancy is considered "term" at 37 to 42 weeks)

**WEEKLY CHART**
14 WEEKS PASSED & STARTING 15

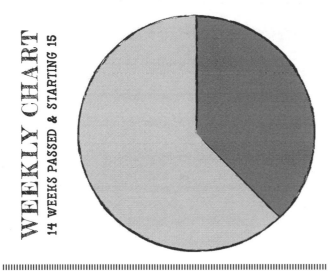

*How big is baby now?*

From crown to rump, baby is between 1.9 inches & 2.5 inches long (average=56.6mm)

(All measurements are approximate, and based on average fetal development)

## APPOINTMENTS & REMINDERS FOR THIS WEEK

_____  _____

_____  _____

_____  _____

{ ON MY MIND }

**DAY 99**

14 WEEKS, 1 DAY (14W1D)

DATE: ____/____

*3 goals for this week*

to-do
☐ ........................
☐ ........................
☐ ........................

SLEEP: [_____]
APPETITE: [_____]
MOOD: [_____]

**181** DAYS UNTIL YOUR DUE DATE (ESTIMATED)

PERCENTAGE COMPLETED **35.4%**

**BABY TALK**

— Your baby's face is starting to look more recognizably human!
— His bones are formed now, and getting stronger and harder each day.
— The bone marrow is starting to make blood.
— If you could peek inside, you might be able to tell now if it's a boy or a girl.

DAY **100**

14 WEEKS, 2 DAYS (14W2D)

DATE:    /

### Life right now

---

**things to research**
- ☐ ....................................
- ☐ ....................................
- ☐ ....................................

SLEEP: ▬▬▬▬▬▬▬▬
APPETITE: ▬▬▬▬▬▬▬▬
MOOD: ▬▬▬▬▬▬▬▬

**180** *days until your due date*

*fraction completed* **5/14**

WEEK 1
WEEK 2
WEEK 3
WEEK 4
WEEK 5
WEEK 6
WEEK 7
WEEK 8
WEEK 9
WEEK 10
WEEK 11
WEEK 12
WEEK 13
WEEK 14
WEEK 15
WEEK 16
WEEK 17
WEEK 18
WEEK 19
WEEK 20
WEEK 21
WEEK 22
WEEK 23
WEEK 24
WEEK 25
WEEK 26
WEEK 27
WEEK 28
WEEK 29
WEEK 30
WEEK 31
WEEK 32
WEEK 33
WEEK 34
WEEK 35
WEEK 36
WEEK 37
WEEK 38
WEEK 39
WEEK 40
WEEK 41
WEEK 42

DAY **101**

14 WEEKS, 3 DAYS (14W3D)

DATE:    /

### This week I feel...

---

**questions for my caregiver**
- ☐ ....................................
- ☐ ....................................
- ☐ ....................................

SLEEP: ▬▬▬▬▬▬▬▬
APPETITE: ▬▬▬▬▬▬▬▬
MOOD: ▬▬▬▬▬▬▬▬

**179** DAYS UNTIL YOUR DUE DATE (ESTIMATED)

PERCENTAGE COMPLETED **63.9%**

**def·i·ni·tion**

**Linea nigra:** A brownish vertical line that may appear on the abdomen, starting at the belly button and continuing down to the pubic area. This dark coloring (*linea nigra* is Latin for "black line") is caused by pregnancy hormones boosting the production of the pigment melanin (which will also darken the nipples). The linea nigra will fade after pregnancy, but might not completely disappear.

There have been few studies on genital piercings during pregnancy. According to research by Myrna L Armstrong, EdD, RN, FAAN, "When we interviewed OB/GYN nurse practitioners about the topic, they stressed removal of both navel & genital piercings during advanced pregnancy due to fears of tissue tears in the respective locations." Consider a temporary plastic replacement instead.

# DAY 102

## 14 WEEKS, 4 DAYS (14W4D)

**DATE:** /

### *Making me a little bit crazy*

*grateful for...*
- ☐ ....................................................
- ☐ ....................................................
- ☐ ....................................................

**SLEEP:**
**APPETITE:**
**MOOD:**

## 178 DAYS UNTIL YOUR DUE DATE (ESTIMATED)

**PERCENTAGE COMPLETED** 36.4%

66 *A mother's joy begins when new life is stirring inside... when a tiny heartbeat is heard for the very first time, and a playful kick reminds her that she is never alone.* 99
— Unknown

# DAY 103

## 14 WEEKS, 5 DAYS (14W5D)

**DATE:** /

### *I am grateful for...*

*to tell my partner*
- ☐ ....................................................
- ☐ ....................................................
- ☐ ....................................................

**SLEEP:**
**APPETITE:**
**MOOD:**

## 177 *days until your due date*

*percentage remaining* 63.2%

**ABOUT YOU**

There are few things in the world as exciting as feeling your baby move inside your belly (called "quickening"). Although your baby has been moving and kicking for many weeks, only at about 16 weeks can you really start to notice those wiggles — and even that depends on where the placenta is and how much padding you have. At first, the kicks may feel like bubbles popping or gentle butterfly wings.

DAY **104**

14 WEEKS, 6 DAYS (14W6D)

DATE:        /

## Pregnancy dreams

to-do
- ☐ ......................................
- ☐ ......................................
- ☐ ......................................

SLEEP:
APPETITE:
MOOD:

**176** days until your due date (estimated)

percentage completed **62.8%**

### GIRLS IN ROMANIA

BABY NAMES

*Maria, Elena, Ioana, Andreea, Sofia, Alexandra, Antonia, Daria, Ana, Gabriela*

---

DAY **105**

15 WEEKS, 0 DAYS (15W0D)

DATE:        /

## Who has noticed my belly

shopping wish list
- ☐ ......................................
- ☐ ......................................
- ☐ ......................................

SLEEP:
APPETITE:
MOOD:

**175** days until your due date (thereabouts)

fraction completed **5/8**

### ~ A LITTLE NOTE TO THE FUTURE ~

☐ WISH  ☐ PREDICTION  ☐ PRAYER  ☐ HOPE  ☐ REMINDER

WEEK 1
WEEK 2
WEEK 3
WEEK 4
WEEK 5
WEEK 6
WEEK 7
WEEK 8
WEEK 9
WEEK 10
WEEK 11
WEEK 12
WEEK 13
WEEK 14
WEEK 15
WEEK 16
WEEK 17
WEEK 18
WEEK 19
WEEK 20
WEEK 21
WEEK 22
WEEK 23
WEEK 24
WEEK 25
WEEK 26
WEEK 27
WEEK 28
WEEK 29
WEEK 30
WEEK 31
WEEK 32
WEEK 33
WEEK 34
WEEK 35
WEEK 36
WEEK 37
WEEK 38
WEEK 39
WEEK 40
WEEK 41
WEEK 42

## START OF WEEK 16

**13** WEEKS SINCE CONCEPTION : WEEKS UNTIL YOUR DUE DATE **24**

(Dates are estimates only | Pregnancy is considered "term" at 37 to 42 weeks)

### WEEKLY CHART
**15 WEEKS PASSED & STARTING 16**

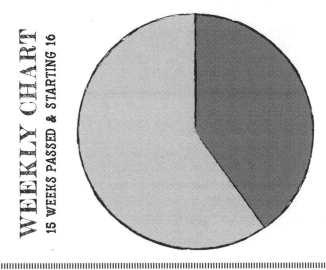

### How big is baby now?

From crown to rump, baby is between 2.3 inches & 3 inches long (average=70mm)

(All measurements are approximate, and based on average fetal development)

### APPOINTMENTS & REMINDERS FOR THIS WEEK

———————   ———————
———————   ———————
———————   ———————

**{ ON MY MIND }**

## DAY 106

**15 WEEKS, 1 DAY (15W1D)**

DATE:        /

*3 wishes for this week*

to-do
☐ ..................................
☐ ..................................
☐ ..................................

SLEEP:
APPETITE:
MOOD:

**174** DAYS UNTIL YOUR DUE DATE (ESTIMATED)

PERCENTAGE COMPLETED **37.9%**

### BABY TALK

— If your baby is a girl, she already has several million eggs in her tiny ovaries... the beginnings of your future grandchildren!

— Baby's fingernails and toenails are well-formed, and hair is growing on that little head.

## DAY 107

**15 WEEKS, 2 DAYS (15W2D)**

DATE:        /

### Recent changes

things to research
- ☐ ............................................
- ☐ ............................................
- ☐ ............................................

SLEEP:

APPETITE:

MOOD:

## 173 days until your due date

percentage remaining **61.8%**

**def·i·ni·tion**

**High-risk pregnancy:** This refers to a woman with pregnancy complications, due to maternal or fetal factors, or a combination thereof. High-risk pregnancies require more frequent prenatal checkups, and may mean additional monitoring, testing and treatment.

---

## DAY 108

**15 WEEKS, 3 DAYS (15W3D)**

DATE:        /

### This week I feel...

questions for my caregiver
- ☐ ............................................
- ☐ ............................................
- ☐ ............................................

SLEEP:

APPETITE:

MOOD:

## 172 DAYS UNTIL YOUR DUE DATE (ESTIMATED)

PERCENTAGE COMPLETED **38.6%**

*Notes*

In a few weeks, if you have an abdominal ultrasound, you will probably be asked to drink lots of water beforehand — and to hold it. By the time you get in the chair, it may feel like your bladder is going to pop. The idea is to use the bladder as a pillow to prop up the lower part of the uterus so the ultrasound tech can see your cervix and the lower regions of your uterus. Fortunately, you should only need it super-full for the first few minutes.

WEEK 1
WEEK 2
WEEK 3
WEEK 4
WEEK 5
WEEK 6
WEEK 7
WEEK 8
WEEK 9
WEEK 10
WEEK 11
WEEK 12
WEEK 13
WEEK 14
WEEK 15
WEEK 16
WEEK 17
WEEK 18
WEEK 19
WEEK 20
WEEK 21
WEEK 22
WEEK 23
WEEK 24
WEEK 25
WEEK 26
WEEK 27
WEEK 28
WEEK 29
WEEK 30
WEEK 31
WEEK 32
WEEK 33
WEEK 34
WEEK 35
WEEK 36
WEEK 37
WEEK 38
WEEK 39
WEEK 40
WEEK 41
WEEK 42

MONTH 1    MONTH 2    MONTH 3        MONTH 4        MONTH 5

DAYS 1-7
8-14
15-21
22-28
29-35
36-42
43-49
50-56
57-63
64-70
71-77
78-84
85-91
92-98
99-105
106-112
113-119
120-126
127-133
134-140
141-147
148-154
155-161
162-168
169-175
176-182
183-189
190-196
197-203
204-210
211-217
218-224
225-231
232-238
239-245
246-252
253-259
260-266
267-273
274-280
281-287
288-294

# DAY 109

## 15 WEEKS, 4 DAYS (15W4D)

DATE:          /

### Finally this happened

grateful for...
☐ ........................................
☐ ........................................
☐ ........................................

SLEEP:
APPETITE:
MOOD:

## 171 DAYS UNTIL YOUR DUE DATE (ESTIMATED)

### PERCENTAGE COMPLETED 38.9%

66 Let us make pregnancy
an occasion when we 99
appreciate our female bodies.

— Merete Leonhardt-Lupa

# DAY 110

## 15 WEEKS, 5 DAYS (15W5D)

DATE:          /

### Not very patient about...

to tell my partner
☐ ........................................
☐ ........................................
☐ ........................................

SLEEP:
APPETITE:
MOOD:

## 170 days until your due date (approximately)

### how far you have come 11/28

**ABOUT YOU**

If you have a low-risk pregnancy, have you considered having a home birth? According to a study reported in 2014 in the JOURNAL OF MIDWIFERY & WOMEN'S HEALTH, 97% of babies born at home were carried to full-term (average birth weight: 8 pounds); and of the 16,924 women, 94% had a vaginal birth, while the VBAC success rate was 87%. Just 11% of women intending to birth at home transferred to the hospital during labor.

DAY **111**

15 WEEKS, 6 DAYS (15W6D)

DATE:        /

## What I do differently now

to-do
- [ ] .........................................
- [ ] .........................................
- [ ] .........................................

SLEEP:
APPETITE:
MOOD:

**169** days until your due date *(estimated)*

percentage still to go **60.4%**

BABY NAMES

### BOYS IN EGYPT

Youssef, Ahmed, Mahmoud
Mustafa, Yassin, Taha, Khaled,
Hamza, Hassan, Karim, Tareq, Ali,
Omar, Halim, Selim

DAY **112**

16 WEEKS, 0 DAYS (16W0D)

DATE:        /

## The hardest thing so far

shopping wish list
- [ ] .........................................
- [ ] .........................................
- [ ] .........................................

SLEEP:
APPETITE:
MOOD:

**168** days until your due date *(thereabouts)*

fraction completed **2/5**

~A LITTLE NOTE TO THE FUTURE~

☐ WISH  ☐ PREDICTION  ☐ PRAYER  ☐ HOPE  ☐ REMINDER

WEEK 1
WEEK 2
WEEK 3
WEEK 4
WEEK 5
WEEK 6
WEEK 7
WEEK 8
WEEK 9
WEEK 10
WEEK 11
WEEK 12
WEEK 13
WEEK 14
WEEK 15
WEEK 16
WEEK 17
WEEK 18
WEEK 19
WEEK 20
WEEK 21
WEEK 22
WEEK 23
WEEK 24
WEEK 25
WEEK 26
WEEK 27
WEEK 28
WEEK 29
WEEK 30
WEEK 31
WEEK 32
WEEK 33
WEEK 34
WEEK 35
WEEK 36
WEEK 37
WEEK 38
WEEK 39
WEEK 40
WEEK 41
WEEK 42

**By the end of this month (week 20), your baby will be about as long as a banana!**

That means when measured from the top of his (very large) head to his (very tiny) bottom, he's about 6½ inches long — but if you go from crown to heel, he is closer to nine inches long. Your baby banana probably weighs about 6 to 8 ounces.

# MONTH 5

### WEEK 17, WEEK 18 WEEK 19 & WEEK 20

## How do you feel?

At the beginning of this month,
rate how you're feeling with a line, X or circle

 **ENERGY AMOUNT**

 **IMPATIENCE DEGREE**

 **EMOTIONAL INTENSITY**

 **GRUMPINESS GRADE**

 **SOCIABILITY SCALE**

 **LOVE+ROMANCE LEVEL**

 **FORGETFULNESS FACTOR**

 **GROWTH GAUGE**

Add a picture of yourself at 5 months here
Photos not your thing? Estimate your pregnancy size and
shape by drawing over the shadowed image below

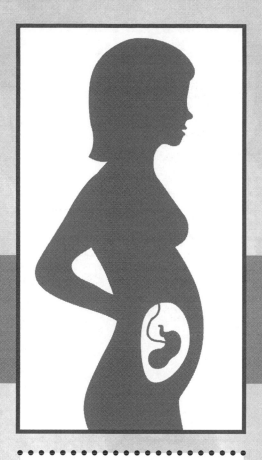

## One year from now
(assuming you give birth around 40 weeks)

Your baby will be about 8 months old!

### YOU & BABY

Weight gain:

Belly circumference:

Fundal height:

Baby's heart rate:

Baby's position:

### 5 WORDS FOR WHAT'S ON YOUR MIND RIGHT NOW

### notes

## START OF WEEK 17

**14** WEEKS SINCE CONCEPTION  :  WEEKS UNTIL YOUR DUE DATE **23**

(Dates are estimates only | Pregnancy is considered "term" at 37 to 42 weeks)

**WEEKLY CHART**
16 WEEKS PASSED & STARTING 17

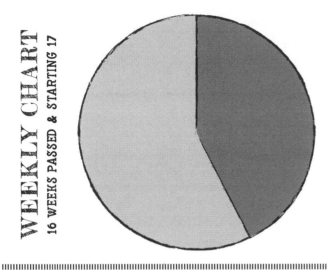

How big is baby now?

From crown to rump, baby is between 2.9 inches & 3.6 inches long (average=84.6mm)

(All measurements are approximate, and based on average fetal development)

## APPOINTMENTS & REMINDERS FOR THIS WEEK

_____  _____

_____  _____

_____  _____

{ ON MY MIND }

**DAY 113**

16 WEEKS, 1 DAY (16W1D)

DATE:          /

### 3 goals for this week

to-do
☐ .................................
☐ .................................
☐ .................................

SLEEP: ▭▬▬▬▬
APPETITE: ▭▬▬▬▬
MOOD: ▭▬▬▬▬

**167** DAYS UNTIL YOUR DUE DATE (ESTIMATED)

PERCENTAGE LEFT TO GO **59.6%**

**BABY TALK**

— When a baby is born at full-term, more than half of his weight will be fat!

— To that end, fat production starts this week, and will help keep your newborn warm while his internal thermostat adjusts to life outside the womb.

## DAY 114

**16 WEEKS, 2 DAYS (16W2D)**

DATE:　　/

### My life right now...

things to research
- [ ] .................................................
- [ ] .................................................
- [ ] .................................................

SLEEP:
APPETITE:
MOOD:

## 166 days until your due date

percentage completed **40.7%**

**def·i·ni·tion**

**Doula:** A professional labor assistant, usually a woman, who provides emotional, physical and sometimes spiritual support to the laboring mother. According to DONA International, studies have found that a doula's presence at birth can result in shorter labors with fewer complications, and reduces the mother's request for pain medication and/or epidurals. (Find out more at dona.org)

## DAY 115

**16 WEEKS, 3 DAYS (16W3D)**

DATE:　　/

### This week I feel...

questions for my caregiver
- [ ] .................................................
- [ ] .................................................
- [ ] .................................................

SLEEP:
APPETITE:
MOOD:

## 165 DAYS UNTIL YOUR DUE DATE (ESTIMATED)

[ each dark | line represents 5 days passed ]

**Notes**

What should you look for in maternity clothing? Experts agree that the most important thing is quality. Your pregnancy wardrobe won't be huge and everything will get regular wear, so make sure the clothes you buy are well-made. (You can resell them or pass on to a friend when you're done.)

TRIMESTER　　　THIRD TRIMESTER

WEEK 1
WEEK 2
WEEK 3
WEEK 4
WEEK 5
WEEK 6
WEEK 7
WEEK 8
WEEK 9
WEEK 10
WEEK 11
WEEK 12
WEEK 13
WEEK 14
WEEK 15
WEEK 16
WEEK 17
WEEK 18
WEEK 19
WEEK 20
WEEK 21
WEEK 22
WEEK 23
WEEK 24
WEEK 25
WEEK 26
WEEK 27
WEEK 28
WEEK 29
WEEK 30
WEEK 31
WEEK 32
WEEK 33
WEEK 34
WEEK 35
WEEK 36
WEEK 37
WEEK 38
WEEK 39
WEEK 40
WEEK 41
WEEK 42

## DAY 116

16 WEEKS, 4 DAYS (16W4D)

DATE:      /

### What makes me smile

grateful for...
- [ ] .............................................
- [ ] .............................................
- [ ] .............................................

SLEEP:
APPETITE:
MOOD:

**164** DAYS UNTIL YOUR DUE DATE (ESTIMATED)

PERCENTAGE COMPLETED **41.4%**

❝ Pregnancy is a process that invites you to surrender to the unseen force behind all life. ❞

*- Judy Ford*

## DAY 117

16 WEEKS, 5 DAYS (16W5D)

DATE:      /

### My reading list

to tell my partner
- [ ] .............................................
- [ ] .............................................
- [ ] .............................................

SLEEP:
APPETITE:
MOOD:

**163** days until your due date (approximately)

percentage remaining **58.2%**

**ABOUT YOU**

Pregnant women tend to delay the treatment of oral disease due to concerns for the baby's safety. However, as Homa Amini, DDS, said in an article in GENERAL DENTISTRY, routine dental treatment can be performed safely at any time during pregnancy. Just be sure your dentist knows that you're expecting.

## DAY 118

### 16 WEEKS, 6 DAYS (16W6D)

DATE: /

*A self-portrait*

to-do
- ☐ ............................................
- ☐ ............................................
- ☐ ............................................

SLEEP:

APPETITE:

MOOD:

**162** days until
your due date
(estimated)

percentage completed **42.1%**

BABY NAMES

### GIRLS IN COLOMBIA

*Mariana, Valentina, Isabella, Sofia, Valeria, María José, Gabriela, Sara, Salomé, Daniela*

## DAY 119

### 17 WEEKS, 0 DAYS (17W0D)

DATE: /

*Relationship changes*

shopping wish list
- ☐ ............................................
- ☐ ............................................
- ☐ ............................................

SLEEP:

APPETITE:

MOOD:

**161** days until
your due date
(thereabouts)

fraction left to go **23/40**

### ~ A LITTLE NOTE TO THE FUTURE ~

☐ WISH ☐ PREDICTION ☐ PRAYER ☐ HOPE ☐ REMINDER

WEEK 1
WEEK 2
WEEK 3
WEEK 4
WEEK 5
WEEK 6
WEEK 7
WEEK 8
WEEK 9
WEEK 10
WEEK 11
WEEK 12
WEEK 13
WEEK 14
WEEK 15
WEEK 16
WEEK 17
WEEK 18
WEEK 19
WEEK 20
WEEK 21
WEEK 22
WEEK 23
WEEK 24
WEEK 25
WEEK 26
WEEK 27
WEEK 28
WEEK 29
WEEK 30
WEEK 31
WEEK 32
WEEK 33
WEEK 34
WEEK 35
WEEK 36
WEEK 37
WEEK 38
WEEK 39
WEEK 40
WEEK 41
WEEK 42

DAYS 1-7
8-14
15-21
22-28
29-35
36-42
43-49
50-56
57-63
64-70
71-77
78-84
85-91
92-98
99-105
106-112
113-119
120-126
127-133
134-140
141-147
148-154
155-161
162-168
169-175
176-182
183-189
190-196
197-203
204-210
211-217
218-224
225-231
232-238
239-245
246-252
253-259
260-266
267-273
274-280
281-287
288-294

## START OF WEEK 18

**15** WEEKS SINCE CONCEPTION      WEEKS UNTIL YOUR DUE DATE **22**

(Dates are estimates only | Pregnancy is considered "term" at 37 to 42 weeks)

**WEEKLY CHART**
17 WEEKS PASSED & STARTING 18

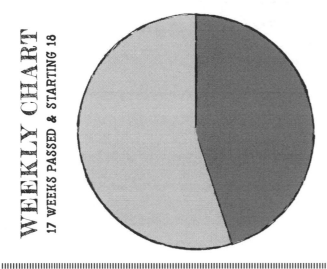

*How big is baby now?*

Weight: 2-1/2 to 4 ounces
Length: 4 to 5 inches (crown to rump)

(All measurements are approximate, and based on average fetal development)

### APPOINTMENTS & REMINDERS FOR THIS WEEK

_____  _____
_____  _____
_____  _____

{ ON MY MIND }

**DAY 120**

17 WEEKS, 1 DAY (17W1D)

DATE: _____ / _____

*3 wishes for this week*

to-do
☐ .......................................................
☐ .......................................................
☐ .......................................................

SLEEP:
APPETITE:
MOOD:

**160** DAYS UNTIL YOUR DUE DATE (ESTIMATED)

FRACTION COMPLETED **3/7**

**BABY TALK**

— Your baby is now starting to hear, and eyesight is forming — her eyes will soon be able to detect light and dark.
— He or she also continues to deposit heat-producing brown fat throughout his body.

## DAY 121

**17 WEEKS, 2 DAYS (17W2D)**

DATE:        /

### Recent changes

**things to research**
- ☐ ........................................
- ☐ ........................................
- ☐ ........................................

SLEEP:

APPETITE:

MOOD:

**159** days until your due date

percentage completed **43.2%**

**def·i·ni·tion**

**Pre-eclampsia:** High blood pressure during pregnancy is part of a complicated condition that arises rather suddenly 5 to 10 percent of the time in the latter half of pregnancy. The condition may also include protein in the urine and/or swelling of the face, hands and feet. (This is also called pregnancy-induced hypertension, or PIH.)

**TRIMESTER**

## DAY 122

**17 WEEKS, 3 DAYS (17W3D)**

DATE:        /

### This week I feel...

**questions for my caregiver**
- ☐ ........................................
- ☐ ........................................
- ☐ ........................................

SLEEP:

APPETITE:

MOOD:

**158** DAYS UNTIL YOUR DUE DATE (ESTIMATED)

PERCENTAGE LEFT TO GO **56.4%**

When you're scheduling your prenatal checkups, you might want to ask your healthcare provider's office staff what is the least busy time for exams. In a busy practice, schedules often get delayed late in the day, so first thing in the morning or right after lunch might be your best bets for quicker visits.

**THIRD TRIMESTER**

WEEK 1
WEEK 2
WEEK 3
WEEK 4
WEEK 5
WEEK 6
WEEK 7
WEEK 8
WEEK 9
WEEK 10
WEEK 11
WEEK 12
WEEK 13
WEEK 14
WEEK 15
WEEK 16
WEEK 17
WEEK 18
WEEK 19
WEEK 20
WEEK 21
WEEK 22
WEEK 23
WEEK 24
WEEK 25
WEEK 26
WEEK 27
WEEK 28
WEEK 29
WEEK 30
WEEK 31
WEEK 32
WEEK 33
WEEK 34
WEEK 35
WEEK 36
WEEK 37
WEEK 38
WEEK 39
WEEK 40
WEEK 41
WEEK 42

## DAY 123

17 WEEKS, 4 DAYS (17W4D)

DATE:          /

### On looking pregnant

grateful for...
- ☐ .....................................
- ☐ .....................................
- ☐ .....................................

SLEEP:
APPETITE:
MOOD:

**157** DAYS UNTIL YOUR DUE DATE (ESTIMATED)

PERCENTAGE COMPLETED **43.9%**

66 There is no other organ quite like the uterus. If men had such an organ, they would brag about it. So should we. 99
— Ina May Gaskin

## DAY 124

17 WEEKS, 5 DAYS (17W5D)

DATE:          /

### Maternity clothes I want

to tell my partner
- ☐ .....................................
- ☐ .....................................
- ☐ .....................................

SLEEP:
APPETITE:
MOOD:

**156** days until your due date (approximately)

percentage remaining **55.7%**

ABOUT YOU

By now, you're probably finally starting to believe that you really are pregnant. Whether it's the tiny bulge in your tummy that makes wearing your jeans impossible, or those first flutters that might feel like someone is tickling you from the inside, you can tell that things are definitely changing. It's about time, right?!

DAY **125**

17 WEEKS, 6 DAYS (17W6D)

DATE:        /

*I wish I'd known*

to-do
☐ ....................................
☐ ....................................
☐ ....................................

SLEEP:
APPETITE:
MOOD:

**155** days until
your due date
(estimated)

[ each dark | line represents 5 days passed ]

**BABY NAMES**

### GIRL NAMES FROM THE 1920S

Mary, Dorothy, Helen, Margaret,
Ruth, Virginia, Doris, Mildred,
Frances, Elizabeth, Evelyn, Anna,
Marie, Alice

DAY **126**

18 WEEKS, 0 DAYS (18W0D)

DATE:        /

*A sweet moment*

shopping wish list
☐ ....................................
☐ ....................................
☐ ....................................

SLEEP:
APPETITE:
MOOD:

**154** days until
your due date
(thereabouts)

fraction
left to go **11/20**

~ A LITTLE NOTE TO THE FUTURE ~
☐ WISH  ☐ PREDICTION  ☐ PRAYER  ☐ HOPE  ☐ REMINDER

WEEK 1
WEEK 2
WEEK 3
WEEK 4
WEEK 5
WEEK 6
WEEK 7
WEEK 8
WEEK 9
WEEK 10
WEEK 11
WEEK 12
WEEK 13
WEEK 14
WEEK 15
WEEK 16
WEEK 17
WEEK 18
WEEK 19
WEEK 20
WEEK 21
WEEK 22
WEEK 23
WEEK 24
WEEK 25
WEEK 26
WEEK 27
WEEK 28
WEEK 29
WEEK 30
WEEK 31
WEEK 32
WEEK 33
WEEK 34
WEEK 35
WEEK 36
WEEK 37
WEEK 38
WEEK 39
WEEK 40
WEEK 41
WEEK 42

## START OF WEEK 19

**16** WEEKS SINCE CONCEPTION : WEEKS UNTIL YOUR DUE DATE **21**

(Dates are estimates only | Pregnancy is considered "term" at 37 to 42 weeks)

**WEEKLY CHART**
**18 WEEKS PASSED & STARTING 19**

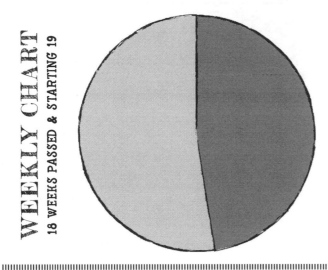

### How big is baby now?

Weight: 4 to 5 ounces
Length: 5-1/4 to 6 inches (crown to rump)

(All measurements are approximate, and based on average fetal development)

## APPOINTMENTS & REMINDERS FOR THIS WEEK

_____  _____
_____  _____
_____  _____
_____  _____

{ ON MY MIND }

---

## DAY 127

**18 WEEKS, 1 DAY (18W1D)**

DATE:          /

### 3 ideas for this week

to-do
☐ .........................................
☐ .........................................
☐ .........................................

SLEEP:
APPETITE:
MOOD:

## 153 DAYS UNTIL YOUR DUE DATE (ESTIMATED)

PERCENTAGE COMPLETED **45.3%**

**BABY TALK**

— Your baby's permanent tooth buds are now forming behind the primary teeth.
— His or her soft cartilage skeleton continues to grow harder each day.
— Your little one otherwise continues to grow, although not at the pace of the last few months.

DAYS 1-7
8-14
15-21
22-28
29-35
36-42
43-49
50-56
57-63
64-70
71-77
78-84
85-91
92-98
99-105
106-112
113-119
120-126
127-133
134-140
141-147
148-154
155-161
162-168
169-175
176-182
183-189
190-196
197-203
204-210
211-217
218-224
225-231
232-238
239-245
246-252
253-259
260-266
267-273
274-280
281-287
288-294

## DAY 128

**18 WEEKS, 2 DAYS (18W2D)**

DATE:        /

### My life right now...

things to research
- [ ] ....................................
- [ ] ....................................
- [ ] ....................................

SLEEP:
APPETITE:
MOOD:

## 152 days until your due date

*fraction remaining* **19/35**

**def·i·ni·tion**

**Melasma:** A patchy brownish discoloration some women get on the skin on the face, caused by pregnancy hormones causing an increased production of the pigment melanin. Also called "the mask of pregnancy" or chloasma, it usually disappears after delivery.

---

## DAY 129

**18 WEEKS, 3 DAYS (18W3D)**

DATE:        /

### This week I feel...

questions for my caregiver
- [ ] ....................................
- [ ] ....................................
- [ ] ....................................

SLEEP:
APPETITE:
MOOD:

## 151 DAYS UNTIL YOUR DUE DATE (ESTIMATED)

**PERCENTAGE LEFT TO GO** **53.9%**

*Notes*

When you're expecting, sometimes you need to sit on the sidelines a little more. There are a few fun things you shouldn't do when pregnant, such as riding on a roller coaster and/or other amusement park thrill rides, downhill skiing and water-skiing, trampolining, trapeze work, surfing, body surfing, and diving. When in doubt about any activity, ask your caregiver if it's safe.

WEEK 1
WEEK 2
WEEK 3
WEEK 4
WEEK 5
WEEK 6
WEEK 7
WEEK 8
WEEK 9
WEEK 10
WEEK 11
WEEK 12
WEEK 13
WEEK 14
WEEK 15
WEEK 16
WEEK 17
WEEK 18
WEEK 19
WEEK 20
WEEK 21
WEEK 22
WEEK 23
WEEK 24
WEEK 25
WEEK 26
WEEK 27
WEEK 28
WEEK 29
WEEK 30
WEEK 31
WEEK 32
WEEK 33
WEEK 34
WEEK 35
WEEK 36
WEEK 37
WEEK 38
WEEK 39
WEEK 40
WEEK 41
WEEK 42

MONTH 1          MONTH 2          MONTH 3          MONTH 4          MONTH 5

DAYS 1-7
8-14
15-21
22-28
29-35
36-42
43-49
50-56
57-63
64-70
71-77
78-84
85-91
92-98
99-105
106-112
113-119
120-126
127-133
134-140
141-147
148-154
155-161
162-168
169-175
176-182
183-189
190-196
197-203
204-210
211-217
218-224
225-231
232-238
239-245
246-252
253-259
260-266
267-273
274-280
281-287
288-294

## DAY 130

**18 WEEKS, 4 DAYS (18W4D)**

DATE:        /

### How I relax

grateful for...
- ☐ .....................................
- ☐ .....................................
- ☐ .....................................

SLEEP:
APPETITE:
MOOD:

## 150

**DAYS UNTIL YOUR DUE DATE**
(ESTIMATED)

**FRACTION COMPLETED** 13/28

66 *Babies are always more trouble than you thought — and more wonderful.* 99

*- Charles Osgood*

## DAY 131

**18 WEEKS, 5 DAYS (18W5D)**

DATE:        /

### What I wonder about

to tell my partner
- ☐ .....................................
- ☐ .....................................
- ☐ .....................................

SLEEP:
APPETITE:
MOOD:

## 149

*days until your due date*
(approximately)

*how far you have come* 46.8%

**ABOUT YOU**

Many women underestimate the time they will need and/or want off for maternity leave. A good basic rule is to imagine about how much time you think you will need — then double it. Six weeks is the minimum recommended leave, but that really only covers your physical recovery from childbirth. You will probably want a bit more time to get to know your baby, and to give yourself space to adjust to your whole new life.

DAY **132**

18 WEEKS, 6 DAYS (18W6D)

DATE:        /

## I'm impatient to...

to-do
- ☐ ....................................
- ☐ ....................................
- ☐ ....................................

SLEEP:
APPETITE:
MOOD:

**148** days until
your due date
(estimated)

percentage remaining **52.8%**

### GIRLS IN IRAN

**BABY NAMES**

Fatemeh, Zahra, Setayesh, Hasti,
Zeinab, Nazanin-Zahra, Reihaneh,
Maryam, Mobina, Narges

---

DAY **133**

19 WEEKS, 0 DAYS (19W0D)

DATE:        /

## Advice I have received

shopping wish list
- ☐ ....................................
- ☐ ....................................
- ☐ ....................................

SLEEP:
APPETITE:
MOOD:

**147** days until
your due date
(thereabouts)

fraction remaining **21/40**

~ A LITTLE NOTE TO THE FUTURE ~
☐ WISH  ☐ PREDICTION  ☐ PRAYER  ☐ HOPE  ☐ REMINDER

WEEK 1
WEEK 2
WEEK 3
WEEK 4
WEEK 5
WEEK 6
WEEK 7
WEEK 8
WEEK 9
WEEK 10
WEEK 11
WEEK 12
WEEK 13
WEEK 14
WEEK 15
WEEK 16
WEEK 17
WEEK 18
WEEK 19
WEEK 20
WEEK 21
WEEK 22
WEEK 23
WEEK 24
WEEK 25
WEEK 26
WEEK 27
WEEK 28
WEEK 29
WEEK 30
WEEK 31
WEEK 32
WEEK 33
WEEK 34
WEEK 35
WEEK 36
WEEK 37
WEEK 38
WEEK 39
WEEK 40
WEEK 41
WEEK 42

TRIMESTER          THIRD TRIMESTER

## START OF WEEK 20

**17** WEEKS SINCE CONCEPTION    WEEKS UNTIL YOUR DUE DATE **20**

(Dates are estimates only | Pregnancy is considered "term" at 37 to 42 weeks)

### WEEKLY CHART
19 WEEKS PASSED & STARTING 20

**HALFWAY THERE!**

### How big is baby now?

Weight: 5 to 7 ounces
Length: 5-1/2 to 6-1/2 inches (crown to rump)

(All measurements are approximate, and based on average fetal development)

### APPOINTMENTS & REMINDERS FOR THIS WEEK

_____  _____

_____  _____

_____  _____  Start thinking about birth plan (see ideas @ end of book)

### { ON MY MIND }

---

## DAY 134

19 WEEKS, 1 DAY (19W1D)

DATE:     /

### 3 wishes for this week

to-do
☐ ...........................
☐ ...........................
☐ ...........................

SLEEP: 😖 ▭▭▭▭▭ 😴
APPETITE: 😋 ▭▭▭▭▭ 🤢
MOOD: 🙂 ▭▭▭▭▭ 😣

**146** DAYS UNTIL YOUR DUE DATE (ESTIMATED)

PERCENTAGE COMPLETED **47.9%**

### BABY TALK

— Baby is now beginning to form vernix caseosa, a waxy white substance that protects his or her skin from amniotic fluid.

— By birth, most of the vernix will probably be gone, except for some in folds and creases (like in the neck, diaper area and underarms).

## DAY 135

**19 WEEKS, 2 DAYS (19W2D)**

DATE:     /

### Recent changes

things to research

☐ ......................
☐ ......................
☐ ......................

SLEEP: ▭
APPETITE: ▭
MOOD: ▭

# 145 *days until your due date*

[ each dark | line represents 5 days passed ]

||||||||||||||||||||||||||||||||||||||||||||||||||||

**def·i·ni·tion**

**Braxton-Hicks contractions:** A usually painless tightening of the uterus. Occasional uterine contractions occur throughout pregnancy, but have no effect on the cervix. Contractions during the ninth month still tend to be brief, irregular, and imperceptible to the mom-to-be, but they are more frequent and coordinated than earlier ones.

---

## DAY 136

**19 WEEKS, 3 DAYS (19W3D)**

DATE:     /

### This week I feel...

questions for my caregiver

☐ ......................
☐ ......................
☐ ......................

SLEEP: ▭
APPETITE: ▭
MOOD: ▭

# 144 DAYS UNTIL YOUR DUE DATE (ESTIMATED)

**FRACTION COMPLETED** 17/35

**Notes**

Kangaroo mother care – in which a premature baby stays in skin-to-skin contact with a parent's chest – has lasting positive impact on brain development, according to Canadian research from 2012. Very premature infants who benefited from this technique had better brain functioning in adolescence than did preemies placed in incubators.

---

WEEK 1
WEEK 2
WEEK 3
WEEK 4
WEEK 5
WEEK 6
WEEK 7
WEEK 8
WEEK 9
WEEK 10
WEEK 11
WEEK 12
WEEK 13
WEEK 14
WEEK 15
WEEK 16
WEEK 17
WEEK 18
WEEK 19
WEEK 20
WEEK 21
WEEK 22
WEEK 23
WEEK 24
WEEK 25
WEEK 26
WEEK 27
WEEK 28
WEEK 29
WEEK 30
WEEK 31
WEEK 32
WEEK 33
WEEK 34
WEEK 35
WEEK 36
WEEK 37
WEEK 38
WEEK 39
WEEK 40
WEEK 41
WEEK 42

# DAY 137

### 19 WEEKS, 4 DAYS (19W4D)

**DATE:** /

## A little stressed about...

grateful for...
- ☐ ..................................................
- ☐ ..................................................
- ☐ ..................................................

**SLEEP:**
**APPETITE:**
**MOOD:**

# 143
### DAYS UNTIL YOUR DUE DATE (ESTIMATED)

**PERCENTAGE COMPLETED** **48.9%**

66 We can't understand when we're pregnant, or when our siblings are expecting, how profound it is to have a shared history with a younger generation: blood, genes, humor. 99
— Anne Lamott

---

# DAY 138

### 19 WEEKS, 5 DAYS (19W5D)

**DATE:** /

## Best things I have read

to tell my partner
- ☐ ..................................................
- ☐ ..................................................
- ☐ ..................................................

**SLEEP:**
**APPETITE:**
**MOOD:**

# 142
### days until your due date (approximately)

**percentage remaining** **50.7%**

**ABOUT YOU**

If you can, try making several of your prenatal appointments in advance, rather than waiting until your appointment or a week or two before. The sooner you schedule these checkups, the better shot you have at getting the most convenient time slot for you. You can also find out about booking any ultrasound exam ahead of time, too. (Keep track of all your appointments at the back of this book!)

DAYS 1-7
8-14
15-21
22-28
29-35
36-42
43-49
50-56
57-63
64-70
71-77
78-84
85-91
92-98
99-105
106-112
113-119
120-126
127-133
134-140
141-147
148-154
155-161
162-168
169-175
176-182
183-189
190-196
197-203
204-210
211-217
218-224
225-231
232-238
239-245
246-252
253-259
260-266
267-273
274-280
281-287
288-294

DAY **139**

19 WEEKS, 6 DAYS (19W6D)

DATE:        /

*What wears me out*

to-do
- ☐ ...........................
- ☐ ...........................
- ☐ ...........................

SLEEP:
APPETITE:
MOOD:

**141** days until
your due date
(estimated)

You're almost halfway through!

BOYS IN BRAZIL

BABY NAMES

*Miguel, Davi, Arthur, Pedro, Gabriel, Bernardo, Lucas, Matheus, Rafael, Heitor*

DAY **140**

20 WEEKS, 0 DAYS (20W0D)

DATE:        /

*Halfway there!*

shopping wish list
- ☐ ...........................
- ☐ ...........................
- ☐ ...........................

SLEEP:
APPETITE:
MOOD:

**140** days until
your due date
(thereabouts)

percentage left to go **50%**

~ A LITTLE NOTE TO THE FUTURE ~

☐ WISH   ☐ PREDICTION   ☐ PRAYER   ☐ HOPE   ☐ REMINDER

WEEK 1
WEEK 2
WEEK 3
WEEK 4
WEEK 5
WEEK 6
WEEK 7
WEEK 8
WEEK 9
WEEK 10
WEEK 11
WEEK 12
WEEK 13
WEEK 14
WEEK 15
WEEK 16
WEEK 17
WEEK 18
WEEK 19
WEEK 20
WEEK 21
WEEK 22
WEEK 23
WEEK 24
WEEK 25
WEEK 26
WEEK 27
WEEK 28
WEEK 29
WEEK 30
WEEK 31
WEEK 32
WEEK 33
WEEK 34
WEEK 35
WEEK 36
WEEK 37
WEEK 38
WEEK 39
WEEK 40
WEEK 41
WEEK 42

**By the end of this month (week 24), your baby will be about as tall as a vintage vinyl record!**

When measured from the top of her head to her heel, she's somewhere around 11 to 13 inches — with 12" being the diameter of a dinner plate. And while that little person is about a foot long, she weighs only a pound or so.

# MONTH 6

## How do you feel?

At the beginning of this month,
rate how you're feeling with a line, X or circle

 **ENERGY AMOUNT**

**IMPATIENCE DEGREE**

**EMOTIONAL INTENSITY**

**GRUMPINESS GRADE**

**SOCIABILITY SCALE**

**LOVE+ROMANCE LEVEL**

**FORGETFULNESS FACTOR**

**GROWTH GAUGE**

Add a picture of yourself at 6 months here
Photos not your thing? Estimate your pregnancy size and shape by drawing over the shadowed image below

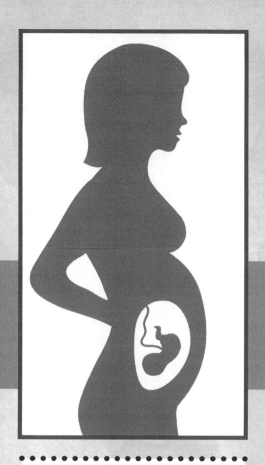

## One year from now
(assuming you give birth around 40 weeks)

Your baby will be
about 9 months old!

### YOU & BABY

Weight gain:

Belly circumference:

Fundal height:

Baby's heart rate:

Baby's position:

### 6 WORDS FOR WHAT'S ON YOUR MIND RIGHT NOW

## notes

1. Craving some fish? To limit your exposure to mercury, choose salmon, catfish and pollock, and limit white tuna to 6 ounces a week.
2. During pregnancy, you can be at increased risk for developing carpal tunnel syndrome. Use wrist rests to while typing, keep good posture, and drink plenty of fluids to help prevent it.
3. The NHTSA says that expectant moms should always wear seat belts (secured below your belly, snug across your hips and pelvic bone) and leave the air bags turned on.

MONTH 1   MONTH 2   MONTH 3   MONTH 4   MONTH 5

DAYS 1-7
8-14
15-21
22-28
29-35
36-42
43-49
50-56
57-63
64-70
71-77
78-84
85-91
92-98
99-106
108-112
113-119
120-126
127-133
134-140
141-147
148-154
155-161
162-168
169-175
176-182
183-189
190-196
197-203
204-210
211-217
218-224
225-231
232-238
239-245
246-252
253-259
260-266
267-273
274-280
281-287
288-294

## START OF **WEEK 21**

**18** WEEKS SINCE CONCEPTION : WEEKS UNTIL YOUR DUE DATE **19**

(Dates are estimates only | Pregnancy is considered "term" at 37 to 42 weeks)

### WEEKLY CHART
**20 WEEKS PASSED & STARTING 21**

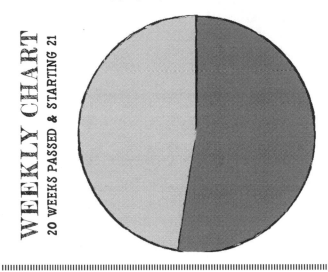

 *How big is baby now?*

Weight: 6 to 8 ounces
Length: 6 to 7 inches (crown to rump)

(All measurements are approximate, and based on average fetal development)

## APPOINTMENTS & REMINDERS FOR THIS WEEK

_____  _____
_____  _____
_____  _____

{ ON MY MIND }

---

### DAY **141**

**20 WEEKS, 1 DAY (20W1D)**

DATE: _____ / _____

*3 goals for this week*

to-do
☐ ...................................................
☐ ...................................................
☐ ...................................................

SLEEP:
APPETITE:
MOOD:

**139** DAYS UNTIL YOUR DUE DATE (ESTIMATED)

PERCENTAGE COMPLETED **50.4%**

- - - - - - - - - - - - - - - - - - - - - -

### BABY TALK

— Your baby is starting to drink the amniotic fluid, and his digestive system is mature enough to absorb nutrients.
— Not only is that mini person starting to drink and taste, but all of his or her sensory systems are maturing.

DAY **142**

20 WEEKS, 2 DAYS (20W2D)

DATE:        /

## My life right now...

WEEK 1
WEEK 2
WEEK 3
WEEK 4
WEEK 5
WEEK 6
WEEK 7
WEEK 8
WEEK 9
WEEK 10
WEEK 11
WEEK 12
WEEK 13
WEEK 14
WEEK 15
WEEK 16
WEEK 17
WEEK 18
WEEK 19
WEEK 20
WEEK 21
WEEK 22
WEEK 23
WEEK 24
WEEK 25
WEEK 26
WEEK 27
WEEK 28
WEEK 29
WEEK 30
WEEK 31
WEEK 32
WEEK 33
WEEK 34
WEEK 35
WEEK 36
WEEK 37
WEEK 38
WEEK 39
WEEK 40
WEEK 41
WEEK 42

**things to research**
- [ ] ....................
- [ ] ....................
- [ ] ....................

SLEEP: ▭▭▭▭▭▭▭
APPETITE: ▭▭▭▭▭▭▭
MOOD: ▭▭▭▭▭▭▭

**138** *days until your due date*

*percentage remaining* **49.3%**

**def·i·ni·tion**

**Round ligaments:** Ligaments that run along both sides of the uterus, connecting it to the groin. They stretch during pregnancy (especially during the second trimester), and as the pressure from the uterus grows, you may feel a pulling pain or cramping sensation. Support your uterus with pillows when in bed, and consider using a maternity belt or girdle.

TRIMESTER

---

DAY **143**

20 WEEKS, 3 DAYS (20W3D)

DATE:        /

## This week I feel...

**questions for my caregiver**
- [ ] ....................
- [ ] ....................
- [ ] ....................

SLEEP: ▭▭▭▭▭▭▭
APPETITE: ▭▭▭▭▭▭▭
MOOD: ▭▭▭▭▭▭▭

**137** DAYS UNTIL YOUR DUE DATE (ESTIMATED)

PERCENTAGE COMPLETED **51.1%**

*Notes*

When shopping for maternity wear, choose as many easy-care items as you can — things that are machine washable and, ideally, need no ironing. (Especially when you have fewer clothing options, you don't want to have half of your wardrobe out at the dry cleaner... or in a pile waiting for you to hand-wash.)

THIRD TRIMESTER

MONTH 1    MONTH 2    MONTH 3    MONTH 4    MONTH 5

DAYS 1-7
8-14
15-21
22-28
29-35
36-42
43-49
50-56
57-63
64-70
71-77
78-84
85-91
92-98
99-105
106-112
113-119
120-126
127-133
134-140
141-147
148-154
155-161
162-168
169-175
176-182
183-189
190-196
197-203
204-210
211-217
218-224
225-231
232-238
239-245
246-252
253-259
260-266
267-273
274-280
281-287
288-294

# DAY 144

## 20 WEEKS, 4 DAYS (20W4D)

DATE:        /

### Finally! 20 weeks

grateful for...
- [ ] ....................................
- [ ] ....................................
- [ ] ....................................

SLEEP: ▱▱▱▱▱▱▱

APPETITE: ▱▱▱▱▱▱▱

MOOD: ▱▱▱▱▱▱▱

# 136 DAYS UNTIL YOUR DUE DATE (ESTIMATED)

FRACTION COMPLETED 18/35

66 For far too many, pregnancy and birth
is still something that happens to them 99
rather than something they set out
consciously and joyfully to do themselves.
- Sheila Kitzinger

---

# DAY 145

## 20 WEEKS, 5 DAYS (20W5D)

DATE:        /

### Baby stuff I have

to tell my partner
- [ ] ....................................
- [ ] ....................................
- [ ] ....................................

SLEEP: ▱▱▱▱▱▱▱

APPETITE: ▱▱▱▱▱▱▱

MOOD: ▱▱▱▱▱▱▱

# 135 days until your due date (approximately)

[ each dark | line represents 5 days passed ]

ABOUT YOU — One of the tastiest medical studies ever evaluated the impact of high-flavanol chocolate on pregnancy. "This study indicates that chocolate could have a positive impact on placenta and fetal growth and development, and that chocolate's effects are not solely and directly due to flavanol content," said researcher Emmanuel Bujold, MD of the Université Laval Québec City, Canada. So now you know what's for dessert tonight!

DAY 146

20 WEEKS, 6 DAYS (20W6D)

DATE: /

*Ultrasound results*

to-do
- ☐ ..........................
- ☐ ..........................
- ☐ ..........................

SLEEP:
APPETITE:
MOOD:

**134** days until your due date (estimated)

percentage completed **52.1%**

BABY NAMES

## GIRLS IN PORTUGAL

*Sofia, Leonor, Matilde, Beatriz, Inês, Maria, Carolina, Mariana, Filipa, Margarida*

DAY 147

21 WEEKS, 0 DAYS (21W0D)

DATE: /

*A moment of zen*

shopping wish list
- ☐ ..........................
- ☐ ..........................
- ☐ ..........................

SLEEP:
APPETITE:
MOOD:

**133** days until your due date (thereabouts)

percentage left to go **47.5%**

~A LITTLE NOTE TO THE FUTURE~

☐ WISH　☐ PREDICTION　☐ PRAYER　☐ HOPE　☐ REMINDER

TRIMESTER　　　THIRD TRIMESTER

WEEK 1
WEEK 2
WEEK 3
WEEK 4
WEEK 5
WEEK 6
WEEK 7
WEEK 8
WEEK 9
WEEK 10
WEEK 11
WEEK 12
WEEK 13
WEEK 14
WEEK 15
WEEK 16
WEEK 17
WEEK 18
WEEK 19
WEEK 20
WEEK 21
WEEK 22
WEEK 23
WEEK 24
WEEK 25
WEEK 26
WEEK 27
WEEK 28
WEEK 29
WEEK 30
WEEK 31
WEEK 32
WEEK 33
WEEK 34
WEEK 35
WEEK 36
WEEK 37
WEEK 38
WEEK 39
WEEK 40
WEEK 41
WEEK 42

## START OF WEEK 22

**19** WEEKS SINCE CONCEPTION ⁞ WEEKS UNTIL YOUR DUE DATE **18**

(Dates are estimates only | Pregnancy is considered "term" at 37 to 42 weeks)

### WEEKLY CHART
21 WEEKS PASSED & STARTING 22

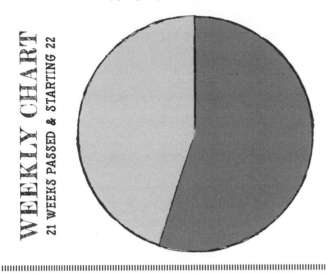

*How big is baby now?*

Weight: 9 to 11 ounces
Length: 6 to 7-1/2 inches (crown to rump)

(All measurements are approximate, and based on average fetal development)

### APPOINTMENTS & REMINDERS FOR THIS WEEK

—————  ———————
—————  ———————
—————  ———————
—————  ———————

{ ON MY MIND }

---

## DAY **148**
**21 WEEKS, 1 DAY (21W1D)**

DATE:        /

*3 wishes for this week*

to-do
☐ ...........................................
☐ ...........................................
☐ ...........................................

SLEEP:
APPETITE:
MOOD:

**132** DAYS UNTIL YOUR DUE DATE (ESTIMATED)

PERCENTAGE COMPLETED **52.9%**

### BABY TALK
— Hair is beginning to appear on baby's head.
— More fine hair, called lanugo, is forming all over his body.
— Your baby's fingernails have now reached the tips of his tiny fingers.

## DAY 149

**21 WEEKS, 2 DAYS (21W2D)**

DATE:        /

### Recent changes

things to research
- [ ] ......................................
- [ ] ......................................
- [ ] ......................................

SLEEP:
APPETITE:
MOOD:

## 131 days until your due date

percentage remaining **46.7%**

**def·i·ni·tion**

**Breastfeeding:** The act of feeding your baby the milk created by your body, just for him or her. A nursing baby suckles on the areola (pigmented part around the nipple) on the breast to get the milk. In the days right after birth, breasts produce small amounts of colostrum, a sticky clear liquid with vital nutrients. This is all your baby needs at first. Mature milk arrives a few days after birth.

TRIMESTER

---

## DAY 150

**21 WEEKS, 3 DAYS (21W3D)**

DATE:        /

### This week I feel...

questions for my caregiver
- [ ] ......................................
- [ ] ......................................
- [ ] ......................................

SLEEP:
APPETITE:
MOOD:

## 130 DAYS UNTIL YOUR DUE DATE (ESTIMATED)

**FRACTION COMPLETED** 15/28

Have you considered hiring a doula for your birth? According to a 2013 study, expectant moms matched with a doula — a trained birth companion — were two times less likely to experience a birth complication involving themselves or their baby, and significantly more likely to initiate breastfeeding.

THIRD TRIMESTER

WEEK 1
WEEK 2
WEEK 3
WEEK 4
WEEK 5
WEEK 6
WEEK 7
WEEK 8
WEEK 9
WEEK 10
WEEK 11
WEEK 12
WEEK 13
WEEK 14
WEEK 15
WEEK 16
WEEK 17
WEEK 18
WEEK 19
WEEK 20
WEEK 21
WEEK 22
WEEK 23
WEEK 24
WEEK 25
WEEK 26
WEEK 27
WEEK 28
WEEK 29
WEEK 30
WEEK 31
WEEK 32
WEEK 33
WEEK 34
WEEK 35
WEEK 36
WEEK 37
WEEK 38
WEEK 39
WEEK 40
WEEK 41
WEEK 42

## DAY 151

21 WEEKS, 4 DAYS (21W4D)

DATE: /

### So grateful for...

grateful for...
☐ ....................
☐ ....................
☐ ....................

SLEEP:
APPETITE:
MOOD:

# 129 DAYS UNTIL YOUR DUE DATE (ESTIMATED)

## PERCENTAGE COMPLETED 53.9%

> 66 It's not all going to be rainbows and butterflies and joy... It can vary from feeling nothing, feeling scared, feeling stressed, to the pure joy of holding your newborn in your arms. - Iffath Hoskins, MD 99

## DAY 152

21 WEEKS, 5 DAYS (21W5D)

DATE: /

### The mom I want to be

to tell my partner
☐ ....................
☐ ....................
☐ ....................

SLEEP:
APPETITE:
MOOD:

# 128 days until your due date

## percentage remaining 45.7%

**ABOUT YOU**

Something interesting about pregnancy weight gain: Boys may be more likely to survive in utero when expectant moms gain enough weight. Kristen Navara, a reproductive endocrinologist at the University of Georgia, analyzed data on 26 million pregnancies.

She wrote in a 2014 journal article, "The correlation was a near perfect relationship where the proportion of males rose with the number of pounds women gained during gestation."

## DAY 153

21 WEEKS, 6 DAYS (21W6D)

DATE:        /

### This is a little annoying

to-do
- ☐ .............................................
- ☐ .............................................
- ☐ .............................................

SLEEP:
APPETITE:
MOOD:

## 127 days until your due date (estimated)

percentage completed **54.6%**

**BABY NAMES**

### BOYS IN PAKISTAN

Mohammad, Ali, Hussain, Omar, Bilal, Usman, Zahid, Shahid, Saqib, Nomaan

## DAY 154

22 WEEKS, 0 DAYS (22W0D)

DATE:        /

### Favorite food & drink

shopping wish list
- ☐ .............................................
- ☐ .............................................
- ☐ .............................................

SLEEP:
APPETITE:
MOOD:

## 126 days until your due date (thereabouts)

fraction completed **11/20**

~A LITTLE NOTE TO THE FUTURE~

☐ WISH  ☐ PREDICTION  ☐ PRAYER  ☐ HOPE  ☐ REMINDER

WEEK 1
WEEK 2
WEEK 3
WEEK 4
WEEK 5
WEEK 6
WEEK 7
WEEK 8
WEEK 9
WEEK 10
WEEK 11
WEEK 12
WEEK 13
WEEK 14
WEEK 15
WEEK 16
WEEK 17
WEEK 18
WEEK 19
WEEK 20
WEEK 21
WEEK 22
WEEK 23
WEEK 24
WEEK 25
WEEK 26
WEEK 27
WEEK 28
WEEK 29
WEEK 30
WEEK 31
WEEK 32
WEEK 33
WEEK 34
WEEK 35
WEEK 36
WEEK 37
WEEK 38
WEEK 39
WEEK 40
WEEK 41
WEEK 42

# START OF WEEK 23

**20** WEEKS SINCE CONCEPTION : WEEKS UNTIL YOUR DUE DATE **17**

(Dates are estimates only | Pregnancy is considered "term" at 37 to 42 weeks)

## WEEKLY CHART
### 22 WEEKS PASSED & STARTING 23

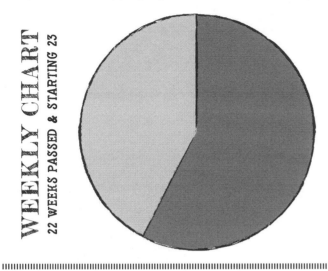

*How big is baby now?*

Weight: 11 to 16 ounces
Length: 10 to 11 inches (head to heel)

(All measurements are approximate, and based on average fetal development)

## APPOINTMENTS & REMINDERS FOR THIS WEEK

_____  _____
_____  _____
_____  _____

*See nursery planning & baby gear checklists @ end of book*

## { ON MY MIND }

## DAY 155

**22 WEEKS, 1 DAY (22W1D)**

DATE:        /

*3 goals for this week*

to-do
☐ ......................................
☐ ......................................
☐ ......................................

SLEEP: _____
APPETITE: _____
MOOD: _____

**125** DAYS UNTIL YOUR DUE DATE (ESTIMATED)

FRACTION COMPLETED **31/56**

## BABY TALK

— You are starting to share immune system antibodies with the baby, which will help protect him or her from illness during the first months.

— The middle ear bones are also forming, meaning that your child will soon be able to hear your voice and your heartbeat.

## DAY 156

22 WEEKS, 2 DAYS (22W2D)

DATE:    /

### My life right now...

**things to research**
- ☐ ..................................................
- ☐ ..................................................
- ☐ ..................................................

SLEEP:
APPETITE:
MOOD:

**124** *days until your due date*

*percentage left to go* **44.3%**

**def·i·ni·tion**

**Couvade:** A "sympathetic pregnancy" (or false pregnancy), usually experienced by the partner/father. From the French term for "to hatch," sometimes the partner experiences symptoms such as morning sickness, weight gain, fatigue and other signs of pregnancy. According to some studies, couvade *may* be an expression of anxiety, identification with the baby, ambivalence about impending parenthood, or caused by certain other psychological stresses.

TRIMESTER

---

## DAY 157

22 WEEKS, 3 DAYS (22W3D)

DATE:    /

### This week I feel...

**questions for my caregiver**
- ☐ ..................................................
- ☐ ..................................................
- ☐ ..................................................

SLEEP:
APPETITE:
MOOD:

**123** **DAYS UNTIL YOUR DUE DATE (ESTIMATED)**

**PERCENTAGE COMPLETED 56.1%**

**Notes**

If you're going to stand for a long time, skip the high heels and go for low-heeled shoes. "Lower heels will provide you with greater stability during a time when newly-gained weight might throw off your balance," notes the American Podiatric Medical Association (APMA). Also, to ease strain on your lower back, try placing one foot on a footstool, switching feet from time to time.

THIRD TRIMESTER

WEEK 1
WEEK 2
WEEK 3
WEEK 4
WEEK 5
WEEK 6
WEEK 7
WEEK 8
WEEK 9
WEEK 10
WEEK 11
WEEK 12
WEEK 13
WEEK 14
WEEK 15
WEEK 16
WEEK 17
WEEK 18
WEEK 19
WEEK 20
WEEK 21
WEEK 22
WEEK 23
WEEK 24
WEEK 25
WEEK 26
WEEK 27
WEEK 28
WEEK 29
WEEK 30
WEEK 31
WEEK 32
WEEK 33
WEEK 34
WEEK 35
WEEK 36
WEEK 37
WEEK 38
WEEK 39
WEEK 40
WEEK 41
WEEK 42

## DAY 158

**22 WEEKS, 4 DAYS (22W4D)**

DATE: 　　/

### Friends tell me

grateful for...
- [ ] .................................................
- [ ] .................................................
- [ ] .................................................

SLEEP:
APPETITE:
MOOD:

# 122 DAYS UNTIL YOUR DUE DATE (ESTIMATED)

PERCENTAGE COMPLETED **56.4%**

66 When you moved, I felt squeezed with a wild infatuation and protectiveness. We are one. Nothing, not even death, can change that. 99
— Suzanne Finnamore

## DAY 159

**22 WEEKS, 5 DAYS (22W5D)**

DATE: 　　/

### One year from now...

to tell my partner
- [ ] .................................................
- [ ] .................................................
- [ ] .................................................

SLEEP:
APPETITE:
MOOD:

# 121 days until your due date

percentage remaining **43.2%**

**ABOUT YOU**

"The purpose of labor is NOT the creation of an opening or a hole," says midwife and childbirth educator Carla Hartley of TrustBirth.com. "The purpose of labor contractions and retractions is to BUILD the fundus [top of the uterine muscle], which will, when it is ready, EJECT the baby, like a piston. Without a nice thick fundus there is no power to get baby out...The cervix is pulled up as a result of the building of the fundus."

DAYS 1-7
8-14
15-21
22-28
29-35
36-42
43-49
50-56
57-63
64-70
71-77
78-84
85-91
92-98
99-105
106-112
113-119
120-126
127-133
134-140
141-147
148-154
155-161
162-168
169-175
176-182
183-189
190-196
197-203
204-210
211-217
218-224
225-231
232-238
239-245
246-252
253-259
260-266
267-273
274-280
281-287
288-294

## DAY 160

### 22 WEEKS, 6 DAYS (22W6D)

DATE:        /

### About my doctor/midwife

to-do
- [ ] ................................................
- [ ] ................................................
- [ ] ................................................

SLEEP:
APPETITE:
MOOD:

## 120
days until
your due date
(estimated)

fraction
completed   4/7

### GIRLS IN ISRAEL

BABY NAMES

Noa, Tamar, Shira, Maya,
Yael, Adele, Talia, Avigail,
Ayala, Sarah

---

## DAY 161

### 23 WEEKS, 0 DAYS (23W0D)

DATE:        /

### What makes me weepy

shopping wish list
- [ ] ................................................
- [ ] ................................................
- [ ] ................................................

SLEEP:
APPETITE:
MOOD:

## 119
days until
your due date
(thereabouts)

percentage
completed   57.5%

### ~ A LITTLE NOTE TO THE FUTURE ~

☐ WISH  ☐ PREDICTION  ☐ PRAYER  ☐ HOPE  ☐ REMINDER

WEEK 1
WEEK 2
WEEK 3
WEEK 4
WEEK 5
WEEK 6
WEEK 7
WEEK 8
WEEK 9
WEEK 10
WEEK 11
WEEK 12
WEEK 13
WEEK 14
WEEK 15
WEEK 16
WEEK 17
WEEK 18
WEEK 19
WEEK 20
WEEK 21
WEEK 22
WEEK 23
WEEK 24
WEEK 25
WEEK 26
WEEK 27
WEEK 28
WEEK 29
WEEK 30
WEEK 31
WEEK 32
WEEK 33
WEEK 34
WEEK 35
WEEK 36
WEEK 37
WEEK 38
WEEK 39
WEEK 40
WEEK 41
WEEK 42

MONTH 1    MONTH 2    MONTH 3    MONTH 4    MONTH 5

DAYS 1-7
8-14
15-21
22-28
29-35
36-42
43-49
50-56
57-63
64-70
71-77
78-84
85-91
92-98
99-105
106-112
113-119
120-126
127-133
134-140
141-147
148-154
155-161
162-168
169-175
176-182
183-189
190-196
197-203
204-210
211-217
218-224
225-231
232-238
239-245
246-252
253-259
260-266
267-273
274-280
281-287
288-294

## START OF WEEK 24

**21** WEEKS SINCE CONCEPTION : WEEKS UNTIL YOUR DUE DATE **16**

(Dates are estimates only | Pregnancy is considered "term" at 37 to 42 weeks)

### WEEKLY CHART
### 23 WEEKS PASSED & STARTING 24

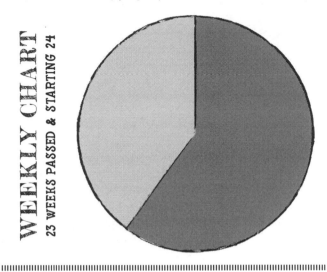

 *How big is baby now?*

Weight: 16 to 19 ounces
Length: 10 to 12 inches

(All measurements are approximate, and based on average fetal development)

### APPOINTMENTS & REMINDERS FOR THIS WEEK

_____  _____
_____  _____
_____  _____
_____  _____

{ ON MY MIND }

---

## DAY 162

### 23 WEEKS, 1 DAY (23W1D)

**DATE:**         /

┌─────────────────────────────┐
│ *3 ideas for this week* ~    │
│                             │
│                             │
│                             │
│                             │
│                             │
└─────────────────────────────┘

**to-do**
☐ ............................................
☐ ............................................
☐ ............................................

SLEEP:
APPETITE:
MOOD:

**118** DAYS UNTIL YOUR DUE DATE (ESTIMATED)

PERCENTAGE REMAINING **57.9%**

- - - - - - - - - - - - - - - - - - - - - -

### BABY TALK

— Your baby's hearing is pretty well-developed already, so go ahead and start singing and talking to him!
— Right now, much of his skin is wrinkled, as he awaits the white fat deposits that will give him that "chubby baby" look.

## DAY 163

### 23 WEEKS, 2 DAYS (23W2D)

DATE:        /

*Recent changes*

things to research
☐ .................................................
☐ .................................................
☐ .................................................

SLEEP:
APPETITE:
MOOD:

## 117 *days until your due date*

*percentage completed* 41.8%

**Contractions:** A tightening of the uterus. During labor, contractions become stronger, longer and closer together, and help the baby progress down the birth canal. Many women describe their early contractions feeling much like strong menstrual cramps, while others use terms like "sharp" and "intense." The power of the contractions increases during labor, particularly after your water breaks.

def·i·ni·tion

## DAY 164

### 23 WEEKS, 3 DAYS (23W3D)

DATE:        /

*This week I feel...*

questions for my caregiver
☐ .................................................
☐ .................................................
☐ .................................................

SLEEP:
APPETITE:
MOOD:

## 116 DAYS UNTIL YOUR DUE DATE (ESTIMATED)

**FRACTION REMAINING** 29/70

At each prenatal exam for the rest of your pregnancy, your caregiver likely will take a urine sample (looking for sugar and protein), get your weight, blood pressure, pulse and oxygen saturation levels (often tested with a pulse oximeter clipped to your finger for a minute) as well as check of your feet/ankles, hands and face for swelling.

TRIMESTER        THIRD TRIMESTER

WEEK 1
WEEK 2
WEEK 3
WEEK 4
WEEK 5
WEEK 6
WEEK 7
WEEK 8
WEEK 9
WEEK 10
WEEK 11
WEEK 12
WEEK 13
WEEK 14
WEEK 15
WEEK 16
WEEK 17
WEEK 18
WEEK 19
WEEK 20
WEEK 21
WEEK 22
WEEK 23
WEEK 24
WEEK 25
WEEK 26
WEEK 27
WEEK 28
WEEK 29
WEEK 30
WEEK 31
WEEK 32
WEEK 33
WEEK 34
WEEK 35
WEEK 36
WEEK 37
WEEK 38
WEEK 39
WEEK 40
WEEK 41
WEEK 42

MONTH 1  MONTH 2  MONTH 3  MONTH 4  MONTH 5

DAYS 1-7
8-14
15-21
22-28
29-35
36-42
43-49
50-56
57-63
64-70
71-77
78-84
85-91
92-98
99-105
106-112
113-119
120-126
127-133
134-140
141-147
148-154
155-161
162-168
169-175
176-182
183-189
190-196
197-203
204-210
211-217
218-224
225-231
232-238
239-245
246-252
253-259
260-266
267-273
274-280
281-287
288-294

## DAY 165

### 23 WEEKS, 4 DAYS (23W4D)

DATE:        /

**Something I can't do anymore**

grateful for...
☐ .............................
☐ .............................
☐ .............................

SLEEP: ▭
APPETITE: ▭
MOOD: ▭

## 115 DAYS UNTIL YOUR DUE DATE (ESTIMATED)

[ each dark | line represents 5 days passed ]

||||||||||||||||||||||||||||||||||||||||||||||||||||||||||||

66 It was the tiniest thing
I ever decided to put
my whole life into. 99

- Terri Guillemets

## DAY 166

### 23 WEEKS, 5 DAYS (23W5D)

DATE:        /

**Connecting with my partner**

to tell my partner
☐ .............................
☐ .............................
☐ .............................

SLEEP: ▭
APPETITE: ▭
MOOD: ▭

## 114 days until your due date

how far you have come **59.3%**

**ABOUT YOU**

The pubic bones are connected by ligaments, which loosen quite noticeably during pregnancy due to the effects of the hormone relaxin. This is to allow your hips to open just a bit as the baby moves through the birth canal, but that looseness can cause occasional pain. A pelvic support belt may help, as will moving your hips, abdomen and legs more slowly and carefully.

DAY **167**

23 WEEKS, 6 DAYS (23W6D)

DATE:        /

## How baby's movement feels

to-do
- [ ] ......................................
- [ ] ......................................
- [ ] ......................................

SLEEP:
APPETITE:
MOOD:

**113** days until
your due date
(estimated)

percentage **40.4%**
remaining

### BABY NAMES

#### BOYS IN ENGLAND

Oliver, Jack, Harry, Jacob,
Charlie, Thomas, George,
Oscar, James, William

---

DAY **168**

24 WEEKS, 0 DAYS (24W0D)

DATE:        /

## Pregnancy would be better if...

shopping wish list
- [ ] ......................................
- [ ] ......................................
- [ ] ......................................

SLEEP:
APPETITE:
MOOD:

**112** days until
your due date
(thereabouts)

fraction **3/5**
completed

~A LITTLE NOTE TO THE FUTURE~
☐ WISH  ☐ PREDICTION  ☐ PRAYER  ☐ HOPE  ☐ REMINDER

WEEK 1
WEEK 2
WEEK 3
WEEK 4
WEEK 5
WEEK 6
WEEK 7
WEEK 8
WEEK 9
WEEK 10
WEEK 11
WEEK 12
WEEK 13
WEEK 14
WEEK 15
WEEK 16
WEEK 17
WEEK 18
WEEK 19
WEEK 20
WEEK 21
WEEK 22
WEEK 23
WEEK 24
WEEK 25
WEEK 26
WEEK 27
WEEK 28
WEEK 29
WEEK 30
WEEK 31
WEEK 32
WEEK 33
WEEK 34
WEEK 35
WEEK 36
WEEK 37
WEEK 38
WEEK 39
WEEK 40
WEEK 41
WEEK 42

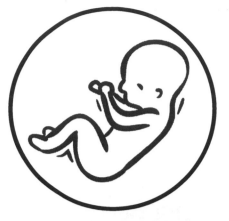

**By the end of this month (week 28), your baby will be about the length of a loaf of bread!**

That little person inside you is now about 14 to 16 inches long — like a long loaf of sliced bread, a baguette, or a hero sandwich. Growing fast, he or she weighs a bit over two pounds.

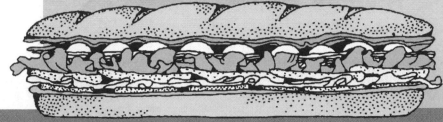

# MONTH 7

## WEEK 25, WEEK 26
## WEEK 27 & WEEK 28

## How do you feel?

At the beginning of this month,
rate how you're feeling with a line, X or circle

 ENERGY AMOUNT

IMPATIENCE DEGREE

EMOTIONAL INTENSITY

GRUMPINESS GRADE

SOCIABILITY SCALE

LOVE+ROMANCE LEVEL

FORGETFULNESS FACTOR

GROWTH GAUGE

Add a picture of yourself at 7 months here
Photos not your thing? Estimate your pregnancy size and
shape by drawing over the shadowed image below

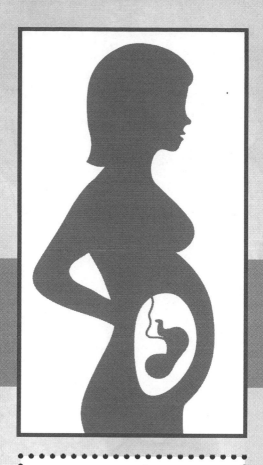

## One year from now
(assuming you give birth around 40 weeks)
Your baby will be about 10 months old!

### YOU & BABY

Weight gain:

Belly circumference:

Fundal height:

Baby's heart rate:

Baby's position:

### 7 WORDS FOR WHAT'S ON YOUR MIND RIGHT NOW

## notes

1. Twice monthly prenatal appointments usually start around week 28.
2. The GTT is a screening for gestational diabetes, a temporary form of diabetes during pregnancy. The idea is to load you up with sugar, then see how your body copes with it. This test is usually performed between 24 and 28 weeks.
3. Your breasts will continue to grow larger as the milk ducts multiply and mature. Your nipples will also get bigger, as will the areolas — the pink area around the nipples (which may also darken).

START OF

# WEEK 25

22 WEEKS SINCE CONCEPTION : WEEKS UNTIL YOUR DUE DATE 15

(Dates are estimates only | Pregnancy is considered "term" at 37 to 42 weeks)

## WEEKLY CHART
### 24 WEEKS PASSED & STARTING 25

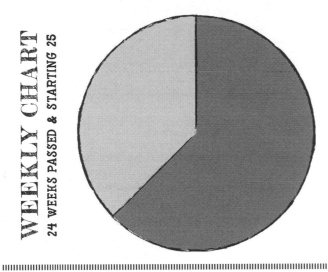

 *How big is baby now?*

Weight: 1-1/4 to 1-1/2 pounds
Length: 11 to 13 inches

(All measurements are approximate, and based on average fetal development)

## APPOINTMENTS & REMINDERS FOR THIS WEEK

_____ _____
_____ _____
_____ _____

{ ON MY MIND }

---

DAY **169**

24 WEEKS, 1 DAY (24W1D)

DATE:        /

*3 goals for this week*

to-do
☐ ..........................
☐ ..........................
☐ ..........................

SLEEP:
APPETITE:
MOOD:

**111** DAYS UNTIL YOUR DUE DATE (ESTIMATED)

PERCENTAGE COMPLETED **60.4%**

BABY TALK
— Your baby is spending much of his or her time swimming around in the amniotic fluid, as well as sleeping and waking up again.
— The complex structure of the spine begins to develop this week, meaning making new bones, ligaments and tendons.

## DAY 170

24 WEEKS, 2 DAYS (24W2D)

DATE:      /

*I need to remind myself...*

things to research
- [ ] ............................................
- [ ] ............................................
- [ ] ............................................

SLEEP: 
APPETITE: 
MOOD: 

### 110 *days until your due date*

*fraction completed* 17/28

**Colostrum:** Early breastmilk, which is rich in nutrients and antibodies, making it the perfect first food for babies. Colostrum may be apparent even second trimester of pregnancy as slightly sticky droplets oozing from your nipples. In 2009, scientists at Queen Mary, University of London discovered that an ingredient in colostrum can even protect and repair the delicate intestines of newborn babies.

def·i·ni·tion

TRIMESTER

## DAY 171

24 WEEKS, 3 DAYS (24W3D)

DATE:      /

*This week I feel...*

questions for my caregiver
- [ ] ............................................
- [ ] ............................................
- [ ] ............................................

SLEEP: 
APPETITE: 
MOOD: 

### 109 DAYS UNTIL YOUR DUE DATE (ESTIMATED)

PERCENTAGE REMAINING 38.9%

Hoping for some professional portraits to remember this pregnancy? Check out portfolios online to find a photographer with a style you like, then contact them to explain exactly what kind of pictures you want and get a quote. This communication will give you a chance to see how responsive they are to your ideas, and will help you find a pro who makes you feel comfortable and relaxed — leading to better keepsake pictures of this amazing time.

THIRD TRIMESTER

WEEK 1
WEEK 2
WEEK 3
WEEK 4
WEEK 5
WEEK 6
WEEK 7
WEEK 8
WEEK 9
WEEK 10
WEEK 11
WEEK 12
WEEK 13
WEEK 14
WEEK 15
WEEK 16
WEEK 17
WEEK 18
WEEK 19
WEEK 20
WEEK 21
WEEK 22
WEEK 23
WEEK 24
WEEK 25
WEEK 26
WEEK 27
WEEK 28
WEEK 29
WEEK 30
WEEK 31
WEEK 32
WEEK 33
WEEK 34
WEEK 35
WEEK 36
WEEK 37
WEEK 38
WEEK 39
WEEK 40
WEEK 41
WEEK 42

MONTH 1  MONTH 2  MONTH 3  MONTH 4  MONTH 5

DAYS 1-7
8-14
15-21
22-28
29-35
36-42
43-49
50-56
57-63
64-70
71-77
78-84
85-91
92-98
99-105
106-112
113-119
120-126
127-133
134-140
141-147
148-154
155-161
162-168
169-175
176-182
183-189
190-196
197-203
204-210
211-217
218-224
225-231
232-238
239-245
246-252
253-259
260-266
267-273
274-280
281-287
288-294

## DAY 172

### 24 WEEKS, 4 DAYS (24W4D)

DATE: /

### The best thing so far is...

grateful for...
- [ ] ............................................
- [ ] ............................................
- [ ] ............................................

SLEEP:
APPETITE:
MOOD:

## 108 DAYS UNTIL YOUR DUE DATE (ESTIMATED)

FRACTION COMPLETED 43/70

66 *Giving birth is an ecstatic jubilant adventure not available to males. It is a woman's crowning creative experience of a lifetime.* 99

— John Stevenson

## DAY 173

### 24 WEEKS, 5 DAYS (24W5D)

DATE: /

### Baby name plans

to tell my partner
- [ ] ............................................
- [ ] ............................................
- [ ] ............................................

SLEEP:
APPETITE:
MOOD:

## 107 days until your due date

how far you have come 61.8%

ABOUT YOU

To avoid some of the (mostly inevitable) pubic bone pain so common in this stage of pregnancy, be especially careful when you get in and out of bed (try turning on your side, then move your legs off the bed) and try not to twist or flex your hips too much. Use pillows to help you get into a comfortable sleeping position that won't over-extend your joints.

# DAY 174

**24 WEEKS, 6 DAYS (24W6D)**

DATE:  /

*Nursery/baby space prep*

to-do
- ☐ ......................................
- ☐ ......................................
- ☐ ......................................

SLEEP:
APPETITE:
MOOD:

# 106
days until
your due date
(estimated)

percentage remaining **37.8%**

## BOY NAMES FROM THE 1920S

**BABY NAMES**

*Robert, William, Charles,
George, Joseph, Richard, Edward,
Donald, Thomas, Frank, Harold,
Paul, Raymond*

---

# DAY 175

**25 WEEKS, 0 DAYS (25W0D)**

DATE:  /

*I already miss...*

shopping wish list
- ☐ ......................................
- ☐ ......................................
- ☐ ......................................

SLEEP:
APPETITE:
MOOD:

# 105
days until
your due date
(thereabouts)

[ each dark | line represents 5 days passed ]

~A LITTLE NOTE TO THE FUTURE~

☐ WISH ☐ PREDICTION ☐ PRAYER ☐ HOPE ☐ REMINDER

WEEK 1
WEEK 2
WEEK 3
WEEK 4
WEEK 5
WEEK 6
WEEK 7
WEEK 8
WEEK 9
WEEK 10
WEEK 11
WEEK 12
WEEK 13
WEEK 14
WEEK 15
WEEK 16
WEEK 17
WEEK 18
WEEK 19
WEEK 20
WEEK 21
WEEK 22
WEEK 23
WEEK 24
WEEK 25
WEEK 26
WEEK 27
WEEK 28
WEEK 29
WEEK 30
WEEK 31
WEEK 32
WEEK 33
WEEK 34
WEEK 35
WEEK 36
WEEK 37
WEEK 38
WEEK 39
WEEK 40
WEEK 41
WEEK 42

START OF

# WEEK 26

**23** WEEKS SINCE CONCEPTION : WEEKS UNTIL YOUR DUE DATE **14**

(Dates are estimates only | Pregnancy is considered "term" at 37 to 42 weeks)

## WEEKLY CHART
### 25 WEEKS PASSED & STARTING 26

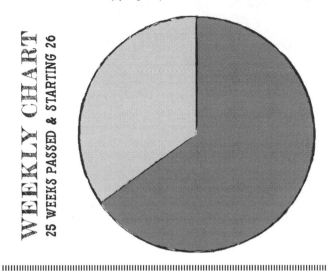

 *How big is baby now?*

Weight: 1-1/4 pounds to 1-3/4 pounds
Length: 13 to 15 inches

(All measurements are approximate, and based on average fetal development)

## APPOINTMENTS & REMINDERS FOR THIS WEEK

_____ _____
_____ _____
_____ _____
_____ _____

{ ON MY MIND }

---

**DAY 176**

25 WEEKS, 1 DAY (25W1D)

DATE:        /

*3 wishes for this week*

to-do
☐ ..................................................
☐ ..................................................
☐ ..................................................

SLEEP:
APPETITE:
MOOD:

**104** DAYS UNTIL YOUR DUE DATE (ESTIMATED)

FRACTION COMPLETED **22/35**

- - - - - - - - - - - - - - - - -

BABY TALK

— Your baby's fingerprints and footprints are beginning to appear now!
— The air sacs (alveoli) are starting to form inside the lungs in preparation for breathing.
— Thanks to medical advances, babies born this early, while considered extremely premature, have better odds than ever of surviving.

## DAY 177
### 25 WEEKS, 2 DAYS (25W2D)
DATE:        /

*My life right now...*

things to research
- [ ] ........................................
- [ ] ........................................
- [ ] ........................................

SLEEP:
APPETITE:
MOOD:

## 103 *days until your due date*

*percentage remaining* **36.7%**

**det·i·ni·tion**

**Breech presentation:** The breech position means baby is set to be born bottom first. It occurs in about 2-4% births. There are several types of breech presentations (presenting = the part of the baby lowered and set to emerge first), including... *Full breech:* Buttocks presenting, flexed hips and knees (cannonball-style); *Frank breech:* Baby's bottom presenting, legs up, with feet up by the head; *Incomplete breech:* Bottom down with one leg extended (sort of a combination of Full and Frank); *Footling breech:* One or both feet presenting.

---

## DAY 178
### 25 WEEKS, 3 DAYS (25W3D)
DATE:        /

*This week I feel...*

questions for my caregiver
- [ ] ........................................
- [ ] ........................................
- [ ] ........................................

SLEEP:
APPETITE:
MOOD:

## 102 DAYS UNTIL YOUR DUE DATE (ESTIMATED)

PERCENTAGE COMPLETED **63.6%**

What is molding? It's the overlapping of fetal skull bones during birth — and may mean that your baby's born with a "cone head." That's what your baby's head is supposed to do in order for it to fit through the birth canal, and is the reason the skull bones are not yet fused.

TRIMESTER              THIRD TRIMESTER

WEEK 1
WEEK 2
WEEK 3
WEEK 4
WEEK 5
WEEK 6
WEEK 7
WEEK 8
WEEK 9
WEEK 10
WEEK 11
WEEK 12
WEEK 13
WEEK 14
WEEK 15
WEEK 16
WEEK 17
WEEK 18
WEEK 19
WEEK 20
WEEK 21
WEEK 22
WEEK 23
WEEK 24
WEEK 25
WEEK 26
WEEK 27
WEEK 28
WEEK 29
WEEK 30
WEEK 31
WEEK 32
WEEK 33
WEEK 34
WEEK 35
WEEK 36
WEEK 37
WEEK 38
WEEK 39
WEEK 40
WEEK 41
WEEK 42

# DAY 179

## 25 WEEKS, 4 DAYS (25W4D)

DATE:        /

### This is perfect

grateful for...
☐ .............................................
☐ .............................................
☐ .............................................

SLEEP: ▢▬▬▬▬▬▬▬▬◼
APPETITE: ▢▬▬▬▬▬▬▬▬◼
MOOD: ▢▬▬▬▬▬▬▬▬◼

# 101
### DAYS UNTIL YOUR DUE DATE
### (ESTIMATED)

PERCENTAGE COMPLETED **63.9%**

66 I begin to love this little creature, and to anticipate his birth as a fresh twist to a knot which I do not wish to untie. 99

- Mary Wollstonecraft

# DAY 180

## 25 WEEKS, 5 DAYS (25W5D)

DATE:        /

### Guilty pleasures

to tell my partner
☐ .............................................
☐ .............................................
☐ .............................................

SLEEP: ▢▬▬▬▬▬▬▬▬◼
APPETITE: ▢▬▬▬▬▬▬▬▬◼
MOOD: ▢▬▬▬▬▬▬▬▬◼

# 100
### days until your due date

fraction completed **5/14**

ABOUT YOU

You might find yourself squirming and fidgeting with a new itch: on your nipples. This is different from the generalized breast and tummy itching you would expect when your skin stretches rapidly. For one thing, this intense, persistent itchiness is highly localized. While intense for a few weeks, the itch often disappears as quickly as it arrived. Try a lanolin nipple cream or a moisturizer for some relief.

176-182
183-189
190-196
197-203
204-210
211-217
218-224
225-231
232-238
239-245
246-252
253-259
260-266
267-273
274-280
281-287
288-294

## DAY 181

### 25 WEEKS, 6 DAYS (25W6D)

DATE:        /

*Getting difficult now to...*

to-do
- [ ] ...................................................
- [ ] ...................................................
- [ ] ...................................................
- [ ] ...................................................

SLEEP:
APPETITE:
MOOD:

**99** days until
your due date
(estimated)

percentage
remaining **35.4%**

BABY NAMES

### GIRLS IN JAPAN

*Sakura, Riko, Aoi, Wakana,*
*Sakura, Rin, Azuna, Himari,*
*Hinata, Yuna, Kaede*

## DAY 182

### 26 WEEKS, 0 DAYS (26W0D)

DATE:        /

*Minor annoyances*

shopping wish list
- [ ] ...................................................
- [ ] ...................................................
- [ ] ...................................................

SLEEP:
APPETITE:
MOOD:

**98** days until
your due date
(thereabouts)

fraction
left to go **7/20**

~A LITTLE NOTE TO THE FUTURE~
- [ ] WISH  [ ] PREDICTION  [ ] PRAYER  [ ] HOPE  [ ] REMINDER

WEEK 1
WEEK 2
WEEK 3
WEEK 4
WEEK 5
WEEK 6
WEEK 7
WEEK 8
WEEK 9
WEEK 10
WEEK 11
WEEK 12
WEEK 13
WEEK 14
WEEK 15
WEEK 16
WEEK 17
WEEK 18
WEEK 19
WEEK 20
WEEK 21
WEEK 22
WEEK 23
WEEK 24
WEEK 25
WEEK 26
WEEK 27
WEEK 28
WEEK 29
WEEK 30
WEEK 31
WEEK 32
WEEK 33
WEEK 34
WEEK 35
WEEK 36
WEEK 37
WEEK 38
WEEK 39
WEEK 40
WEEK 41
WEEK 42

MONTH 1    MONTH 2    MONTH 3    MONTH 4    MONTH 5

DAYS 1-7
8-14
15-21
22-28
29-35
36-42
43-49
50-56
57-63
64-70
71-77
78-84
85-91
92-98
99-105
106-112
113-119
120-126
127-133
134-140
141-147
148-154
155-161
162-168
169-175
176-182
**183-189**
190-196
197-203
204-210
211-217
218-224
225-231
232-238
239-245
246-252
253-259
260-266
267-273
274-280
281-287
288-294

## START OF WEEK 27

**24** WEEKS SINCE CONCEPTION ⋮ WEEKS UNTIL YOUR DUE DATE **13**

(Dates are estimates only | Pregnancy is considered "term" at 37 to 42 weeks)

### WEEKLY CHART
**26 WEEKS PASSED & STARTING 27**

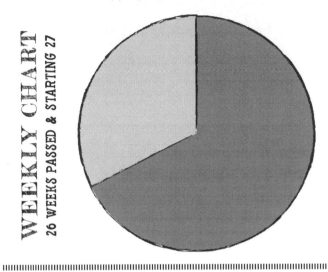

 *How big is baby now?*

Weight: 1-1/2 pounds to 2 pounds
Length: 12 to 14 inches

(All measurements are approximate, and based on average fetal development)

### APPOINTMENTS & REMINDERS FOR THIS WEEK

_____ _____
_____ _____
_____ _____
_____ _____

{ ON MY MIND }

---

## DAY 183

**26 WEEKS, 1 DAY (26W1D)**

DATE: /

*3 goals for this week*

**to-do**
☐ ......................................
☐ ......................................
☐ ......................................

SLEEP: ⊏━━━━━━━━━━━⊐
APPETITE: ⊏━━━━━━━━━━━⊐
MOOD: ⊏━━━━━━━━━━━⊐

**97** DAYS UNTIL YOUR DUE DATE (ESTIMATED)

PERCENTAGE LEFT TO GO **34.6%**

### BABY TALK

— Your baby's taste buds are now forming, and he or she will start sampling flavors from the foods you eat, delivered via amniotic fluid (which, well, he pees into and then drinks again).

— Sometimes your little one will get hiccups, which you will feel as regular thumps in your belly.

## DAY 184

### 26 WEEKS, 2 DAYS (26W2D)

DATE:        /

*I need to remind myself...*

things to research
- [ ] ......................................................
- [ ] ......................................................
- [ ] ......................................................

SLEEP:
APPETITE:
MOOD:

**96** *days until your due date*

*percentage completed* **65.7%**

## DAY 185

### 26 WEEKS, 3 DAYS (26W3D)

DATE:        /

*This week I feel...*

questions for my caregiver
- [ ] ......................................................
- [ ] ......................................................
- [ ] ......................................................

SLEEP:
APPETITE:
MOOD:

**95** DAYS UNTIL YOUR DUE DATE (ESTIMATED)

[ each dark | line represents 5 days passed ]

|||||||||||||||||||||||||||||||||||||||||||||||||||||||||||||||||||

---

**de·fi·ni·tion**

**Perineum:** The area between the vagina and the anus. The perineum is stretched during a vaginal delivery, and may tear, or be cut if your caregiver performs an episiotomy. Perineal massage may help the vaginal opening widen and gently stretch as much as needed to accommodate the baby's head and body.

*Notes*

Many airlines won't allow you to fly if you are past 34 weeks of pregnancy unless your caregiver has given you written approval or the situation is urgent. (Individual airlines vary, so check before booking your flight.) It would be smart to bring a note with you on your flight any time you're visibly pregnant — just in case a very cautious staff member asks.

WEEK 1
WEEK 2
WEEK 3
WEEK 4
WEEK 5
WEEK 6
WEEK 7
WEEK 8
WEEK 9
WEEK 10
WEEK 11
WEEK 12
WEEK 13
WEEK 14
WEEK 15
WEEK 16
WEEK 17
WEEK 18
WEEK 19
WEEK 20
WEEK 21
WEEK 22
WEEK 23
WEEK 24
WEEK 25
WEEK 26
WEEK 27
WEEK 28
WEEK 29
WEEK 30
WEEK 31
WEEK 32
WEEK 33
WEEK 34
WEEK 35
WEEK 36
WEEK 37
WEEK 38
WEEK 39
WEEK 40
WEEK 41
WEEK 42

MONTH 1    MONTH 2    MONTH 3    MONTH 4    MONTH 5

DAYS 1-7
8-14
15-21
22-28
29-35
36-42
43-49
50-56
57-63
64-70
71-77
78-84
85-91
92-98
99-105
106-112
113-119
120-126
127-133
134-140
141-147
148-154
155-161
162-168
169-175
176-182
183-189
190-196
197-203
204-210
211-217
218-224
225-231
232-238
239-245
246-252
253-259
260-266
267-273
274-280
281-287
288-294

## DAY 186
### 26 WEEKS, 4 DAYS (26W4D)

DATE:        /

*New & unusual*

grateful for...
☐ ................................
☐ ................................
☐ ................................

SLEEP: ▬▬▬▬▬▬▬▬▬
APPETITE: ▬▬▬▬▬▬▬▬▬
MOOD: ▬▬▬▬▬▬▬▬▬

## 94
### DAYS UNTIL YOUR DUE DATE
### (ESTIMATED)

FRACTION COMPLETED **2/3**

66 *We never know the love of a parent till we become parents ourselves.* 99

— Henry Ward Beecher

## DAY 187
### 26 WEEKS, 5 DAYS (26W5D)

DATE:        /

*I love to imagine...*

to tell my partner
☐ ................................
☐ ................................
☐ ................................

SLEEP: ▬▬▬▬▬▬▬▬▬
APPETITE: ▬▬▬▬▬▬▬▬▬
MOOD: ▬▬▬▬▬▬▬▬▬

## 93
*days until your due date*

*how far you have come* **66.7%**

**ABOUT YOU**

If your blood is Rh Negative (Rh-), you may be given an injection of RhoGAM at your next medical visit. This can help prevent problems in case your blood is incompatible with your baby's — something that could mean major complications. You will get another injection of this immune globulin right after you give birth.

DAY **188**

26 WEEKS, 6 DAYS (26W6D)

DATE:      /

## When I see babies now...

to-do
- [ ] .................................................
- [ ] .................................................
- [ ] .................................................

SLEEP:
APPETITE:
MOOD:

**92** days until
your due date
(estimated)

percentage
remaining **32.9%**

**BABY NAMES**

### BOYS IN MEXICO

Santiago, Mateo, Matías, Diego,
Sebastián, Nicolás, Miguel Ángel,
Iker, Alejandro, Samuel

DAY **189**

27 WEEKS, 0 DAYS (27W0D)

DATE:      /

## Song lyrics I love

shopping wish list
- [ ] .................................................
- [ ] .................................................
- [ ] .................................................

SLEEP:
APPETITE:
MOOD:

**91** days until
your due date
(thereabouts)

fraction
left to go **13/40**

~ A LITTLE NOTE TO THE FUTURE ~
- [ ] WISH  [ ] PREDICTION  [ ] PRAYER  [ ] HOPE  [ ] REMINDER

WEEK 1
WEEK 2
WEEK 3
WEEK 4
WEEK 5
WEEK 6
WEEK 7
WEEK 8
WEEK 9
WEEK 10
WEEK 11
WEEK 12
WEEK 13
WEEK 14
WEEK 15
WEEK 16
WEEK 17
WEEK 18
WEEK 19
WEEK 20
WEEK 21
WEEK 22
WEEK 23
WEEK 24
WEEK 25
WEEK 26
WEEK 27
WEEK 28
WEEK 29
WEEK 30
WEEK 31
WEEK 32
WEEK 33
WEEK 34
WEEK 35
WEEK 36
WEEK 37
WEEK 38
WEEK 39
WEEK 40
WEEK 41
WEEK 42

TRIMESTER                    THIRD TRIMESTER

# TRIMESTER 3

DATE BABY TURNED HEAD DOWN: _____          FINISHED CHILDBIRTH CLASSES: _____

| THE THIRD TRIMESTER | MONTH | WEEKS |
|---|---|---|
| | SEVEN | 28 - 31 |
| | EIGHT | 32 - 36 |
| | NINE+TEN | 37 - 42 |

## PREGNANCY NO-NOS: THINGS TO AVOID

Soft cheeses + deli meats     Alcohol + caffeine
Raw/undercooked meat          Some artificial sweeteners
Raw eggs (dough/batter)       Medications/drugs/herbs
Unpasteurized juice + milk    Bug spray, cleaners, solvents
Raw/undercooked sprouts       Cat litter boxes
Shark, swordfish, tilefish    Cigarettes, smoke + e-cigs

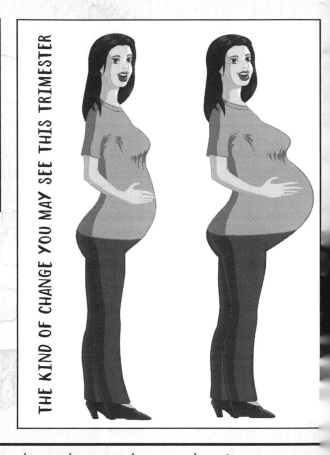

THE KIND OF CHANGE YOU MAY SEE THIS TRIMESTER

### A quick reminder

Be sure to talk to your healthcare provider if you plan to travel more than an hour or two from home, or to anywhere with extreme conditions (heat, cold, high altitude, remote location, war zone, outbreaks or other health alerts in place). If you have a high-risk pregnancy or are nearing the end or your term, you will probably be asked to stay close to home.

Attach an ultrasound picture here!
(Don't have one? Add a pregnancy photo or draw your baby instead.)

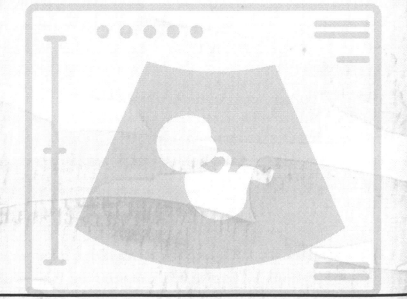

# Week 28 until baby is born

## HEALTH & MEDICAL TESTS IN TRIMESTER THREE

*This is a basic overview of some typical prenatal care offered in the US*

**Most of the prenatal tests done during the third trimester are to assure the well-being of your baby.**

**Group B Strep (GBS) Culture:** GBS can be detected during pregnancy by taking a swab of both the vagina and rectum for special culture. IV antibiotics administered to mom during labor should protect the newborn from any problems.

**Ultrasound:** Can approximate baby's size, determine position, check fluid levels, confirm the placental attachment site, etc.

**Nonstress Test (NST):** Checks to see if baby's heart beats faster moving (and/or in response to sound or your movement).

**Biophysical Profile (BPP):** A NST plus an ultrasound.

**Stress Test:** AKA the "oxytocin challenge test" involves giving you the hormone oxytocin to stimulate contractions to be sure baby's heart doesn't slow down after a contraction.

**Amniocentesis:** During the third trimester, it can help assess fetal lung maturity when preterm birth is imminent.

**Fetal Fibronectin (fFN) Test:** A simple cervical swab test that can predict if you are about to go into labor. This test is used to help prevent/prepare for preterm delivery, and to avoid unnecessary labor induction when you go past your due date.

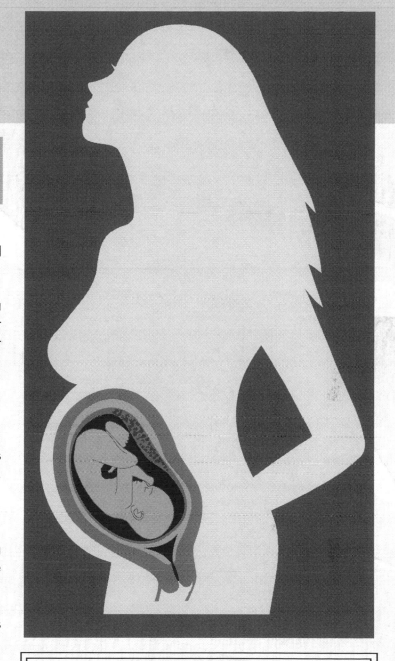

### 7 hints to figure out baby's position

1. Head: Hard and round
2. Hands/feet/elbows/knees: Small, lumpy, soft
3. Back and bottom: Soft, smooth and curved
4. Hands and fingers: Flutters
5. Kicks: Feet and knees
6. Kicks above your belly button: Head down
7. Hiccups above belly button: Head up

## TRIMESTER 3 PARALLELS

My theme song:

Sitcom title:

Superhero identity:

Actress in my life story:

Product I could endorse:

The animal I would be:

# Notes from the third trimester

MONTH 1     MONTH 2     MONTH 3     MONTH 4     MONTH 5

DAYS 1-7
6-14
15-21
22-28
29-35
36-42
43-49
50-56
57-63
64-70
71-77
78-84
85-91
92-98
99-105
106-112
113-119
120-126
127-133
134-140
141-147
148-154
155-161
162-168
169-175
176-182
183-189
190-196
197-203
204-210
211-217
218-224
225-231
232-238
239-245
246-252
253-259
260-266
267-273
274-280
281-287
288-294

## START OF WEEK 28

**25** WEEKS SINCE CONCEPTION    WEEKS UNTIL YOUR DUE DATE **12**

(Dates are estimates only | Pregnancy is considered "term" at 37 to 42 weeks)

### WEEKLY CHART
**27 WEEKS PASSED & STARTING 28**

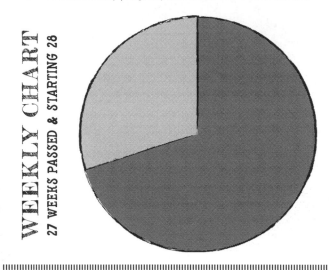

### How big is baby now?

Weight: 1-3/4 pounds to 2 pounds
Length: 13 to 15 inches

(All measurements are approximate, and based on average fetal development)

## APPOINTMENTS & REMINDERS FOR THIS WEEK

_____  _____
_____  _____
_____  _____
_____  _____

### { ON MY MIND }

---

## DAY 190

**27 WEEKS, 1 DAY (27W1D)**

DATE:   /

### 3 wishes for this week

to-do
- ☐ ......................................
- ☐ ......................................
- ☐ ......................................

SLEEP:
APPETITE:
MOOD:

**90** DAYS UNTIL YOUR DUE DATE (ESTIMATED)

FRACTION COMPLETED **19/28**

### BABY TALK

- This is a time of rapid brain and nervous system development.
- He or she is also starting a sleep-wake cycle, and is getting to know your voice!
- Those tiny lungs still have a long way to mature, but if born now — and with the right care — your baby has a very good chance of survival.

## DAY 191

**27 WEEKS, 2 DAYS (27W2D)**

DATE:     /

### Life right now

*things to research*
- ☐ ......................................
- ☐ ......................................
- ☐ ......................................

SLEEP:

APPETITE:

MOOD:

## 89 days until your due date

percentage completed **68.2%**

**Effacement:** During the first stage of labor, the cervix shortens ("thins"), a process called effacement. Effacement can usually be visualized by blowing up a balloon: as the balloon gets bigger, the neck actually stretches, shortens, and becomes incorporated into the body of the balloon. Effacement is expressed in terms of percentages: no effacement is called 0 percent, full effacement is 100 percent.

def·i·ni·tion

---

## DAY 192

**27 WEEKS, 3 DAYS (27W3D)**

DATE:     /

### This week I feel...

*questions for my caregiver*
- ☐ ......................................
- ☐ ......................................
- ☐ ......................................

SLEEP:

APPETITE:

MOOD:

## 88 DAYS UNTIL YOUR DUE DATE (ESTIMATED)

PERCENTAGE LEFT TO GO **31.4%**

According to Guinness World Records, the heaviest baby born to a healthy mother weighed 22 pounds, 8 ounces. A woman in Italy named Carmelina Fedele gave birth to this toddler-sized newborn boy back in 1955.

On that topic, this is probably a great time to get a maternity support belt or pregnancy belly band to help hold up your own burgeoning bump!

WEEK 1
WEEK 2
WEEK 3
WEEK 4
WEEK 5
WEEK 6
WEEK 7
WEEK 8
WEEK 9
WEEK 10
WEEK 11
WEEK 12
WEEK 13
WEEK 14
WEEK 15
WEEK 16
WEEK 17
WEEK 18
WEEK 19
WEEK 20
WEEK 21
WEEK 22
WEEK 23
WEEK 24
WEEK 25
WEEK 26
WEEK 27
WEEK 28
WEEK 29
WEEK 30
WEEK 31
WEEK 32
WEEK 33
WEEK 34
WEEK 35
WEEK 36
WEEK 37
WEEK 38
WEEK 39
WEEK 40
WEEK 41
WEEK 42

DAYS 1-7
8-14
15-21
22-28
29-35
36-42
43-49
50-56
57-63
64-70
71-77
78-84
85-91
92-98
99-105
106-112
113-119
120-126
127-133
134-140
141-147
148-154
155-161
162-168
169-175
176-182
183-189
190-196
197-203
204-210
211-217
218-224
225-231
232-238
239-245
246-252
253-259
260-266
267-273
274-280
281-287
288-294

## DAY 193

### 27 WEEKS, 4 DAYS (27W4D)

DATE:    /

### Aches and pains

grateful for...
- ☐ ...........................................
- ☐ ...........................................
- ☐ ...........................................

SLEEP:
APPETITE:
MOOD:

**87** DAYS UNTIL YOUR DUE DATE (ESTIMATED)

PERCENTAGE COMPLETED **68.9%**

66 *Everything grows rounder and wider and weirder, and I sit here in the middle of it all and wonder who in the world you will turn out to be.* 99
— Carrie Fisher

## DAY 194

### 27 WEEKS, 5 DAYS (27W5D)

DATE:    /

### I can't believe...

to tell my partner
- ☐ ...........................................
- ☐ ...........................................
- ☐ ...........................................

SLEEP:
APPETITE:
MOOD:

**86** days until your due date

percentage remaining **31.7%**

ABOUT YOU

You may notice Braxton-Hicks contractions — a (mostly) painless tightening of your uterus that may leave you a tiny bit breathless for a moment. These flex and exercise the uterus, while ensuring good blood flow to all parts of this muscle. Although these 'practice' contractions may seem like early labor, they don't dilate your cervix — nor will they help to predict when you will give birth.

DAY **195**

27 WEEKS, 6 DAYS (27W6D)

DATE:        /

## Something I just learned

to-do
- [ ]
- [ ]
- [ ]

SLEEP:
APPETITE:
MOOD:

**85** days until your due date
(estimated)

[ each dark | line represents 5 days passed ]

 **BABY NAMES**

### GIRLS IN CHILE

Isidora, Florencia, Amanda,
Emilia, Sofia, Martina, Maite,
Josefa, Agustina, Antonella

---

DAY **196**

28 WEEKS, 0 DAYS (28W0D)

DATE:        /

## What baby seems to like

shopping wish list
- [ ]
- [ ]
- [ ]

SLEEP:
APPETITE:
MOOD:

**84** days until your due date
(thereabouts)

fraction completed **7/10**

~A LITTLE NOTE TO THE FUTURE~

☐ WISH  ☐ PREDICTION  ☐ PRAYER  ☐ HOPE  ☐ REMINDER

WEEK 1
WEEK 2
WEEK 3
WEEK 4
WEEK 5
WEEK 6
WEEK 7
WEEK 8
WEEK 9
WEEK 10
WEEK 11
WEEK 12
WEEK 13
WEEK 14
WEEK 15
WEEK 16
WEEK 17
WEEK 18
WEEK 19
WEEK 20
WEEK 21
WEEK 22
WEEK 23
WEEK 24
WEEK 25
WEEK 26
WEEK 27
WEEK 28
WEEK 29
WEEK 30
WEEK 31
WEEK 32
WEEK 33
WEEK 34
WEEK 35
WEEK 36
WEEK 37
WEEK 38
WEEK 39
WEEK 40
WEEK 41
WEEK 42

**By the end of this month (week 32), your baby will be about as long as two pieces of paper — like the width of these two pages!**

Rolling into the home stretch now, your little one is long but very skinny. Although he or she is around 16 to 18 inches tall, that miniature person probably weighs no more than four pounds.

# MONTH 8

WEEK 29, WEEK 30 WEEK 31 & WEEK 32

## How do you feel?

At the beginning of this month, rate how you're feeling with a line, X or circle

 **ENERGY AMOUNT**

 **IMPATIENCE DEGREE**

 **EMOTIONAL INTENSITY**

 **GRUMPINESS GRADE**

**SOCIABILITY SCALE**

 **LOVE+ROMANCE LEVEL**

 **FORGETFULNESS FACTOR**

 **GROWTH GAUGE**

Add a picture of yourself at 8 months here
Photos not your thing? Estimate your pregnancy size and shape by drawing over the shadowed image below

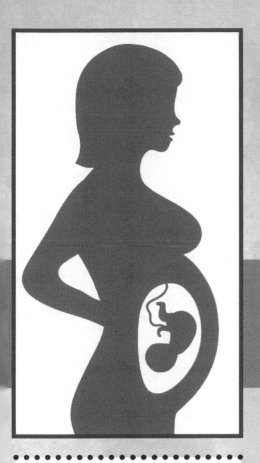

## One year from now

(assuming you give birth around 40 weeks)

Your baby will be about 11 months old!

### YOU & BABY

Weight gain:

Belly circumference:

Fundal height:

Baby's heart rate:

Baby's position:

### 8 WORDS FOR WHAT'S ON YOUR MIND RIGHT NOW

### 4 things to know this month

1. You will probably have prenatal appointments twice a month until week 36.
2. Always hungry? Try to snack on nutrient-dense foods – fruits and veggies, lean poultry and meat, whole grains, nuts and seeds. Also plan meals in advance, so you don't want everything in sight.
3. Your childbirth class (or refresher class) will probably start soon! Usually, they run 2-3 hours a night, one night a week for about six weeks.
4. Avoid carrying unbalanced loads and don't move or carry anything you cannot handle easily. (This includes toddlers.)

### notes

DAYS 1-7
8-14
15-21
22-28
29-35
36-42
43-49
50-56
57-63
64-70
71-77
78-84
85-91
92-98
99-105
106-112
113-119
120-126
127-133
134-140
141-147
148-154
155-161
162-168
169-175
176-182
183-189
190-196
197-203
204-210
211-217
218-224
225-231
232-238
239-245
246-252
253-259
260-266
267-273
274-280
281-287
288-294

## START OF WEEK 29

**26** WEEKS SINCE CONCEPTION    WEEKS UNTIL YOUR DUE DATE **11**

(Dates are estimates only | Pregnancy is considered "term" at 37 to 42 weeks)

### WEEKLY CHART
28 WEEKS PASSED & STARTING 29

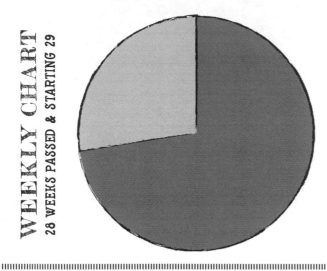

 **How big is baby now?**

Weight: 2 to 2-1/4 pounds
Length: 14 to 16 inches

(All measurements are approximate, and based on average fetal development)

### APPOINTMENTS & REMINDERS FOR THIS WEEK

_____

_____

_____

*See nursery planning & baby gear checklists @ end of book*

**{ ON MY MIND }**

---

### DAY 197
**28 WEEKS, 1 DAY (28W1D)**
DATE:        /

#### 3 goals for this week

to-do
☐ ..............................
☐ ..............................
☐ ..............................

SLEEP: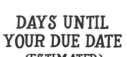
APPETITE:
MOOD:

**83** DAYS UNTIL YOUR DUE DATE (ESTIMATED)

PERCENTAGE COMPLETED **70.4%**

### BABY TALK
— Although the baby's lungs are not completely mature, he or she has already started rhythmic breathing movements — "practice breathing."
— His or her bones are now fully-developed (and the bone marrow is producing red blood cells), but they're still soft and cartilaginous.

# DAY 198
### 28 WEEKS, 2 DAYS (28W2D)
DATE:        /

## What I'm doing differently

things to research
- [ ] ................................................
- [ ] ................................................
- [ ] ................................................

SLEEP:
APPETITE:
MOOD:

## 82 days until your due date
### percentage remaining 29.3%

**Dilation:** During the first stage of labor, the opening of the cervix — the bottom of the uterus — widens enough for the baby to emerge. Dilation is measured in centimeters (0 to 10), with 10 being considered "complete" or fully dilated. This is a major turning point in labor, and means the pushing stage is about to begin.

de·fi·ni·tion

TRIMESTER

---

# DAY 199
### 28 WEEKS, 3 DAYS (28W3D)
DATE:        /

## This week I feel...

questions for my caregiver
- [ ] ................................................
- [ ] ................................................
- [ ] ................................................

SLEEP:
APPETITE:
MOOD:

## 81 DAYS UNTIL YOUR DUE DATE (ESTIMATED)
### PERCENTAGE COMPLETED 71.1%

Notes

How long will your doctor be with you at the hospital? In general, MDs will check on you when you first get to the hospital and every few hours during labor. They're on call for medical procedures, if there are complications, and when the baby's minutes away from birth. That's just one of many reasons to be extra nice to the hospital staff, because they're who will be looking after you.

THIRD TRIMESTER

WEEK 1
WEEK 2
WEEK 3
WEEK 4
WEEK 5
WEEK 6
WEEK 7
WEEK 8
WEEK 9
WEEK 10
WEEK 11
WEEK 12
WEEK 13
WEEK 14
WEEK 15
WEEK 16
WEEK 17
WEEK 18
WEEK 19
WEEK 20
WEEK 21
WEEK 22
WEEK 23
WEEK 24
WEEK 25
WEEK 26
WEEK 27
WEEK 28
WEEK 29
WEEK 30
WEEK 31
WEEK 32
WEEK 33
WEEK 34
WEEK 35
WEEK 36
WEEK 37
WEEK 38
WEEK 39
WEEK 40
WEEK 41
WEEK 42

# DAY 200

### 28 WEEKS, 4 DAYS (28W4D)

**DATE:** /

## Surprising & strange

grateful for...
- ☐ ........................................
- ☐ ........................................
- ☐ ........................................

**SLEEP:**

**APPETITE:**

**MOOD:**

## 80 DAYS UNTIL YOUR DUE DATE
### (ESTIMATED)

**FRACTION COMPLETED** 5/7

> " Think of stretch marks as pregnancy service stripes. "
>
> — Joyce Armor

# DAY 201

### 28 WEEKS, 5 DAYS (28W5D)

**DATE:** /

## I hope I won't forget...

to tell my partner
- ☐ ........................................
- ☐ ........................................
- ☐ ........................................

**SLEEP:**

**APPETITE:**

**MOOD:**

## 79 days until your due date

*percentage remaining* **28.2%**

**ABOUT YOU**

These days, you may need to be careful when sneezing, coughing — or even laughing! This is the trimester known for annoying urine leaks, also known as stress incontinence. Keeping up on your Kegels will help a lot, as will clenching as needed, and taking frequent bathroom breaks. (Panty liners might also be a really good idea.)

DAYS 1-7
8-14
15-21
22-28
29-35
36-42
43-49
50-56
57-63
64-70
71-77
78-84
85-91
92-98
99-105
106-112
113-119
120-126
127-133
134-140
141-147
148-154
155-161
162-168
169-175
176-182
183-189
190-196
197-203
204-210
211-217
218-224
225-231
232-238
239-245
246-252
253-259
260-266
267-273
274-280
281-287
288-294

## DAY 202

**28 WEEKS, 6 DAYS (28W6D)**

DATE:         /

### How I am staying healthy

to-do
☐ ........................................
☐ ........................................
☐ ........................................

SLEEP:
APPETITE:
MOOD:

**78** days until your due date *(estimated)*

percentage completed **72.1%**

### GIRLS IN TAHITI

BABY NAMES

*Tiare, Hinano, Poema, Maeva, Hina, Vaea, Titaua, Moea, Moeata, Tarita, Titaina, Teura, Heikapu, Mareva*

---

## DAY 203

**29 WEEKS, 0 DAYS (29W0D)**

DATE:         /

### Something I will miss

shopping wish list
☐ ........................................
☐ ........................................
☐ ........................................

SLEEP:
APPETITE:
MOOD:

**77** days until your due date *(thereabouts)*

FRACTION REMAINING **11/40**

~A LITTLE NOTE TO THE FUTURE~
☐ WISH  ☐ PREDICTION  ☐ PRAYER  ☐ HOPE  ☐ REMINDER

WEEK 1
WEEK 2
WEEK 3
WEEK 4
WEEK 5
WEEK 6
WEEK 7
WEEK 8
WEEK 9
WEEK 10
WEEK 11
WEEK 12
WEEK 13
WEEK 14
WEEK 15
WEEK 16
WEEK 17
WEEK 18
WEEK 19
WEEK 20
WEEK 21
WEEK 22
WEEK 23
WEEK 24
WEEK 25
WEEK 26
WEEK 27
WEEK 28
WEEK 29
WEEK 30
WEEK 31
WEEK 32
WEEK 33
WEEK 34
WEEK 35
WEEK 36
WEEK 37
WEEK 38
WEEK 39
WEEK 40
WEEK 41
WEEK 42

DAYS 1-7
8-14
15-21
22-28
29-35
36-42
43-49
50-56
57-63
64-70
71-77
78-84
85-91
92-98
99-105
106-112
113-119
120-126
127-133
134-140
141-147
148-154
155-161
162-168
169-175
176-182
183-189
190-196
197-203
204-210
211-217
218-224
225-231
232-238
239-245
246-252
253-259
260-266
267-273
274-280
281-287
288-294

START OF **WEEK 30**

**27** WEEKS SINCE CONCEPTION : WEEKS UNTIL YOUR DUE DATE **10**

(Dates are estimates only | Pregnancy is considered "term" at 37 to 42 weeks)

## WEEKLY CHART
### 29 WEEKS PASSED & STARTING 30

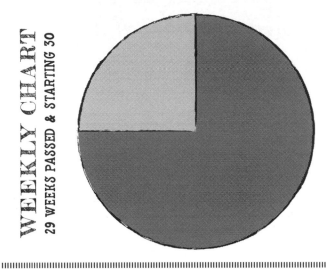

 *How big is baby now?*

Weight: 2-1/4 to 2-3/4 pounds
Length: 15 to 17 inches

(All measurements are approximate, and based on average fetal development)

## APPOINTMENTS & REMINDERS FOR THIS WEEK

_____   _____
_____   _____
_____   _____
_____   _____

{ ON MY MIND }

---

**DAY 204**

**29 WEEKS, 1 DAY (29W1D)**

DATE:        /

*3 wishes for this week*

to-do
☐ ...............................................
☐ ...............................................
☐ ...............................................

SLEEP:
APPETITE:
MOOD:      

**76** DAYS UNTIL YOUR DUE DATE (ESTIMATED)

PERCENTAGE LEFT TO GO **27.1%**

**BABY TALK**
— In the eyes, the retinas continue to develop, and baby will soon turn towards the light that filters in through your abdomen.
— Fat stores under his or her skin are increasing, as your little person starts to really look like a newborn. (Aww!)

WEEK 1
WEEK 2
WEEK 3
WEEK 4
WEEK 5
WEEK 6
WEEK 7
WEEK 8
WEEK 9
WEEK 10
WEEK 11
WEEK 12
WEEK 13
WEEK 14
WEEK 15
WEEK 16
WEEK 17
WEEK 18
WEEK 19
WEEK 20
WEEK 21
WEEK 22
WEEK 23
WEEK 24
WEEK 25
WEEK 26
WEEK 27
WEEK 28
WEEK 29
WEEK 30
WEEK 31
WEEK 32
WEEK 33
WEEK 34
WEEK 35
WEEK 36
WEEK 37
WEEK 38
WEEK 39
WEEK 40
WEEK 41
WEEK 42

## DAY 205

29 WEEKS, 2 DAYS (29W2D)

DATE:    /

### Life right now

*things to research*
- [ ] ............................
- [ ] ............................
- [ ] ............................

SLEEP:
APPETITE:
MOOD:

**75** *days until your due date*

[ each dark | line represents 5 days passed ]

**Epidural:** A regional anesthetic (painkiller) used during labor. By the use of a needle, a narrow tube (catheter) is inserted, through which anesthesia is injected into the outer lining of the spinal cord (epidural space). While it's considered the gold standard of pain relief, it's also been associated with prolonged labor and certain other complications. Research it more before you're due.

*de·fi·ni·tion*

## DAY 206

29 WEEKS, 3 DAYS (29W3D)

DATE:    /

### This week I feel...

*questions for my caregiver*
- [ ] ............................
- [ ] ............................
- [ ] ............................

SLEEP:
APPETITE:
MOOD:

**74** DAYS UNTIL YOUR DUE DATE (ESTIMATED)

PERCENTAGE COMPLETED **73.6%**

*Notes*

Now is a great time to make some creative pregnancy memories! Some ideas to consider: A: Get a kit to make a belly cast – a 3D mold of your pregnant torso. (Fun to do with your partner.) B: Try painting the skin on your bump. Use non-toxic face paints to make any design you like! (Older kids love this one.) C: Book a portrait session with a local photographer. (Fun for all!)

MONTH 1    MONTH 2    MONTH 3    MONTH 4    MONTH 5

DAYS 1-7
8-14
15-21
22-28
29-35
36-42
43-49
50-56
57-63
64-70
71-77
78-84
85-91
92-98
99-105
106-112
113-119
120-126
127-133
134-140
141-147
148-154
155-161
162-168
169-175
176-182
183-189
190-196
197-203
204-210
211-217
218-224
225-231
232-238
239-245
246-252
253-259
260-266
267-273
274-280
281-287
288-294

# DAY 207

**29 WEEKS, 4 DAYS (29W4D)**

DATE:        /

### When mood swings strike

grateful for...
- ☐ ....................................
- ☐ ....................................
- ☐ ....................................

SLEEP:
APPETITE:
MOOD:

**73** DAYS UNTIL YOUR DUE DATE (ESTIMATED)

PERCENTAGE COMPLETED **73.9%**

66 Every woman carries pregnancy differently... I carry big. It doesn't matter how much I eat or exercise, I make big babies.
- Tamera Mowry-Housley 99

(Son Aden weighed 9 lbs., 5 oz; daughter Ariah weighed 10 lbs., 2 oz.)

# DAY 208

**29 WEEKS, 5 DAYS (29W5D)**

DATE:        /

### Wouldn't it be nice if...

to tell my partner
- ☐ ....................................
- ☐ ....................................
- ☐ ....................................

SLEEP:
APPETITE:
MOOD:

**72** days until your due date

percentage remaining **25.7%**

**ABOUT YOU**

Call you Bigfoot? University of Iowa researchers measured women's feet at the beginning of pregnancy and 5 months after delivery. They confirmed what many have long suspected: pregnancy can permanently change the size and shape of feet. Your arch height may get shorter, and your foot will get longer... meaning that mama will soon need some new pairs of shoes!

## DAY 209

**29 WEEKS, 6 DAYS (29W6D)**

DATE:        /

*So excited about this*

WEEK 1
WEEK 2
WEEK 3
WEEK 4
WEEK 5
WEEK 6
WEEK 7
WEEK 8
WEEK 9
WEEK 10
WEEK 11
WEEK 12
WEEK 13
WEEK 14
WEEK 15
WEEK 16
WEEK 17
WEEK 18
WEEK 19
WEEK 20
WEEK 21
WEEK 22
WEEK 23
WEEK 24
WEEK 25
WEEK 26
WEEK 27
WEEK 28
WEEK 29
WEEK 30
WEEK 31
WEEK 32
WEEK 33
WEEK 34
WEEK 35
WEEK 36
WEEK 37
WEEK 38
WEEK 39
WEEK 40
WEEK 41
WEEK 42

## DAY 210

**30 WEEKS, 0 DAYS (30W0D)**

DATE:        /

*This was really strange*

**to-do**
- ☐ ............................
- ☐ ............................
- ☐ ............................

**shopping wish list**
- ☐ ............................
- ☐ ............................
- ☐ ............................

SLEEP: ▭▭▭▭▭▭
APPETITE: ▭▭▭▭▭▭
MOOD: ▭▭▭▭▭▭

SLEEP: ▭▭▭▭▭▭
APPETITE: ▭▭▭▭▭▭
MOOD: ▭▭▭▭▭▭

**71** days until your due date (estimated)

percentage completed **74.6%**

**70** days until your due date (thereabouts)

fraction left to go **1/4!**

### BOYS IN DENMARK

*William, Noah, Lucas, Oscar, Frederik, Victor, Malthe, Emil, Oliver, Elias*

**BABY NAMES**

~ A LITTLE NOTE TO THE FUTURE ~
☐ WISH  ☐ PREDICTION  ☐ PRAYER  ☐ HOPE  ☐ REMINDER

## START OF WEEK 31

**28** WEEKS SINCE CONCEPTION : WEEKS UNTIL YOUR DUE DATE **09**

(Dates are estimates only | Pregnancy is considered "term" at 37 to 42 weeks)

### WEEKLY CHART
#### 30 WEEKS PASSED & STARTING 31

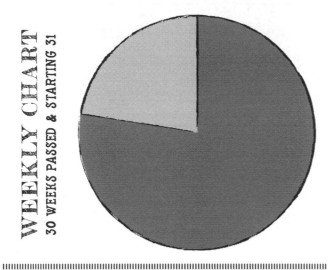

### How big is baby now?

Weight: 2-3/4 to 3-1/4 pounds
Length: 15 to 17 inches

(All measurements are approximate, and based on average fetal development)

### APPOINTMENTS & REMINDERS FOR THIS WEEK

——————  ——————
——————  ——————
——————  ——————

### { ON MY MIND }

---

## DAY **211**

### 30 WEEKS, 1 DAY (30W1D)

DATE: /

### 3 ideas for this week

**to-do**
☐ ......................................
☐ ......................................
☐ ......................................

SLEEP:
APPETITE:
MOOD:

**69** DAYS UNTIL YOUR DUE DATE (ESTIMATED)

PERCENTAGE COMPLETED **75.3%**

### BABY TALK

— Up to this point, baby was growing longer more than round — but from now on, your son or daughter will start to fill out and gain more weight.
— Meanwhile, the body systems are continuing to develop. You can monitor his or her health by recording movements on the kick count charts at the back of the book!

DAY **212**

30 WEEKS, 2 DAYS (30W2D)

DATE:        /

*I need to remind myself...*

**things to research**
- ☐ ..........................................................
- ☐ ..........................................................
- ☐ ..........................................................

SLEEP:

APPETITE:

MOOD:

**68** *days until your due date*

*fraction remaining* **17/70**

**det·i·ni·tion**

**Presentation:** The part of the fetus that enters the birth canal first. Some presentations include variations of cephalic (head), breech (bottom, legs or feet) or shoulder. A posterior presentation occurs when a baby faces toward the mother's front instead of toward her back. How the baby is presenting can have a major impact on the duration and intensity of labor.

---

DAY **213**

31 WEEKS, 3 DAYS (31W3D)

DATE:        /

*This week I feel...*

**questions for my caregiver**
- ☐ ..........................................................
- ☐ ..........................................................
- ☐ ..........................................................

SLEEP:

APPETITE:

MOOD:

**67** DAYS UNTIL YOUR DUE DATE (ESTIMATED)

PERCENTAGE REMAINING **23.9%**

*Notes*

Impatient to meet your baby? Unfortunately, early labor induction carries with it numerous pitfalls, including increasing your chance of having a cesarean section. "Letting low-risk pregnant patients go into spontaneous labor and delaying non-medically indicated deliveries until 39 weeks' gestation benefit both mothers and babies," noted The American College of Obstetricians and Gynecologists in 2013.

WEEK 1
WEEK 2
WEEK 3
WEEK 4
WEEK 5
WEEK 6
WEEK 7
WEEK 8
WEEK 9
WEEK 10
WEEK 11
WEEK 12
WEEK 13
WEEK 14
WEEK 15
WEEK 16
WEEK 17
WEEK 18
WEEK 19
WEEK 20
WEEK 21
WEEK 22
WEEK 23
WEEK 24
WEEK 25
WEEK 26
WEEK 27
WEEK 28
WEEK 29
WEEK 30
WEEK 31
WEEK 32
WEEK 33
WEEK 34
WEEK 35
WEEK 36
WEEK 37
WEEK 38
WEEK 39
WEEK 40
WEEK 41
WEEK 42

# DAY 214

### 30 WEEKS, 4 DAYS (30W4D)

DATE:　　/

## What is so very wonderful

grateful for...
- [ ] ......................................
- [ ] ......................................
- [ ] ......................................

SLEEP:
APPETITE:
MOOD:

## 66 DAYS UNTIL YOUR DUE DATE (ESTIMATED)

### PERCENTAGE COMPLETED 76.4%

66 *Making a decision to have a child — it's momentous. It is to decide forever to have your heart go walking around outside your body.* 99
— Elizabeth Stone

---

# DAY 215

### 30 WEEKS, 5 DAYS (30W5D)

DATE:　　/

## This is a little annoying

to tell my partner
- [ ] ......................................
- [ ] ......................................
- [ ] ......................................

SLEEP:
APPETITE:
MOOD:

## 65 *days until your due date*

[ each dark | line represents 5 days passed ]

|||||||||||||||||||||||||||||||||||||||||||||||||||||||||||

**ABOUT YOU**

You may get some painful cramps in your lower legs — often in the middle of the night when you're sound asleep. When these "Charley horse" cramps hit in your calf, for example, it can help to flex your ankle and firmly massage the muscle.

Getting more calcium and magnesium in your diet, wearing support hose and stretching before bed might help prevent these annoyances.

DAYS 1-7
8-14
15-21
22-28
29-35
36-42
43-49
50-56
57-63
64-70
71-77
78-84
85-91
92-98
99-105
106-112
113-119
120-126
127-133
134-140
141-147
148-154
155-161
162-168
169-175
176-182
183-189
190-196
197-203
204-210
211-217
218-224
225-231
232-238
239-245
246-252
253-259
260-266
267-273
274-280
281-287
288-294

## DAY 216

**30 WEEKS, 6 DAYS (30W6D)**

DATE:        /

### My birth predictions

WEEK 1
WEEK 2
WEEK 3
WEEK 4
WEEK 5
WEEK 6
WEEK 7
WEEK 8
WEEK 9
WEEK 10
WEEK 11
WEEK 12
WEEK 13
WEEK 14
WEEK 15
WEEK 16
WEEK 17
WEEK 18
WEEK 19
WEEK 20
WEEK 21
WEEK 22
WEEK 23
WEEK 24
WEEK 25
WEEK 26
WEEK 27
WEEK 28
WEEK 29
WEEK 30
WEEK 31
WEEK 32
WEEK 33
WEEK 34
WEEK 35
WEEK 36
WEEK 37
WEEK 38
WEEK 39
WEEK 40
WEEK 41
WEEK 42

**to-do**
- [ ] ............................
- [ ] ............................
- [ ] ............................

SLEEP:
APPETITE:
MOOD:

**64** days until your due date *(estimated)*

percentage left to go **22.9%**

**BABY NAMES**

### GIRLS IN MEXICO

Ximena, Valentina, María Fernanda, Sofía, María José, Martina, Emilia, Zoe, Mia, Dulce María

## DAY 217

**31 WEEKS, 0 DAYS (31W0D)**

DATE:        /

### Just can't get enough

**shopping wish list**
- [ ] ............................
- [ ] ............................
- [ ] ............................

SLEEP:
APPETITE:
MOOD:

**63** days until your due date *(thereabouts)*

percentage completed **77.5%**

~ A LITTLE NOTE TO THE FUTURE ~

☐ WISH  ☐ PREDICTION  ☐ PRAYER  ☐ HOPE  ☐ REMINDER

START OF **WEEK 32**

**29** WEEKS SINCE CONCEPTION : WEEKS UNTIL YOUR DUE DATE **08**

(Dates are estimates only | Pregnancy is considered "term" at 37 to 42 weeks)

**WEEKLY CHART**
31 WEEKS PASSED & STARTING 32

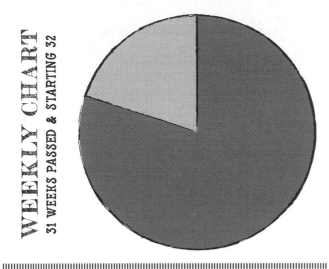

 *How big is baby now?*

Weight: 3-1/4 to 3-3/4 pounds
Length: 16 to 17-1/2 inches

(All measurements are approximate, and based on average fetal development)

## APPOINTMENTS & REMINDERS FOR THIS WEEK

_____ _____
_____ _____
_____ _____
_____ _____

{ ON MY MIND }

**DAY 218**

31 WEEKS, 1 DAY (31W1D)

DATE:        /

*3 wishes for this week*

to-do
☐ .........................................
☐ .........................................
☐ .........................................

SLEEP: ▱▱▱▱▱▱▱▱
APPETITE: ▱▱▱▱▱▱▱▱
MOOD: ▱▱▱▱▱▱▱▱

**62** DAYS UNTIL YOUR DUE DATE (ESTIMATED)

PERCENTAGE LEFT TO GO **22.1%**

**BABY TALK**
— Baby's movements start to feel a little bit different as he grows, since there isn't as much room to play inside the uterus.
— You may notice more bumps inside your belly from elbows and knees as he or she becomes more confined, and if baby turns around, your bump will visibly change shape and size!

# DAY 219

31 WEEKS, 2 DAYS (31W2D)

DATE:        /

## My life right now...

things to research
- [ ] ......................
- [ ] ......................
- [ ] ......................

SLEEP:
APPETITE:
MOOD:

**61** days until your due date

percentage completed **78.2%**

**Blessingway:** A blessingway is a traditional Native American spiritual ceremony, held during pregnancy to celebrate a woman's transition into motherhood. The expectant mother's closest friends attend, and the ritual is meant to also help the mom-to-be prepare for her child's birth. Find out more online at blessingwaybook.com.

def·i·ni·tion

# DAY 220

31 WEEKS, 3 DAYS (31W3D)

DATE:        /

## This week I feel...

questions for my caregiver
- [ ] ......................
- [ ] ......................
- [ ] ......................

SLEEP:
APPETITE:
MOOD:

**60** DAYS UNTIL YOUR DUE DATE (ESTIMATED)

FRACTION COMPLETED **11/14**

Notes

"No longer do I try to define birth by how it 'should' be," says Lesley Everest of Motherwit Doula Care. "Dark rooms, privacy and silence may be one birth giver's healing, and for another it may be their trauma. For some, being told to take their baby as it emerges is a most majestic glory. For another, that message disrupts her to the point of negative physiological impact."

WEEK 1
WEEK 2
WEEK 3
WEEK 4
WEEK 5
WEEK 6
WEEK 7
WEEK 8
WEEK 9
WEEK 10
WEEK 11
WEEK 12
WEEK 13
WEEK 14
WEEK 15
WEEK 16
WEEK 17
WEEK 18
WEEK 19
WEEK 20
WEEK 21
WEEK 22
WEEK 23
WEEK 24
WEEK 25
WEEK 26
WEEK 27
WEEK 28
WEEK 29
WEEK 30
WEEK 31
WEEK 32
WEEK 33
WEEK 34
WEEK 35
WEEK 36
WEEK 37
WEEK 38
WEEK 39
WEEK 40
WEEK 41
WEEK 42

# DAY 221

### 31 WEEKS, 4 DAYS (31W4D)

DATE:        /

## "Mommy brain" strikes

grateful for...
- [ ] ........................................
- [ ] ........................................
- [ ] ........................................

SLEEP:

APPETITE:

MOOD:

# 59

### DAYS UNTIL YOUR DUE DATE
(ESTIMATED)

PERCENTAGE COMPLETED 78.9%

66 It's an established fact. Some women can't stand being pregnant, getting big and bloated, and hauling around a giant stomach, and some women, for reasons probably understood by Darwin, love it. - Rich Cohen 99

# DAY 222

### 31 WEEKS, 5 DAYS (31W5D)

DATE:        /

## What relaxes me most

to tell my partner
- [ ] ........................................
- [ ] ........................................
- [ ] ........................................

SLEEP:

APPETITE:

MOOD:

# 58

### days until your due date

percentage remaining 20.7%

**ABOUT YOU**

Are you feeling a little (ahem) stopped up? Constipation is a very common delight of pregnancy. To help, try boosting your fluid intake, get more fiber (like from raw fruits & veggies and whole grains), and have some prunes or sip some prune juice. Trying to keep your bowel habits regular can help, as can walking, swimming, and getting other exercise. If it gets bad, talk to your caregiver about safe solutions.

# DAY 223

**31 WEEKS, 6 DAYS (31W6D)**

DATE:        /

## Body changes so far

to-do
☐ ............................................
☐ ............................................
☐ ............................................

SLEEP:
APPETITE:
MOOD:

**57** days until your due date (estimated)

percentage completed **79.6%**

## BABY NAMES

### BOYS IN TURKEY

Yusuf, Berat, Mustafa, Emir, Ahmet, Ömer, Mehmet, Muhammed, Emirhan, Eymen

# DAY 224

**32 WEEKS, 0 DAYS (32W0D)**

DATE:        /

## I hope never to forget...

shopping wish list
☐ ............................................
☐ ............................................
☐ ............................................

SLEEP:
APPETITE:
MOOD:

**56** days until your due date (thereabouts)

fraction left to go **1/5**

~ A LITTLE NOTE TO THE FUTURE ~

☐ WISH  ☐ PREDICTION  ☐ PRAYER  ☐ HOPE  ☐ REMINDER

WEEK 1
WEEK 2
WEEK 3
WEEK 4
WEEK 5
WEEK 6
WEEK 7
WEEK 8
WEEK 9
WEEK 10
WEEK 11
WEEK 12
WEEK 13
WEEK 14
WEEK 15
WEEK 16
WEEK 17
WEEK 18
WEEK 19
WEEK 20
WEEK 21
WEEK 22
WEEK 23
WEEK 24
WEEK 25
WEEK 26
WEEK 27
WEEK 28
WEEK 29
WEEK 30
WEEK 31
WEEK 32
WEEK 33
WEEK 34
WEEK 35
WEEK 36
WEEK 37
WEEK 38
WEEK 39
WEEK 40
WEEK 41
WEEK 42

By the end of this month (week 36), your baby will be about as tall as two milk cartons stacked on top of each other (which is not actually not a practical storage technique).

He or she is somewhere around 18 to 19-1/2 inches long. Your little one won't be growing too much longer before birth, but will be busy these next few weeks putting on some adorable baby fat.

# MONTH 9

## How do you feel?

At the beginning of this month,
rate how you're feeling with a line, X or circle

 **ENERGY AMOUNT**

 **IMPATIENCE DEGREE**

 **EMOTIONAL INTENSITY**

 **GRUMPINESS GRADE**

 **SOCIABILITY SCALE**

 **LOVE+ROMANCE LEVEL**

 **FORGETFULNESS FACTOR**

 **GROWTH GAUGE**

Add a picture of yourself at 9 months here
Photos not your thing? Estimate your pregnancy size and
shape by drawing over the shadowed image below

## One year from now

(assuming you give birth around 40 weeks)

*Your baby will be almost a year old!*

### YOU & BABY

Weight gain:

Belly circumference:

Fundal height:

Baby's heart rate:

Baby's position:

### 9 WORDS FOR WHAT'S ON YOUR MIND RIGHT NOW

## 3 things to know this month

1. If you're going somewhere more than an hour or two from home, consider looking up the nearest hospital to your destination that handles births. Just in case.
2. You probably want to pee all the time now, mostly because the baby is sitting on your bladder. Keep up the Kegels, and try drinking a little less at night.
3. Extra weight is concentrated in your front, but don't arch your back to compensate for a shifting center of gravity. Poor posture will stress the muscles, leading to back pain.

*notes*

## START OF WEEK 33

**30** WEEKS SINCE CONCEPTION ⋮ WEEKS UNTIL YOUR DUE DATE **07**

(Dates are estimates only | Pregnancy is considered "term" at 37 to 42 weeks)

**WEEKLY CHART**
**32 WEEKS PASSED & STARTING 33**

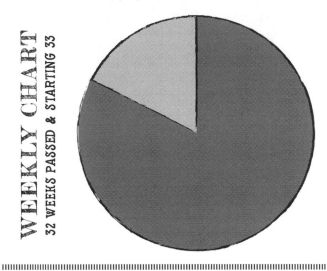

 *How big is baby now?*

Weight: 3-1/2 to 4 pounds
Length: 16 to 18 inches

(All measurements are approximate, and based on average fetal development)

### APPOINTMENTS & REMINDERS FOR THIS WEEK

_____  _____

_____  _____

_____  _____

_____  *Get ready! See the labor bag checklist @ end of book*

### { ON MY MIND }

**DAY 225**

**32 WEEKS, 1 DAY (32W1D)**

DATE:      /

*3 goals for this week*

to-do
☐ .........................................
☐ .........................................
☐ .........................................

SLEEP:       [════════════════]
APPETITE:    [════════════════]
MOOD:        [════════════════]

**51** DAYS UNTIL YOUR DUE DATE (ESTIMATED)

[ each dark | line represents 5 days passed ]

**BABY TALK**

— Your baby will probably turn head-down sometime around now in preparation for birth. It might not be totally obvious to you which end is up, but your caregiver should be able to tell.

— His or her growth (both in weight and in length) begins to slow down a bit.

— New fat makes your little one look more filled out.

WEEK 1
WEEK 2
WEEK 3
WEEK 4
WEEK 5
WEEK 6
WEEK 7
WEEK 8
WEEK 9
WEEK 10
WEEK 11
WEEK 12
WEEK 13
WEEK 14
WEEK 15
WEEK 16
WEEK 17
WEEK 18
WEEK 19
WEEK 20
WEEK 21
WEEK 22
WEEK 23
WEEK 24
WEEK 25
WEEK 26
WEEK 27
WEEK 28
WEEK 29
WEEK 30
WEEK 31
WEEK 32
WEEK 33
WEEK 34
WEEK 35
WEEK 36
WEEK 37
WEEK 38
WEEK 39
WEEK 40
WEEK 41
WEEK 42

## DAY 226

**32 WEEKS, 2 DAYS (32W2D)**

DATE:   /

### What I'm doing differently

**things to research**
- [ ] ......................................
- [ ] ......................................
- [ ] ......................................

SLEEP: ▮▮▮▮▮▮▮▮▮▮
APPETITE: ▮▮▮▮▮▮▮▮▮▮
MOOD: ▮▮▮▮▮▮▮▮▮▮

**54** days until your due date

percentage completed **80.7%**

**Fontanelles:** The "soft spots" between the bony plates on the baby's head. These are gaps in the skull where bones have not yet fused. At birth, this allows the bones to overlap, making it easier for the baby to pass through the birth canal. Later, they allow for the brain's quick growth. The cranial bones are usually fused by 12 to 18 months.

---

## DAY 227

**32 WEEKS, 3 DAYS (32W3D)**

DATE:   /

### This week I feel...

**questions for my caregiver**
- [ ] ......................................
- [ ] ......................................
- [ ] ......................................

SLEEP: ▮▮▮▮▮▮▮▮▮▮
APPETITE: ▮▮▮▮▮▮▮▮▮▮
MOOD: ▮▮▮▮▮▮▮▮▮▮

**53** DAYS UNTIL YOUR DUE DATE (ESTIMATED)

PERCENTAGE LEFT TO GO **18.9%**

**Notes**

Have you found the perfect name? The next step is to write out the initials. If you're lucky, you haven't spelled something you won't want associated with your child... you know, like ASS, BAD, DOG, EWW, HEL, MAD, NAG, NUT, OMG, PEE, PMS, PUS, RAT, WAR, BUG and no doubt many others the kids on the playground would discover.

# DAY 228

32 WEEKS, 4 DAYS (32W4D)

DATE:     /

## Dreams I've been having

grateful for...
- [ ] ................................................
- [ ] ................................................
- [ ] ................................................

SLEEP:
APPETITE:
MOOD:

**52** DAYS UNTIL YOUR DUE DATE (ESTIMATED)

PERCENTAGE COMPLETED **81.4%**

" Babies are bits of stardust, blown from the hand of God. "
- Larry Barretto

# DAY 229

32 WEEKS, 5 DAYS (32W5D)

DATE:     /

## After baby's here, I want to...

to tell my partner
- [ ] ................................................
- [ ] ................................................
- [ ] ................................................

SLEEP:
APPETITE:
MOOD:

**51** days until your due date

percentage remaining **18.2%**

**ABOUT YOU**

The cervix can be compared to a thick rubber band: as it stretches, it widens and thins. To allow passage of the baby, the cervix must both widen (dilate) to 10 cm and thin (efface).

Pre-pregnancy, it is about as hard as the end of your nose — by the end of your term, it's as soft as your earlobe.

# DAY 230

**32 WEEKS, 6 DAYS (32W6D)**

DATE:   /

## My birth philosophy

WEEK 1
WEEK 2
WEEK 3
WEEK 4
WEEK 5
WEEK 6
WEEK 7
WEEK 8
WEEK 9
WEEK 10
WEEK 11
WEEK 12
WEEK 13
WEEK 14
WEEK 15
WEEK 16
WEEK 17
WEEK 18
WEEK 19
WEEK 20
WEEK 21
WEEK 22
WEEK 23
WEEK 24
WEEK 25
WEEK 26
WEEK 27
WEEK 28
WEEK 29
WEEK 30
WEEK 31
WEEK 32

**to-do**
- ☐ ......................
- ☐ ......................
- ☐ ......................

SLEEP: ▭
APPETITE: ▭
MOOD: ▭

# 50
days until
your due date
(estimated)

fraction
completed **23/28**

## BABY NAMES

### ASTRONOMY NAMES - GIRLS

Aurora, Andromeda, Celeste,
Callisto, Elara, Halley, Ophelia,
Pandora, Portia, Vega, Phoebe,
Luna, Larissa, Lyra

---

# DAY 231

**33 WEEKS, 0 DAYS (33W0D)**

DATE:   /

## Current cravings

**shopping wish list**
- ☐ ......................
- ☐ ......................
- ☐ ......................

SLEEP: ▭
APPETITE: ▭
MOOD: ▭

# 49
days until
your due date
(thereabouts)

percentage
completed **82.5%**

### ~A LITTLE NOTE TO THE FUTURE~

☐ WISH ☐ PREDICTION ☐ PRAYER ☐ HOPE ☐ REMINDER

WEEK 33
WEEK 34
WEEK 35
WEEK 36
WEEK 37
WEEK 38
WEEK 39
WEEK 40
WEEK 41
WEEK 42

START OF

# WEEK 34

**31** WEEKS SINCE CONCEPTION    WEEKS UNTIL YOUR DUE DATE **06**

(Dates are estimates only | Pregnancy is considered "term" at 37 to 42 weeks)

## WEEKLY CHART
### 33 WEEKS PASSED & STARTING 34

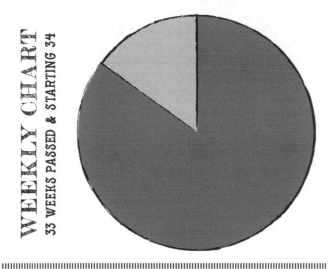

 *How big is baby now?*

Weight: 4 to 4-1/2 pounds
Length: 17 to 19 inches

(All measurements are approximate, and based on average fetal development)

## APPOINTMENTS & REMINDERS FOR THIS WEEK

_____

_____

_____

*Finalize birth plan (see ideas @ end of book)*

{ ON MY MIND }

---

**DAY 232**

33 WEEKS, 1 DAY (33W1D)

DATE:     /

*3 wishes for this week*

to-do
☐ ....................................
☐ ....................................
☐ ....................................

SLEEP:   😣 ▭▭▭▭▭▭▭ 😴
APPETITE:   😋 ▭▭▭▭▭▭▭ 🤢
MOOD:   🙂 ▭▭▭▭▭▭▭ 😠

**48** DAYS UNTIL YOUR DUE DATE (ESTIMATED)

FRACTION COMPLETED **29/35**

- - - - - - - - - - - - - - - - - -

## BABY TALK

— Starting to behave more like a newborn, your baby's eyes can now detect light and dark.

— Because of that development, he or she will close her eyes while sleeping and open them when awake.

— You can help monitor your little one's health each day by counting and recording movements on the kick count charts at the back of the book.

WEEK 1
WEEK 2
WEEK 3
WEEK 4
WEEK 5
WEEK 6
WEEK 7
WEEK 8
WEEK 9
WEEK 10
WEEK 11
WEEK 12
WEEK 13
WEEK 14
WEEK 15
WEEK 16
WEEK 17
WEEK 18
WEEK 19
WEEK 20
WEEK 21
WEEK 22
WEEK 23
WEEK 24
WEEK 25
WEEK 26
WEEK 27
WEEK 28
WEEK 29
WEEK 30
WEEK 31
WEEK 32
WEEK 33
WEEK 34
WEEK 35
WEEK 36
WEEK 37
WEEK 38
WEEK 39
WEEK 40
WEEK 41
WEEK 42

DAY 233

33 WEEKS, 2 DAYS (33W2D)

DATE:    /

## My life right now...

**things to research**
- [ ] ......................................
- [ ] ......................................
- [ ] ......................................

SLEEP:
APPETITE:
MOOD:

**47** days until your due date

percentage completed **83.2%**

**det·i·ni·tion**

**Crowning:** When the baby's head (or other presenting part — such as the bottom in the case of a breech presentation) appears at the vaginal opening, without slipping back inside between contractions. This usually happens moments before delivery. If you're up for it, you can try to reach down to feel that little (wet and slightly smooshy) head at that point!

---

DAY 234

33 WEEKS, 3 DAYS (33W3D)

DATE:    /

## This week I feel...

**questions for my caregiver**
- [ ] ......................................
- [ ] ......................................
- [ ] ......................................

SLEEP:
APPETITE:
MOOD:

**46** DAYS UNTIL YOUR DUE DATE (ESTIMATED)

PERCENTAGE LEFT TO GO **16.4%**

*Notes*

Feeling huge? Here's a comparison that might make you feel better: An African elephant mama is pregnant for about 645 days, and a newborn elephant tips the scale at around 230 pounds. Not too far off, a giraffe pregnancy is around 15 months long. That "baby" calf will be roughly 6 feet tall at birth, and will weigh more than 100 pounds.

## DAY 235

**33 WEEKS, 4 DAYS (33W4D)**

DATE: /

### Advice I've been given

grateful for...
- [ ] .................................
- [ ] .................................
- [ ] .................................

SLEEP:
APPETITE:
MOOD:

**45** DAYS UNTIL
YOUR DUE DATE
(ESTIMATED)

PERCENTAGE COMPLETED **83.9%**

. . . . . . . . . . . . . . . . . . . . . . . . . . . .

" A grand adventure
is about to begin. "

*- A. A. Milne, Winnie the Pooh*

## DAY 236

**33 WEEKS, 5 DAYS (33W5D)**

DATE: /

### How my partner's helping me

to tell my partner
- [ ] .................................
- [ ] .................................
- [ ] .................................

SLEEP:
APPETITE:
MOOD:

**44** days until
your due date

fraction remaining **11/70**

MONTH 1   MONTH 2   MONTH 3   MONTH 4   MONTH 5

DAYS 1-7
8-14
15-21
22-28
29-35
36-42
43-49
50-56
57-63
64-70
71-77
78-84
85-91
92-98
99-105
106-112
113-119
120-126
127-133
134-140
141-147
148-154
155-161
162-168
169-175
176-182
183-189
190-196
197-203
204-210
211-217
218-224
225-231
232-238
239-245
246-252
253-259
260-266
267-273
274-280
281-287
288-294

**ABOUT YOU**

If you have bad heartburn, try to avoid lying down for several hours after you have eaten. But if it's already bedtime, lie on your right side to help your stomach to empty. Also be careful about using pillows or short wedges to prop yourself up, because those can make reflux worse if they bend your midsection. If you need more relief, ask your caregiver about some safe medications.

DAY **237**

33 WEEKS, 6 DAYS (33W6D)

DATE:        /

## Who will be at the birth

to-do
- ☐ .........................................
- ☐ .........................................
- ☐ .........................................

SLEEP: ▭
APPETITE: ▭
MOOD: ▭

**43** days until
your due date
(estimated)

percentage
to go **15.4%**

BABY NAMES

### GIRLS IN DENMARK

*Emma, Ida, Laura, Sofia, Freja, Isabella, Karla, Clara, Anna, Ella*

---

DAY **238**

34 WEEKS, 0 DAYS (34W0D)

DATE:        /

## I can't wait to...

shopping wish list
- ☐ .........................................
- ☐ .........................................
- ☐ .........................................

SLEEP: ▭
APPETITE: ▭
MOOD: ▭

**42** days until
your due date
(thereabouts)

fraction
completed **17/20**

~ A LITTLE NOTE TO THE FUTURE ~

☐ WISH  ☐ PREDICTION  ☐ PRAYER  ☐ HOPE  ☐ REMINDER

THIRD TRIMESTER

WEEK 1
WEEK 2
WEEK 3
WEEK 4
WEEK 5
WEEK 6
WEEK 7
WEEK 8
WEEK 9
WEEK 10
WEEK 11
WEEK 12
WEEK 13
WEEK 14
WEEK 15
WEEK 16
WEEK 17
WEEK 18
WEEK 19
WEEK 20
WEEK 21
WEEK 22
WEEK 23
WEEK 24
WEEK 25
WEEK 26
WEEK 27
WEEK 28
WEEK 29
WEEK 30
WEEK 31
WEEK 32
WEEK 33
WEEK 34
WEEK 35
WEEK 36
WEEK 37
WEEK 38
WEEK 39
WEEK 40
WEEK 41
WEEK 42

## START OF WEEK 35

**32** WEEKS SINCE CONCEPTION　　WEEKS UNTIL YOUR DUE DATE **05**

(Dates are estimates only | Pregnancy is considered "term" at 37 to 42 weeks)

**WEEKLY CHART**
34 WEEKS PASSED & STARTING 35

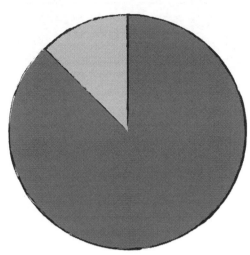

### How big is baby now?

Weight: 4-1/2 to 5 pounds
Length: 17-1/2 to 19 inches

(All measurements are approximate, and based on average fetal development)

## APPOINTMENTS & REMINDERS FOR THIS WEEK

_____  _____

_____  _____

_____  _____

*Take a look at the postpartum promise @ end of book*

### { ON MY MIND }

## DAY 239

**34 WEEKS, 1 DAY (34W1D)**

DATE:　　　/

*3 goals for this week*

to-do
☐ ......................................
☐ ......................................
☐ ......................................

SLEEP: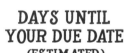
APPETITE:
MOOD:

**41** DAYS UNTIL YOUR DUE DATE (ESTIMATED)

PERCENTAGE REMAINING **14.6%**

**BABY TALK**

— Most babies born at this time will survive, as the final preparations are well underway to keep your little one healthy outside the womb.
— Most bodily systems are fully-developed now, too, except for the lungs. Woo!
— Monitor baby's activity levels with the kick count charts at the back of the book.

# DAY 240

### 34 WEEKS, 2 DAYS (34W2D)

DATE:        /

*I need to remind myself...*

things to research
- [ ] ........................
- [ ] ........................
- [ ] ........................

SLEEP:
APPETITE:
MOOD:

## 40 *days until your due date*

*fraction remaining* **1/7**

**det·i·ni·tion**

**Engagement:** When the widest part of the baby's head has settled deep into the pelvis, the baby is said to be engaged. For you, this means your little one won't be up in your ribs so much, so you should have a little more room to breathe! (This is also called "lightening" or "dropping.") Timing of engagement varies, and doesn't have any clear bearing on when you will give birth.

# DAY 241

### 34 WEEKS, 3 DAYS (34W3D)

DATE:        /

*This week I feel...*

questions for my caregiver
- [ ] ........................
- [ ] ........................
- [ ] ........................

SLEEP:
APPETITE:
MOOD:

## 39 DAYS UNTIL YOUR DUE DATE (ESTIMATED)

PERCENTAGE COMPLETED **86.1%**

*Notes*

Have you and your family thought about what will the grandparents be called? Here are some ideas! Names for Grandmothers: Grammie, Gran, Grandmama, Eema, Mammie, Mimi, Marmi, Nana, Nonni and Oma. Names for Grandfathers: Beepa, Dodie, Granchi, Gumpy, Opa, Pappaw, Pappie, Paw-Paw and Wompa.

WEEK 1
WEEK 2
WEEK 3
WEEK 4
WEEK 5
WEEK 6
WEEK 7
WEEK 8
WEEK 9
WEEK 10
WEEK 11
WEEK 12
WEEK 13
WEEK 14
WEEK 15
WEEK 16
WEEK 17
WEEK 18
WEEK 19
WEEK 20
WEEK 21
WEEK 22
WEEK 23
WEEK 24
WEEK 25
WEEK 26
WEEK 27
WEEK 28
WEEK 29
WEEK 30
WEEK 31
WEEK 32
WEEK 33
WEEK 34
WEEK 35
WEEK 36
WEEK 37
WEEK 38
WEEK 39
WEEK 40
WEEK 41
WEEK 42

MONTH 1    MONTH 2    MONTH 3    MONTH 4    MONTH 5

DAYS 1-7
8-14
15-21
22-28
29-35
36-42
43-49
50-56
57-63
64-70
71-77
78-84
85-91
92-98
99-105
106-112
113-119
120-126
127-133
134-140
141-147
148-154
155-161
162-168
169-175
176-182
183-189
190-196
197-203
204-210
211-217
218-224
225-231
232-238
239-245
246-252
253-259
260-266
267-273
274-280
281-287
288-294

# DAY 242

## 34 WEEKS, 4 DAYS (34W4D)

DATE:        /

### Preparing for postpartum

grateful for...
- [ ] ......................................................
- [ ] ......................................................
- [ ] ......................................................

SLEEP:
APPETITE:
MOOD:

**38** DAYS UNTIL YOUR DUE DATE (ESTIMATED)

PERCENTAGE COMPLETED **86.4%**

66 *Just as a woman's heart knows how and when to pump, her lungs to inhale, and her hand to pull back from fire, so she knows when and how to give birth.* 99

*- Virginia DiOrio*

# DAY 243

## 34 WEEKS, 5 DAYS (34W5D)

DATE:        /

### I wish I could...

to tell my partner
- [ ] ......................................................
- [ ] ......................................................
- [ ] ......................................................

SLEEP:
APPETITE:
MOOD:

**37** days until your due date

percentage remaining **13.2%**

**ABOUT YOU**

"When women are quietly and patiently encouraged and supported in exquisite privacy by friends, family, and professionals who trust birth and trust each woman's inherent ability to give birth, when women stop being 'disturbed' in labor, many more women will give birth normally and ecstatically," wrote Judith A. Lothian, RN, PhD, LCCE, FACCE in THE JOURNAL OF PERINATAL EDUCATION (2004).

## DAY 244

**34 WEEKS, 6 DAYS (34W6D)**

DATE:          /

### How I am "nesting"

to-do
- [ ]
- [ ]
- [ ]

SLEEP:
APPETITE:
MOOD:

## 36 days until your due date
*(estimated)*

fraction completed **61/70**

### BABY NAMES

#### BOYS IN MALAYSIA

*Muhamad, Ahmad, Amar, Adam, Ethan, Umar, Aqil, Danish, Iz Aidan*

## DAY 245

**35 WEEKS, 0 DAYS (35W0D)**

DATE:          /

### Something unexpected

shopping wish list
- [ ]
- [ ]
- [ ]

SLEEP:
APPETITE:
MOOD:

## 35 days until your due date
*(thereabouts)*

[ each dark | line represents 5 days passed ]

‖‖‖‖‖‖‖‖‖‖‖‖‖‖‖‖‖‖‖‖‖‖‖‖‖‖‖‖‖‖‖‖‖‖‖‖‖‖‖‖‖‖‖‖‖‖‖‖

### ~A LITTLE NOTE TO THE FUTURE~

☐ WISH  ☐ PREDICTION  ☐ PRAYER  ☐ HOPE  ☐ REMINDER

WEEK 1
WEEK 2
WEEK 3
WEEK 4
WEEK 5
WEEK 6
WEEK 7
WEEK 8
WEEK 9
WEEK 10
WEEK 11
WEEK 12
WEEK 13
WEEK 14
WEEK 15
WEEK 16
WEEK 17
WEEK 18
WEEK 19
WEEK 20
WEEK 21
WEEK 22
WEEK 23
WEEK 24
WEEK 25
WEEK 26
WEEK 27
WEEK 28
WEEK 29
WEEK 30
WEEK 31
WEEK 32
WEEK 33
WEEK 34
WEEK 35
WEEK 36
WEEK 37
WEEK 38
WEEK 39
WEEK 40
WEEK 41
WEEK 42

## START OF WEEK 36

**33** WEEKS SINCE CONCEPTION   WEEKS UNTIL YOUR DUE DATE **04**

(Dates are estimates only | Pregnancy is considered "term" at 37 to 42 weeks)

### WEEKLY CHART
35 WEEKS PASSED & STARTING 36

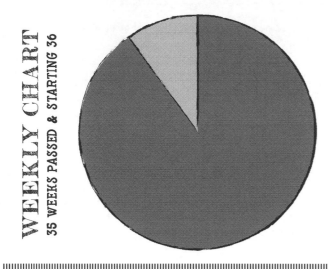

*How big is baby now?*

Weight: 5 to 5-1/2 pounds
Length: 18 to 19 inches

(All measurements are approximate, and based on average fetal development)

## APPOINTMENTS & REMINDERS FOR THIS WEEK

_____   _____
_____   _____
_____   _____

### { ON MY MIND }

---

## DAY 246

35 WEEKS, 1 DAY (35W1D)

DATE:        /

### 3 wishes for this week

**to-do**
☐ ........................................
☐ ........................................
☐ ........................................

SLEEP:
APPETITE:
MOOD:

**34** DAYS UNTIL YOUR DUE DATE (ESTIMATED)

PERCENTAGE REMAINING **12.1%**

### BABY TALK

— As you can no doubt tell, baby is getting pretty snug in there, and it's harder for him or her to turn around.

— While he or she gets ready to join the world, your little person keeps busy doing fun things like wiggling tiny toes into your ribs, kicking your bladder, and head-butting your belly button from the inside.

# DAY 247

## 35 WEEKS, 2 DAYS (35W2D)

DATE:        /

### My life right now...

things to research
- ☐ ........................
- ☐ ........................
- ☐ ........................

SLEEP: 😴 ▬▬▬▬▬▬ 🐾
APPETITE: 😋 ▬▬▬▬▬▬ 😖
MOOD: 🙂 ▬▬▬▬▬▬ 😣

## 33 days until your due date

percentage completed **88.2%**

WEEK 1
WEEK 2
WEEK 3
WEEK 4
WEEK 5
WEEK 6
WEEK 7
WEEK 8
WEEK 9
WEEK 10
WEEK 11
WEEK 12
WEEK 13
WEEK 14
WEEK 15
WEEK 16
WEEK 17
WEEK 18
WEEK 19
WEEK 20
WEEK 21
WEEK 22
WEEK 23
WEEK 24
WEEK 25
WEEK 26
WEEK 27
WEEK 28
WEEK 29
WEEK 30
WEEK 31
WEEK 32
WEEK 33
WEEK 34
WEEK 35
WEEK 36
WEEK 37
WEEK 38
WEEK 39
WEEK 40
WEEK 41
WEEK 42

**de·fi·ni·tion**

**Lochia:** The bloody vaginal discharge you will have after giving birth. Lochia is often compared to a long and heavy menstrual period. It appears in three stages: *Lochia rubra* (a bright red discharge that lasts for approximately three days), *Lochia serosa* (a pinkish discharge that appears next and lasts until about day 10), and finally *Lochia alba* (a thinner whitish-brown discharge which can last anywhere from 1 to 4 weeks). Lochia should be completely gone around 6 weeks postpartum.

---

# DAY 248

## 35 WEEKS, 3 DAYS (35W3D)

DATE:        /

### This week I feel...

questions for my caregiver
- ☐ ........................
- ☐ ........................
- ☐ ........................

SLEEP: 😴 ▬▬▬▬▬▬ 🐾
APPETITE: 😋 ▬▬▬▬▬▬ 😖
MOOD: 🙂 ▬▬▬▬▬▬ 😣

## 32 DAYS UNTIL YOUR DUE DATE (ESTIMATED)

FRACTION COMPLETED **31/35**

*Notes*

The APGAR score is a quick measurement of a newborn's response to birth and life outside the womb. Zero, 1 or 2 point ratings are based on Appearance (color); Pulse (heartbeat); Grimace (reflex); Activity (muscle tone) and Respiration (breathing). Babies are checked at both one minute and 5 minutes after birth, with total scores ranging from 0 (worst) to 10 (best).

MONTH 1          MONTH 2          MONTH 3          MONTH 4          MONTH 5

DAYS 1-7
8-14
15-21
22-28
29-35
36-42
43-49
50-56
57-63
64-70
71-77
78-84
85-91
92-98
99-105
106-112
113-119
120-126
127-133
134-140
141-147
148-154
155-161
162-168
169-175
176-182
183-189
190-196
197-203
204-210
211-217
218-224
225-231
232-238
239-245
246-252
253-259
260-266
267-273
274-280
281-287
288-294

# DAY 249

## 35 WEEKS, 4 DAYS (35W4D)

DATE:        /

### How life will be changing

grateful for...
- ☐ ..............................................
- ☐ ..............................................
- ☐ ..............................................

SLEEP: ▭
APPETITE: ▭
MOOD: ▭

**31** DAYS UNTIL YOUR DUE DATE (ESTIMATED)

PERCENTAGE COMPLETED **88.9%**

❝ The childbirth class neglected to teach you a critical skill: How to swear, breathe and count all at the same time. ❞
— Linda Fiterman

# DAY 250

## 35 WEEKS, 5 DAYS (35W5D)

DATE:        /

### Time is passing very...

to tell my partner
- ☐ ..............................................
- ☐ ..............................................
- ☐ ..............................................

SLEEP: ▭
APPETITE: ▭
MOOD: ▭

**30** days until your due date (approximately)

[ each dark | line represents 5 days passed ]

||||||||||||||||||||||||||||||||||||||||||||||||||||

**ABOUT YOU**

File this under "gross but good": If you notice blood-tinged mucus (bloody show) from the vagina — which may be clear or tinged red, pink or brown — you may be losing the mucus plug that has sealed off the cervix up to this point. This is one of the more visible signs that your body is preparing for birth, but it can happen weeks before labor, or just as it all begins.

## DAY 251

**35 WEEKS, 6 DAYS (35W6D)**

DATE:        /

### Easier than I expected

to-do
- [ ] ..............................................
- [ ] ..............................................
- [ ] ..............................................

SLEEP: ▮▮▮▮▮▮▮▮▮▮▮▮▮▮▮▮▮▮
APPETITE: ▮▮▮▮▮▮▮▮▮▮▮▮▮▮▮▮▮▮
MOOD: ▮▮▮▮▮▮▮▮▮▮▮▮▮▮▮▮▮▮

## 29 days until your due date (estimated)

percentage left to go **10.4%**

### BOYS IN PARIS

**BABY NAMES**

Gabriel, Adam, Raphaël, Paul, Arthur, Victor, Mohammed, Louis, Alexandre, Maxime

---

## DAY 252

**36 WEEKS, 0 DAYS (36W0D)**

DATE:        /

### Harder than I expected

shopping wish list
- [ ] ..............................................
- [ ] ..............................................
- [ ] ..............................................

SLEEP: ▮▮▮▮▮▮▮▮▮▮▮▮▮▮▮▮▮▮
APPETITE: ▮▮▮▮▮▮▮▮▮▮▮▮▮▮▮▮▮▮
MOOD: ▮▮▮▮▮▮▮▮▮▮▮▮▮▮▮▮▮▮

## 28 days until your due date (thereabouts)

fraction completed **9/10**

~ A LITTLE NOTE TO THE FUTURE ~
- [ ] WISH  [ ] PREDICTION  [ ] PRAYER  [ ] HOPE  [ ] REMINDER

WEEK 1
WEEK 2
WEEK 3
WEEK 4
WEEK 5
WEEK 6
WEEK 7
WEEK 8
WEEK 9
WEEK 10
WEEK 11
WEEK 12
WEEK 13
WEEK 14
WEEK 15
WEEK 16
WEEK 17
WEEK 18
WEEK 19
WEEK 20
WEEK 21
WEEK 22
WEEK 23
WEEK 24
WEEK 25
WEEK 26
WEEK 27
WEEK 28
WEEK 29
WEEK 30
WEEK 31
WEEK 32
WEEK 33
WEEK 34
WEEK 35
WEEK 36
WEEK 37
WEEK 38
WEEK 39
WEEK 40
WEEK 41
WEEK 42

By the end of this month (week 40), your baby will be about 20 inches long! That's about two-thirds the width of a standard interior door.

The average birthweight for a baby in the US is about 7-1/2 pounds, but healthy newborns can weigh much more or a little less. Your body and baby's body are working together to make him or her the ideal size.

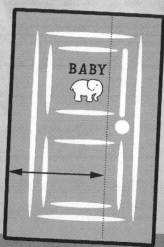

BABY

# MONTH 10

WEEK 37, WEEK 38
WEEK 39 & BEYOND

## How do you feel?

At the beginning of this month, rate how you're feeling with a line, X or circle

 **ENERGY AMOUNT**

 **IMPATIENCE DEGREE**

 **EMOTIONAL INTENSITY**

 **GRUMPINESS GRADE**

 **SOCIABILITY SCALE**

 **LOVE+ROMANCE LEVEL**

 **FORGETFULNESS FACTOR**

 **GROWTH GAUGE**

Add a picture of yourself at 10 months here
Photos not your thing? Estimate your pregnancy size and shape by drawing over the shadowed image below

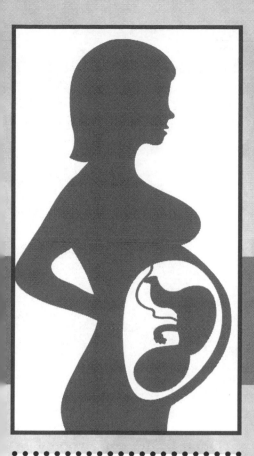

## One year from now
(assuming you give birth around 40 weeks)

Your baby will be
having a birthday party!

### YOU & BABY

Weight gain:

Belly circumference:

Fundal height:

Baby's heart rate:

Baby's position:

### 10 WORDS FOR WHAT'S ON YOUR MIND RIGHT NOW

## 4 things to know this month

1. Most women have weekly prenatal appointments now.
2. In the last few weeks, your weight gain may slow or stop – but your baby is still putting on the pounds!
3. Heartburn? Try eating fresh papaya, pineapple or their juices. Those enzymes speed up the digestion of protein.
4. Postpartum depression is very common, affecting 8 to 19% of women, according to the CDC. If you feel numb or disconnected from your baby, or have scary and/or negative thoughts about your newborn, don't wait: call a doctor or therapist.

## notes

# LABOR & BIRTH

"There is clear and important evidence that walking and upright positions in the first stage of labour reduces the duration of labour, the risk of caesarean birth, the need for epidural, and does not seem to be associated with increased intervention or negative effects on mothers' and babies' well being."

*From* Cochrane Database of Systematic Reviews *(August 2013), reporting on a review of 25 trials with 5218 women*

"All natural birth has a purpose and a plan; who would think of tearing open the chrysalis as the butterfly is emerging? Who would break the shell to pull the chick out?" - Marie Mongon, *Hypnobirthing*

## How pain relief can help some moms & babies bond

Giving birth without pain medication can be a profound and rewarding experience for many women — but that doesn't mean going anesthesia-free suits every birthing mama.

A study reported in 2014 found that women who had epidural anesthesia during a vaginal delivery had a much lower risk for postpartum depression than women who didn't.

Noting a link between acute/chronic pain and depression, Northwestern Medicine perinatal psychiatrist Katherine Wisner, MD, suggests that managing acute pain during and after birth supports the new mother's ability to emotionally attach and care for her baby.

"Pain control gets the mother off to a good beginning rather than starting off defeated and exhausted," Wisner says. "The objective here is to avoid severe pain. Controlling that delivery pain so a woman can comfortably develop as a mother is something that makes a lot of sense."

## BIRTH PLAN BENEFITS: THE BASICS

**This baby has to come out sooner or later, so now is the time to get a birth plan ready.**

Wait... what's a birth plan? The goal of this clever feat of preparation is to help everyone involved in your birth — your healthcare provider, your coach, your doula and anyone else — understand your hopes and desires for labor, delivery, newborn care and postpartum care.

While a birth plan should be considered a clear, simplified statement of your preferences, it is also a great place to begin discussions with your caregiver(s) at a hospital or medical center.

On the birth plan ideas pages at the back of this book, you will find some ideas about what you may want to consider when creating your own plan. Check off the statements that align with your needs, write down any other ideas you would like to add, and combine them all in your own customized birth plan.

No matter your preferences, birth plans are best kept short and to the point — too many extra details may be lost on busy medical support staff. You may even wish to create two plans: one for yourself and your support team, and another, more concise document (no more than a page long) for your caregiver and the hospital staff.

# A PERFECT 10

You know your cervix has to dilate to about 10 centimeters before the pushing phase of labor begins, but just how big is that? To give you an idea, here are some comparisons to familiar objects!

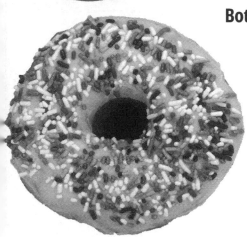

Pea: 1cm
Cheerio: 1.2cm
Penny: 1.9cm
Peppermint candy: 2.2cm
Bottle cap (flat part): 2.6cm
Mini cupcake: 3.5cm
Ping pong ball: 4cm
Peanut butter cup: 5cm
Soda can top: 5.4cm
Big cupcake: 6cm
Baseball: 7cm
Donut: 8cm
Grapefruit: 10cm

# #2 on the worry list

What stresses expectant moms almost as much as the thought of pushing a grapefruit-sized baby head out of a hole that usually is much, much smaller? Here's a hint: It's *another* thing that tends to come out when the baby's head starts pushing in that area.

To put it another way: Imagine a bowling ball and a tube of toothpaste. Picture rolling the ball over the tube, from the sealed end toward the hole.

Well... the bowling ball here equals baby's head, the toothpaste tube is a stand-in for your rectum.

If you haven't cleared out the far end of your digestive system before labor, something is probably going to be in there. That's normal! But if you try holding it in, you're going to be holding back the baby, too. (On

the bright side, a little poop means that you're pushing correctly.)

Many times, the contractions of early labor will stimulate and encourage your bowels to empty themselves out before you even hit the hospital. But if that doesn't happen for you, and you're still concerned about the poop issue, you can ask about getting an enema during early labor.

Really, though, it's nothing the labor & delivery nurses, doctors and midwives haven't seen over and over again. Not only will they be unfazed, they probably have a little towel ready to wipe it away before you even know it.

So try not to stress out and remember that, any moment now, something *much* more exciting things will be emerging nearby.

## Making the cut

An episiotomy is a surgical cut made through the muscle in the perineum, the area between the vagina and the anus.

For many years, it was believed the procedure would widen the birth canal while helping protect women from tearing and other pelvic floor damage — but recent studies have shown the opposite is true. In fact, in 2008, the National Quality Forum suggested limiting routine episiotomy, noting increased risks of pain, laceration and anal incontinence with the procedure.

Fortunately, over the past decade or so, episiotomy rates in the U.S. have declined, so now only 10-20% of women get the cut.

Talk to your caregiver to find out how often he or she performs this procedure. If you want to avoid it unless medically necessary, make your desires clear — and find out what "medically necessary" means to him or her.

### The 10 most relaxing songs

Want soothing tunes for labor? A sound therapist and a stress specialist worked with musicians to create a list of 10 relaxing songs, according to science.

1. Weightless: Marconi Union
2. Airstream: Electra
3. DJ Shah: Mellomaniac
4. Enya: Watermark
5. Coldplay: Strawberry Swing
6. Barcelona: Please Don't Go
7. All Saints: Pure Shores
8. Adele: Someone like You
9. Mozart: Canzonetta Sull'aria
10. Cafe Del Mar: We Can Fly

### Ready to go?

Is your labor bag all ready so you can go to the hospital or birth center without worrying about it? If you're not sure what to bring, you can get a complete checklist at the end of this book.

### START OF WEEK 37

**34** WEEKS SINCE CONCEPTION    WEEKS UNTIL YOUR DUE DATE **03**

(Dates are estimates only | Pregnancy is considered "term" at 37 to 42 weeks)

**WEEKLY CHART**
36 WEEKS PASSED & STARTING 37

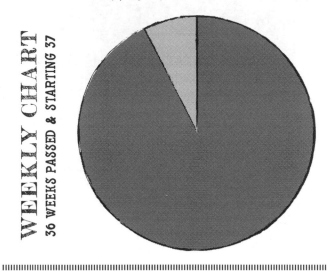

 **How big is baby now?**

Weight: 5-1/2 to 6 pounds
Length: 18 to 19-1/2 inches

(All measurements are approximate, and based on average fetal development)

### APPOINTMENTS & REMINDERS FOR THIS WEEK

_____  _____

_____  _____

_____  _____

*All set with your labor bag checklist @ end of book*

**{ ON MY MIND }**

---

**DAY 253**

**36 WEEKS, 1 DAY (36W1D)**

DATE:   /

*3 ideas for this week*

**to-do**
☐ ......................................
☐ ......................................
☐ ......................................

SLEEP:
APPETITE:
MOOD:

**27** DAYS UNTIL YOUR DUE DATE (ESTIMATED)

PERCENTAGE COMPLETED **90.4%**

**BABY TALK**

— The last weeks of in the womb are called the "finishing period." The baby's weight gain now is white fat, and he or she is considered "term."
— Lanugo (the downy hair all over his or her body) is disappearing.
— Baby's fingernails finally extend beyond his or her fingertips, so can now scratch a little.

WEEK 1
WEEK 2
WEEK 3
WEEK 4
WEEK 5
WEEK 6
WEEK 7
WEEK 8
WEEK 9
WEEK 10
WEEK 11
WEEK 12
WEEK 13
WEEK 14
WEEK 15
WEEK 16
WEEK 17
WEEK 18
WEEK 19
WEEK 20
WEEK 21
WEEK 22
WEEK 23
WEEK 24
WEEK 25
WEEK 26
WEEK 27
WEEK 28
WEEK 29
WEEK 30
WEEK 31
WEEK 32
WEEK 33
WEEK 34
WEEK 35
WEEK 36
WEEK 37
WEEK 38
WEEK 39
WEEK 40
WEEK 41
WEEK 42

## DAY 254

**36 WEEKS, 2 DAYS (36W2D)**

DATE:        /

### Constantly on my mind

things to research
- [ ] ............................
- [ ] ............................
- [ ] ............................

SLEEP:
APPETITE:
MOOD:

**26** days until your due date

percentage remaining **9.3%**

**det·i·ni·tion**

**Transition:** The phase of labor just before the pushing stage, when the cervix opens completely. Some signs of transition: contractions become very strong, and their duration and frequency may be less predictable. It's generally considered the most emotionally overwhelming part of birth. In fact, wanting to cry or give up is a classic sign of this phase. Hang on just a bit little longer!

## DAY 255

**36 WEEKS, 3 DAYS (36W3D)**

DATE:        /

### This week I feel...

questions for my caregiver
- [ ] ............................
- [ ] ............................
- [ ] ............................

SLEEP:
APPETITE:
MOOD:

**25** DAYS UNTIL YOUR DUE DATE (ESTIMATED)

[ each dark | line represents 5 days passed ]

**Notes**

It's time to get ready to add your newborn(s) to your health insurance! Many insurance companies require you add new family members within 30 days of birth. Check with your insurer now to find out what you need to do to add someone to your policy, so you don't have to figure it out later while simultaneously soothing a newborn who is spitting up on your shoulder.

## DAY 256
### 36 WEEKS, 4 DAYS (36W4D)
DATE:        /

### My birth predictions

grateful for...
- ☐ ...........................
- ☐ ...........................
- ☐ ...........................

SLEEP: ▭▭▭▭▭▭▭▭
APPETITE: ▭▭▭▭▭▭▭▭
MOOD: ▭▭▭▭▭▭▭▭

## 24 DAYS UNTIL YOUR DUE DATE (ESTIMATED)

FRACTION COMPLETED **32/35**

❝ There are three reasons for breastfeeding: the milk is always at the right temperature; ❞ it comes in attractive containers; and the cat can't get it
*- Irena Chalmers*

## DAY 257
### 36 WEEKS, 5 DAYS (36W5D)
DATE:        /

### This amazed me

to tell my partner
- ☐ ...........................
- ☐ ...........................
- ☐ ...........................

SLEEP: ▭▭▭▭▭▭▭▭
APPETITE: ▭▭▭▭▭▭▭▭
MOOD: ▭▭▭▭▭▭▭▭

## 23 days until your due date

how far you have come **91.8%**

**ABOUT YOU**

Breastfeeding is natural, yes, but it isn't always easy. To help get ready to nurse your baby, consider taking a class, finding a lactation consultant, and chatting with to breastfeeding moms (online or off). Learn all you can in advance to make your experience as smooth as possible, and always try to correct any problems or cope with any concerns sooner rather than later.

0875 1-7
8-14
15-21
22-28
29-35
36-42
43-49
50-56
57-63
64-70
71-77
78-84
85-91
92-98
99-105
106-112
113-119
120-126
127-133
274-140
121-142
144-154
155-161
162-158
169-175
176-182
183-189
191-196
197-203
204-210
211-217
218-224
225-231
232-238
239-245
246-252
253-259
260-266
267-273
274-280
281-287
288-294

## DAY 258
36 WEEKS, 6 DAYS (36W6D)

DATE: /

### A self-portrait

to-do
- [ ] .................................
- [ ] .................................
- [ ] .................................

SLEEP:
APPETITE:
MOOD:

**22** days until your due date (estimated)

percentage remaining **7.9%**

### BABY NAMES
**BOY NAMES FROM THE 1960S**

Michael, David, James, Robert, Mark, William, Richard, Thomas, Jeffrey, Steven, Joseph, Timothy, Kevin, Scott, Brian, Kenneth

## DAY 259
37 WEEKS, 0 DAYS (37W0D)

DATE: /

### What keeps me up at night

shopping wish list
- [ ] .................................
- [ ] .................................
- [ ] .................................

SLEEP:
APPETITE:
MOOD:

**21** days until your due date (thereabouts)

percentage completed **92.5%**

~ A LITTLE NOTE TO THE FUTURE ~
- [ ] WISH　- [ ] PREDICTION　- [ ] PRAYER　- [ ] HOPE　- [ ] REMINDER

START OF **WEEK 38**

**35** WEEKS SINCE CONCEPTION : WEEKS UNTIL YOUR DUE DATE **02**

(Dates are estimates only | Pregnancy is considered "term" at 37 to 42 weeks)

## WEEKLY CHART
### 37 WEEKS PASSED & STARTING 38

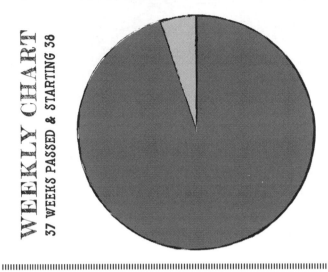

 *How big is baby now?*

Weight: 6 to 7 pounds
Length: 19 to 20 inches

(All measurements are approximate, and based on average fetal development)

## APPOINTMENTS & REMINDERS FOR THIS WEEK

_____  _____
_____  _____
_____  _____

### { ON MY MIND }

---

**DAY 260**

**37 WEEKS, 1 DAY (37W1D)**

DATE:          /

*3 goals for this week*

to-do
- ☐ ................................
- ☐ ................................
- ☐ ................................

SLEEP:       😴 ▭▭▭▭▭▭ 🌀
APPETITE:   😋 ▭▭▭▭▭▭ 🤢
MOOD:       🙂 ▭▭▭▭▭▭ 😣

**20** DAYS UNTIL YOUR DUE DATE (ESTIMATED)

FRACTION LEFT TO GO **1/14**

### BABY TALK

— Your wee one is ready to be born any time now!
— In order for a baby to travel through the birth canal, the head must be small enough and flexible enough to fit. What helps is that a newborn's brain is only a fraction of its adult size, and the skull bones can mold into different positions to help him or her glide through your hips.

## DAY 261

37 WEEKS, 2 DAYS (37W2D)

DATE:   /

### Recent changes

**things to research**
- [ ] ....................................
- [ ] ....................................
- [ ] ....................................

SLEEP: ▮▮▮▮▮▮▮▮▮▮
APPETITE: ▮▮▮▮▮▮▮▮▮▮
MOOD: ▮▮▮▮▮▮▮▮▮▮

## 19 days until your due date

percentage completed **93.2%**

**det·i·ni·tion**

**Lactation consultant:** A lactation consultant aids breastfeeding moms and their babies. They may or may not be certified in order to call themselves a "lactation consultant" and their education and training levels vary. An ICBLC, or Internationally Certified Breastfeeding and Lactation Consultant, has passed an exam given by the International Board of Lactation Consultant Examiners and has received training to help nursing mothers and their little ones.

## DAY 262

37 WEEKS, 3 DAYS (37W3D)

DATE:   /

### This week I feel...

**questions for my caregiver**
- [ ] ....................................
- [ ] ....................................
- [ ] ....................................

SLEEP: ▮▮▮▮▮▮▮▮▮▮
APPETITE: ▮▮▮▮▮▮▮▮▮▮
MOOD: ▮▮▮▮▮▮▮▮▮▮

## 18 DAYS UNTIL YOUR DUE DATE (ESTIMATED)

PERCENTAGE REMAINING **6.4%**

Spontaneous labor (versus induced labor) triggers hormones that provide natural pain relief, helps calm mom during labor, increases mother-baby attachment after birth, enhances breastfeeding, clear fetal lung fluid, and ensures the transfer of maternal antibodies to the newborn. (Source: Association of Women's Health, Obstetric and Neonatal Nurses)

WEEK 1
WEEK 2
WEEK 3
WEEK 4
WEEK 5
WEEK 6
WEEK 7
WEEK 8
WEEK 9
WEEK 10
WEEK 11
WEEK 12
WEEK 13
WEEK 14
WEEK 15
WEEK 16
WEEK 17
WEEK 18
WEEK 19
WEEK 20
WEEK 21
WEEK 22
WEEK 23
WEEK 24
WEEK 25
WEEK 26
WEEK 27
WEEK 28
WEEK 29
WEEK 30
WEEK 31
WEEK 32
WEEK 33
WEEK 34
WEEK 35
WEEK 36
WEEK 37
WEEK 38
WEEK 39
WEEK 40
WEEK 41
WEEK 42

MONTH 1    MONTH 2    MONTH 3    MONTH 4    MONTH 5

DAYS 1-7
8-14
15-21
22-28
29-35
36-42
43-49
50-56
57-63
64-70
71-77
78-84
85-91
92-98
99-105
106-112
113-119
120-126
127-133
134-140
141-147
148-154
155-161
162-168
169-175
176-182
183-189
190-196
197-203
204-210
211-217
218-224
225-231
232-238
239-245
246-252
253-259
260-266
267-273
274-280
281-287
288-294

## DAY 263

### 37 WEEKS, 4 DAYS (37W4D)

DATE:        /

**Breastfeed or bottle feed?**

grateful for...
- ☐ ......................................................
- ☐ ......................................................
- ☐ ......................................................

SLEEP:
APPETITE:
MOOD:

**17** DAYS UNTIL YOUR DUE DATE (ESTIMATED)

PERCENTAGE COMPLETED **93.9%**

❝ *My wife is my hero... It was amazing. Someone else is doing all the hard work, and you're there for them... You sit there and go, 'I would do anything to make this easier for you.'* ❞

— Alec Baldwin on wife Hilaria

## DAY 264

### 37 WEEKS, 5 DAYS (37W5D)

DATE:        /

**How I am keeping busy**

to tell my partner
- ☐ ......................................................
- ☐ ......................................................
- ☐ ......................................................

SLEEP:
APPETITE:
MOOD:

**16** days until your due date

percentage remaining **5.7%**

**ABOUT YOU**

Your body created an entire person, and you never even needed to remember things like, "I have to make eyes today" or "Liver construction this week!" With that in mind, have faith that your baby will arrive when he or she is ready. The human body is made to procreate, and isn't likely to fumble in the end zone. Yes, it's hard, but try to be patient. You are so close!

# DAY 265

**37 WEEKS, 6 DAYS (37W6D)**

**DATE:** /

### *Getting nervous about...*

to-do
- ☐ .................................................
- ☐ .................................................
- ☐ .................................................

**SLEEP:**
**APPETITE:**
**MOOD:**

## 15 days until
your due date
(estimated)

[ each dark | line represents 5 days passed ]

∥∥∥∥∥∥∥∥∥∥∥∥∥∥∥∥∥∥∥∥∥∥∥∥∥∥∥∥∥∥∥∥

## BABY NAMES
### GIRL NAMES MEANING SUNSHINE

*Áine, Apollonia, Cymbeline,
Helen, Idalia, Kalinda, Malina,
Siria, Solana, Soleil*

---

# DAY 266

**38 WEEKS, 0 DAYS (38W0D)**

**DATE:** /

### *I am impatient to...*

shopping wish list
- ☐ .................................................
- ☐ .................................................
- ☐ .................................................

**SLEEP:**
**APPETITE:**
**MOOD:**

## 14 days until
your due date
(thereabouts)

fraction
completed **19/20**

### ~ A LITTLE NOTE TO THE FUTURE ~
☐ WISH　☐ PREDICTION　☐ PRAYER　☐ HOPE　☐ REMINDER

WEEK 1
WEEK 2
WEEK 3
WEEK 4
WEEK 5
WEEK 6
WEEK 7
WEEK 8
WEEK 9
WEEK 10
WEEK 11
WEEK 12
WEEK 13
WEEK 14
WEEK 15
WEEK 16
WEEK 17
WEEK 18
WEEK 19
WEEK 20
WEEK 21
WEEK 22
WEEK 23
WEEK 24
WEEK 25
WEEK 26
WEEK 27
WEEK 28
WEEK 29
WEEK 30
WEEK 31
WEEK 32
WEEK 33
WEEK 34
WEEK 35
WEEK 36
WEEK 37
WEEK 38
WEEK 39
WEEK 40
WEEK 41
WEEK 42

# START OF WEEK 39

**36** WEEKS SINCE CONCEPTION · WEEKS UNTIL YOUR DUE DATE **01**

(Dates are estimates only | Pregnancy is considered "term" at 37 to 42 weeks)

## WEEKLY CHART
### 38 WEEKS PASSED & STARTING 39

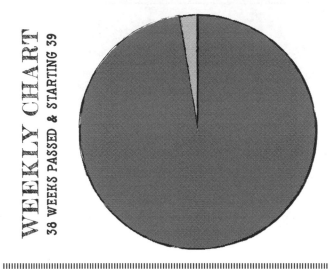

*How big is baby now?*

Weight: 6-3/4 to 7-1/2 pounds
Length: 19 to 20 inches

(All measurements are approximate, and based on average fetal development)

## APPOINTMENTS & REMINDERS FOR THIS WEEK

_____  _____

_____  _____

_____  _____

### { ON MY MIND }

---

## DAY 267

**38 WEEKS, 1 DAY (38W1D)**

DATE: /

### 3 goals for this week

**to-do**
- ☐ ..........................................
- ☐ ..........................................
- ☐ ..........................................

SLEEP:
APPETITE:
MOOD:

**13** DAYS UNTIL YOUR DUE DATE (ESTIMATED)

PERCENTAGE REMAINING **4.6%**

### BABY TALK

— The final systems to develop are the lungs and respiratory system, and they're maturing this week.
— Baby still gains weight in the last few weeks of pregnancy. In addition to giving your little one that cute and cuddly look, the fat under the skin acts as insulation, and will be important to help keep him or her warm after birth.

MONTH 6     MONTH 7     MONTH 8     MONTH 9     **MONTH 10**

WEEK 1
WEEK 2
WEEK 3
WEEK 4
WEEK 5
WEEK 6
WEEK 7
WEEK 8
WEEK 9
WEEK 10
WEEK 11
WEEK 12
WEEK 13
WEEK 14
WEEK 15
WEEK 16
WEEK 17
WEEK 18
WEEK 19
WEEK 20
WEEK 21
WEEK 22
WEEK 23
WEEK 24
WEEK 25
WEEK 26
WEEK 27
WEEK 28
WEEK 29
WEEK 30
WEEK 31
WEEK 32
WEEK 33
WEEK 34
WEEK 35
WEEK 36
WEEK 37
WEEK 38
WEEK 39
WEEK 40
WEEK 41
WEEK 42

## DAY 268

### 38 WEEKS, 2 DAYS (38W2D)

DATE:    /

*I need some help with...*

things to research
- [ ] ................................
- [ ] ................................
- [ ] ................................

SLEEP:
APPETITE:
MOOD:

**12** *days until your due date*

*fraction completed* **67/70**

**Afterpains:** Mild contractions or cramping which help return the uterus returning to its non-pregnant size and state. They are triggered by the release of oxytocin when breastfeeding, although pitocin (synthetic oxytocin) may be given to help the uterus "clamp down" (tighten and stop bleeding). While afterpains can be more painful after the birth of a second or later baby, for all women, they should become milder each day following delivery.

*de·fi·ni·tion*

## DAY 269

### 38 WEEKS, 3 DAYS (38W3D)

DATE:    /

*This week I feel...*

questions for my caregiver
- [ ] ................................
- [ ] ................................
- [ ] ................................

SLEEP:
APPETITE:
MOOD:

**10** **DAYS UNTIL YOUR DUE DATE** (ESTIMATED)

**PERCENTAGE COMPLETED** **96.1%**

It's normal for a breastfed baby to lose a little weight after birth. University researchers note on Penn State's NewbornWeight.org site, "Mothers at first secrete small amounts of colostrum, which contains high concentrations of nutrients and antibodies for the baby. During this period, almost all babies experience some initial weight loss." If you're worried, ask your baby's doctor.

MONTH 1    MONTH 2    MONTH 3    MONTH 4    MONTH 5

DAYS 1-7
8-14
15-21
22-28
29-35
36-42
43-49
50-56
57-63
64-70
71-77
78-84
85-91
92-98
99-105
106-112
113-119
120-126
127-133
134-140
141-147
148-154
155-161
162-168
169-175
176-182
183-189
190-196
197-203
204-210
211-217
218-224
225-231
232-238
239-245
246-252
253-259
260-266
267-273
274-280
281-287
288-294

# DAY 270

## 38 WEEKS, 4 DAYS (38W4D)

DATE:        /

### Can't wait to...with my baby

grateful for...
☐ ............................................
☐ ............................................
☐ ............................................
☐ ............................................

SLEEP: 
APPETITE: 
MOOD: 

## 10 DAYS UNTIL YOUR DUE DATE (ESTIMATED)

FRACTION COMPLETED **27/28**

" There is power that comes to women when they give birth. They don't ask for it, it simply invades them. Accumulates like clouds on the horizon and passes through, carrying the child with it. "
— Sheryl Feldman

# DAY 271

## 38 WEEKS, 5 DAYS (38W5D)

DATE:        /

### A question I always hear

to tell my partner
☐ ............................................
☐ ............................................
☐ ............................................
☐ ............................................

SLEEP: 
APPETITE: 
MOOD: 

## 9 days until your due date

how far you have come **96.8%**

ABOUT YOU

Unfortunately, cervical progress (dilation and effacement) cannot reliably predict when you will — or won't — go into labor. Some caregivers think they're offering you hope when, after an internal exam, they say that you are dilated to 3cm and will probably deliver within a certain number of days. Be prepared, of course, but don't expect your body (or baby) to offer too many obvious clues.

## DAY 272

38 WEEKS, 6 DAYS (38W6D)

DATE:          /

*How I'm staying sane*

WEEK 1
WEEK 2
WEEK 3
WEEK 4
WEEK 5
WEEK 6
WEEK 7
WEEK 8
WEEK 9
WEEK 10
WEEK 11
WEEK 12
WEEK 13
WEEK 14
WEEK 15
WEEK 16
WEEK 17
WEEK 18
WEEK 19
WEEK 20
WEEK 21
WEEK 22
WEEK 23
WEEK 24
WEEK 25
WEEK 26
WEEK 27
WEEK 28
WEEK 29
WEEK 30
WEEK 31
WEEK 32
WEEK 33
WEEK 34
WEEK 35
WEEK 36
WEEK 37
WEEK 38
WEEK 39
WEEK 40
WEEK 41
WEEK 42

to-do
- ☐ ...................................
- ☐ ...................................
- ☐ ...................................

SLEEP: ▭
APPETITE: ▭
MOOD: ▭

**8** days until your due date (estimated)

percentage remaining **2.9%**

**BABY NAMES**

### GIRLS IN VENEZUELA

*Camila, Isabella, Sofia, Victoria, Valentina, Valeria, Nicole, Samantha, Mariana, Antonella*

---

## DAY 273

39 WEEKS, 0 DAYS (39W0D)

DATE:          /

*How people say I'm carrying*

shopping wish list
- ☐ ...................................
- ☐ ...................................
- ☐ ...................................

SLEEP: ▭
APPETITE: ▭
MOOD: ▭

**7** days until your due date (thereabouts)

Just about a week left!

~ A LITTLE NOTE TO THE FUTURE ~

☐ WISH  ☐ PREDICTION  ☐ PRAYER  ☐ HOPE  ☐ REMINDER

## START OF WEEK 40

**37** WEEKS SINCE CONCEPTION : WEEKS UNTIL YOUR DUE DATE **00**

Dates are estimates only | Pregnancy is considered "term" at 37 to 42 weeks

### WEEKLY CHART
**39 WEEKS PASSED & STARTING 40**

(Right about now, it may seem like there's a basketball down your shirt.)

 *How big is baby now?*

Weight: 7-1/4 to 8 pounds
Length: 19 to 21 inches

(All measurements are approximate, and based on average fetal development)

### APPOINTMENTS & REMINDERS FOR THIS WEEK

_____  _____
_____  _____
_____  _____

### { ON MY MIND }

---

## DAY 274

**39 WEEKS, 1 DAY (39W1D)**

DATE: /

### *3 ideas for this week*

### FETAL KICK COUNT TRACKER

☐ ☐ ☐ ☐ ☐ ☐ ☐ ☐ ☐ ☐

Start time : | Stop time : | Time to 10 :

**to-do**
☐ ................................
☐ ................................
☐ ................................

SLEEP: 
APPETITE: 
MOOD: 

**6** DAYS UNTIL YOUR DUE DATE (ESTIMATED)

PERCENTAGE REMAINING **2.1%**

### BABY TALK

— Your baby is ready to be born, but don't forget: Only 5% of kiddos arrive on their due date.
— As the ACOG says, "Babies born between 39 weeks 0 days and 40 weeks 6 days gestation have the best health outcomes, compared with babies born before or after this period."
— Baby's head should be down, all set for delivery.

MONTH 6     MONTH 7     MONTH 8     MONTH 9     **MONTH 10**

WEEK 1
WEEK 2
WEEK 3
WEEK 4
WEEK 5
WEEK 6
WEEK 7
WEEK 8
WEEK 9
WEEK 10
WEEK 11
WEEK 12
WEEK 13
WEEK 14
WEEK 15
WEEK 16
WEEK 17
WEEK 18
WEEK 19
WEEK 20
WEEK 21
WEEK 22
WEEK 23
WEEK 24
WEEK 25
WEEK 26
WEEK 27
WEEK 28
WEEK 29
WEEK 30
WEEK 31
WEEK 32
WEEK 33
WEEK 34
WEEK 35
WEEK 36
WEEK 37
WEEK 38
WEEK 39
WEEK 40
WEEK 41
WEEK 42

## DAY 275

**39 WEEKS, 2 DAYS (39W2D)**

DATE:    /

### My life right now...

FETAL KICK COUNT TRACKER

☐ ☐ ☐ ☐ ☐ ☐ ☐ ☐ ☐ ☐ ☐ ☐

Start time  :   |   Stop time  :   |   Time to 10  :

**things to research**
☐ ......................................
☐ ......................................
☐ ......................................

SLEEP: 😖 �_____ 😴

APPETITE: 😋 _____ 🤢

MOOD: 🙂 _____ 🙁

**5** *days until your due date*

[ each dark | line represents 5 days passed ]

||||||||||||||||||||||||||||||||||||||||||||||

**Prolonged labor:** This is clinically defined as an "abnormally slow progress of labor," lasting more than 20 hours. However, a study reported in the AMERICAN JOURNAL OF OBSTETRICS AND GYNECOLOGY in 2016 found that when women in labor are given more time to deliver their baby than current guidelines recommend, their incidence of cesarean delivery drops by 55 percent. Many babies just aren't interested in following a timetable!

*def·i·ni·tion*

## DAY 276

**39 WEEKS, 3 DAYS (39W3D)**

DATE:    /

### This week I feel...

FETAL KICK COUNT TRACKER

☐ ☐ ☐ ☐ ☐ ☐ ☐ ☐ ☐ ☐ ☐ ☐

Start time  :   |   Stop time  :   |   Time to 10  :

**questions for my caregiver**
☐ ......................................
☐ ......................................
☐ ......................................

SLEEP: 😖 _____ 😴

APPETITE: 😋 _____ 🤢

MOOD: 🙂 _____ 🙁

**4** DAYS UNTIL YOUR DUE DATE (ESTIMATED)

PERCENTAGE COMPLETED **98.6%**

*Notes*

You may feel an almost overwhelming urge to clean your home, prepare meals or finish the nursery. This is called "nesting," and happens to many moms-to-be close to delivery. Go with it, but don't wear yourself out! Take breaks frequently, and force yourself to make rest your top priority. Really — that's way more important than dusting the fridge or alphabetizing the spice rack.

### DAY 277
**39 WEEKS, 4 DAYS (39W4D)**

DATE:       /

*The thought of giving birth...*

## FETAL KICK COUNT TRACKER

☐ ☐ ☐ ☐ ☐ ☐ ☐ ☐ ☐ ☐

Start time   :   | Stop time   :   | Time to 10   :

grateful for...
☐ ......................................
☐ ......................................
☐ ......................................

SLEEP: 
APPETITE: 
MOOD: 

## 3 DAYS UNTIL YOUR DUE DATE (ESTIMATED)

## PERCENTAGE COMPLETED 98.9%

· · · · · · · · · · · · · · · · · · · · · · · · · · · · · · · · · · ·

> 66 Women's bodies have near-perfect knowledge of childbirth;
> it's when their brains get involved that things can go wrong. 99
> — Peggy Vincent

### DAY 278
**39 WEEKS, 5 DAYS (39W5D)**

DATE:       /

*One month from today...*

## FETAL KICK COUNT TRACKER

☐ ☐ ☐ ☐ ☐ ☐ ☐ ☐ ☐ ☐

Start time   :   | Stop time   :   | Time to 10   :

to tell my partner
☐ ......................................
☐ ......................................
☐ ......................................

SLEEP: 
APPETITE: 
MOOD: 

## 2 days until your due date

## percentage remaining 0.7%

**ABOUT YOU**

When labor starts — or you <u>think</u> it's starting — time your contractions with an app, or by using the second hand on a clock or watch, to measure both the duration of the contraction and the amount of time in between contractions. These are important indicators of the progress of labor, so your caregiver or the nurses at the hospital will want to know.

# DAY 279

39 WEEKS, 6 DAYS (39W6D)

DATE: /

## *Am I ready?*

FETAL KICK COUNT TRACKER

☐ ☐ ☐ ☐ ☐ ☐ ☐ ☐ ☐ ☐

Start time : | Stop time : | Time to 10 :

to-do
☐ ..........
☐ ..........
☐ ..........

SLEEP:
APPETITE:
MOOD:

**1** day until your due date (estimated)

Tomorrow you're officially due!
Your baby can show up any time now.

BABY NAMES

### BOYS IN GERMANY

*Ben, Leon, Elias, Finn/Fynn, Jonas, Noah, Paul, Luis/Louis, Lukas/Lucas, Luca & Luka*

# DAY 280

40 WEEKS, 0 DAYS (40W0D)

DATE: /

## *This is it!*

FETAL KICK COUNT TRACKER

☐ ☐ ☐ ☐ ☐ ☐ ☐ ☐ ☐ ☐

Start time : | Stop time : | Time to 10 :

shopping wish list
☐ ..........
☐ ..........
☐ ..........

SLEEP:
APPETITE:
MOOD:

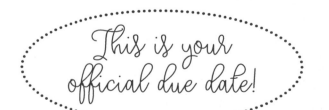

*This is your official due date!*

~A LITTLE NOTE TO THE FUTURE~

☐ WISH ☐ PREDICTION ☐ PRAYER ☐ HOPE ☐ REMINDER

START OF

# WEEK 41

## You made it!

(Your due date is just an approximation, but no doubt your baby gauge is on FULL)

WEEKLY CHART
40 WEEKS PASSED & STARTING 41

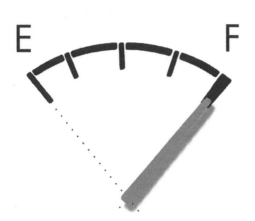

E                    F

*How big is baby now?*

Weight: 7-1/2 to 9 pounds
Length: 19 to 21 inches

(All measurements are approximate, and based on average fetal development)

### APPOINTMENTS & REMINDERS FOR THIS WEEK

_____ _____

_____ _____

_____ _____

_____ _____

{ ON MY MIND }

---

DAY 281

40 WEEKS, 1 DAY (40W1D)

DATE:        /

*3 goals for this week*

to-do
☐ ................................
☐ ................................
☐ ................................

## FETAL KICK COUNT TRACKER

☐ ☐ ☐ ☐ ☐ ☐ ☐ ☐ ☐ ☐

Start time   :   | Stop time   :   | Time to 10   :

SLEEP:
APPETITE:
MOOD:

**1** DAY SINCE
YOUR DUE DATE
(ESTIMATED)

BABY TALK

— If you're still pregnant after 40 weeks, your healthcare provider will want to frequently check on the health of both you and the baby.

— Medical tests might include an ultrasound, non-stress testing, measuring the amniotic fluid levels, and you can track the fetal "kick count."

## DAY 282

40 WEEKS, 2 DAYS (40W2D)

DATE:    /

### Constantly on my mind

WEEK 1
WEEK 2
WEEK 3
WEEK 4
WEEK 5
WEEK 6
WEEK 7
WEEK 8
WEEK 9
WEEK 10
WEEK 11
WEEK 12
WEEK 13
WEEK 14
WEEK 15
WEEK 16
WEEK 17
WEEK 18
WEEK 19
WEEK 20
WEEK 21
WEEK 22
WEEK 23
WEEK 24
WEEK 25
WEEK 26
WEEK 27
WEEK 28
WEEK 29
WEEK 30
WEEK 31
WEEK 32

**things to research**
- [ ] .............................................
- [ ] .............................................
- [ ] .............................................

## FETAL KICK COUNT TRACKER

[ ] [ ] [ ] [ ] [ ] [ ] [ ] [ ] [ ] [ ]

Start time  :  | Stop time  :  | Time to 10  :

SLEEP:       [_____]
APPETITE:   [_____]
MOOD:      [_____]

## 2 DAYS PAST YOUR OFFICIAL DUE DATE

**Non-stress test:** The NST is a prenatal test used in the third trimester to check how the baby is reacting to life in the womb. It is often used to confirm the well-being of the baby based on the concept that a healthy fetus will respond to movement/activity or loud sounds with an increased heart rate.

---

## DAY 283

40 WEEKS, 3 DAYS (40W3D)

DATE:    /

### This week I feel...

**questions for my caregiver**
- [ ] .............................................
- [ ] .............................................
- [ ] .............................................

## FETAL KICK COUNT TRACKER

[ ] [ ] [ ] [ ] [ ] [ ] [ ] [ ] [ ] [ ]

Start time  :  | Stop time  :  | Time to 10  :

SLEEP:       [_____]
APPETITE:   [_____]
MOOD:      [_____]

## 3 DAYS SINCE YOUR DUE DATE (ESTIMATED)

Woo – you made it! Granted, your baby may not have decided to make his or her big entrance yet, but will be doing so any day now. In the meantime, you may think there is no conceivable (ha!) way to get any bigger, and might rightfully wonder if this phase of life will <u>ever</u> end. But know this: It is physically impossible to stay pregnant forever. Really.

MONTH 1    MONTH 2    MONTH 3    MONTH 4    MONTH 5

DAYS 1-7
8-11
15-21
22-28
29-35
36-42
43-49
50-56
57-63
64-70
71-77
78-84
85-91
92-98
99-105
106-112
113-119
120-126
127-133
134-140
141-147
148-154
155-161
162-168
169-175
176-182
183-189
190-196
197-205
206-210
211-217
218-224
225-231
232-238
239-245
246-252
253-259
260-266
267-273
274-280
281-287
288-294

**DAY 284**

**40 WEEKS, 4 DAYS (40W4D)**

DATE: /

*Most impatient friends & family*

grateful for...
☐ ...........................................
☐ ...........................................
☐ ...........................................

**FETAL KICK COUNT TRACKER**

☐ ☐ ☐ ☐ ☐ ☐ ☐ ☐ ☐ ☐

Start time  :  | Stop time  :  | Time to 10  :

SLEEP:
APPETITE:
MOOD:

**4** DAYS SINCE YOUR DUE DATE

66 *In the moments of labor and birth,
all the forces of the universe
are flowing through a woman's body.*
*- Sandra K. Morning Star* 99

**DAY 285**

**40 WEEKS, 5 DAYS (40W5D)**

DATE: /

*Any false alarms?*

to tell my partner
☐ ...........................................
☐ ...........................................
☐ ...........................................

**FETAL KICK COUNT TRACKER**

☐ ☐ ☐ ☐ ☐ ☐ ☐ ☐ ☐ ☐

Start time  :  | Stop time  :  | Time to 10  :

SLEEP:
APPETITE:
MOOD:

**5** *days since your due date*

ABOUT YOU

Once you pass your due date, most caregivers will check in with you every two to three days. Many pregnancies — especially first ones — go post dates, so don't be worried. Be sure your baby is moving every day, and follow your caregiver's instructions on when to contact him or her. (But when in doubt, always give your doctor or midwife a shout, or reach out to your hospital or birth center staff.)

**DAY 286**

40 WEEKS, 6 DAYS (40W6D)

DATE:        /

*How I'm keeping busy*

to-do
- ☐ ............................
- ☐ ............................
- ☐ ............................

### FETAL KICK COUNT TRACKER

☐ ☐ ☐ ☐ ☐ ☐ ☐ ☐ ☐ ☐

Start time   :   | Stop time   :   | Time to 10   :

SLEEP:

APPETITE:

MOOD:

**6** days since your estimated due date

## BABY NAMES

### GIRL NAMES MEANING "HAPPY"

*Blythe, Felicity, Felicia, Hilary, Bonnie, Joy, Ilaria, Gwyneth, Leta, Merry, Nara, Allegra, Halona*

---

**DAY 287**

41 WEEKS, 0 DAYS (41W0D)

DATE:        /

*I never thought...*

shopping wish list
- ☐ ............................
- ☐ ............................
- ☐ ............................

### FETAL KICK COUNT TRACKER

☐ ☐ ☐ ☐ ☐ ☐ ☐ ☐ ☐ ☐

Start time   :   | Stop time   :   | Time to 10   :

SLEEP:

APPETITE:

MOOD:

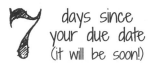 **7** days since your due date (it will be soon!)

### ~ A LITTLE NOTE TO THE FUTURE ~

☐ WISH   ☐ PREDICTION   ☐ PRAYER   ☐ HOPE   ☐ REMINDER

WEEK 1
WEEK 2
WEEK 3
WEEK 4
WEEK 5
WEEK 6
WEEK 7
WEEK 8
WEEK 9
WEEK 10
WEEK 11
WEEK 12
WEEK 13
WEEK 14
WEEK 15
WEEK 16
WEEK 17
WEEK 18
WEEK 19
WEEK 20
WEEK 21
WEEK 22
WEEK 23
WEEK 24
WEEK 25
WEEK 26
WEEK 27
WEEK 28
WEEK 29
WEEK 30
WEEK 31
WEEK 32
WEEK 33
WEEK 34
WEEK 35
WEEK 36
WEEK 37
WEEK 38
WEEK 39
WEEK 40
WEEK 41
WEEK 42

## START OF WEEK 42

**38** WEEKS SINCE CONCEPTION | WEEKS UNTIL YOUR DUE DATE **-1**

Dates are estimates only | Pregnancy is considered "term" at 37 to 42 weeks

**WEEKLY CHART**
41 WEEKS PASSED & STARTING 42

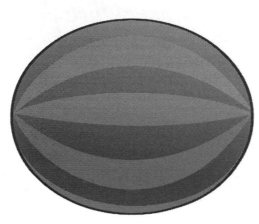

 *How big is baby now?*

Weight: 7-1/2 to 9 pounds
Length: 19 to 21 inches

(All measurements are approximate, and based on average fetal development)

### APPOINTMENTS & REMINDERS FOR THIS WEEK

_____  _____

_____  _____

_____  _____

### { ON MY MIND }

---

 DAY **288**

41 WEEKS, 1 DAY (41W1D)

**DATE:** /

*3 wishes for this week*

**to-do**
- ☐ ................................
- ☐ ................................
- ☐ ................................

## FETAL KICK COUNT TRACKER

☐ ☐ ☐ ☐ ☐ ☐ ☐ ☐ ☐ ☐

Start time : | Stop time : | Time to 10 :

**SLEEP:**
**APPETITE:**
**MOOD:**

**8** DAYS SINCE YOUR DUE DATE

**BABY TALK**

— If you're still pregnant after 41 weeks, your healthcare provider will want to regularly check on the health of both you and the baby.
— Tests your caregiver might run right around now include an ultrasound, non-stress testing (checking heart rate and activity levels), and measuring the amniotic fluid.

WEEK 1
WEEK 2
WEEK 3
WEEK 4
WEEK 5
WEEK 6
WEEK 7
WEEK 8
WEEK 9
WEEK 10
WEEK 11
WEEK 12
WEEK 13
WEEK 14
WEEK 15
WEEK 16
WEEK 17
WEEK 18
WEEK 19
WEEK 20
WEEK 21
WEEK 22
WEEK 23
WEEK 24
WEEK 25
WEEK 26
WEEK 27
WEEK 28
WEEK 29
WEEK 30
WEEK 31
WEEK 32
WEEK 33
WEEK 34
WEEK 35
WEEK 36
WEEK 37
WEEK 38
WEEK 39
WEEK 40
WEEK 41
WEEK 42

## DAY 289

### 41 WEEKS, 2 DAYS (41W2D)

DATE:        /

### Wish I could keep...

things to research
- ☐ ................................
- ☐ ................................
- ☐ ................................

### FETAL KICK COUNT TRACKER

☐ ☐ ☐ ☐ ☐ ☐ ☐ ☐ ☐ ☐

Start time    :    | Stop time    :    | Time to 10    :

SLEEP:

APPETITE:

MOOD:

## 9 DAYS PAST YOUR OFFICIAL DUE DATE

**definition**

Macrosomia: Refers to a newborn who is very large at birth. According to the ACOG, "the term fetal macrosomia implies fetal growth beyond a specific weight, usually 4,000 g (8 pounds, 13 ounces) or 4,500 g (9 pounds, 4 ounces), regardless of the fetal gestational age." Know that size doesn't always signal a problem, or mean you won't be able to give birth vaginally. There are thousands of macrosomic babies born each year who are perfectly healthy.

---

## DAY 290

### 41 WEEKS, 3 DAYS (41W3D)

DATE:        /

### Can't wait to stop...

questions for my caregiver
- ☐ ................................
- ☐ ................................
- ☐ ................................

### FETAL KICK COUNT TRACKER

☐ ☐ ☐ ☐ ☐ ☐ ☐ ☐ ☐ ☐

Start time    :    | Stop time    :    | Time to 10    :

SLEEP:

APPETITE:

MOOD:

## 10 DAYS SINCE YOUR DUE DATE

**Notes**

It probably seems a lot like you have been training for a marathon! Now the race is about to begin, but they won't tell you when it starts, or how the course will be set up. You just have to be ready to run the race, no matter what, with only a moment's notice. And you can.

MONTH 1    MONTH 2    MONTH 3    MONTH 4    MONTH 5

DAYS 1-7
8-14
15-21
22-28
29-35
36-42
43-49
50-56
57-63
64-70
71-77
78-84
85-91
92-98
99-105
106-112
113-119
120-126
127-133
134-140
141-147
148-154
155-161
162-168
169-175
176-182
183-189
190-196
197-203
204-210
211-217
218-224
225-231
232-238
239-245
246-252
253-259
260-266
267-273
274-280
281-287
288-294

## DAY 291

### 41 WEEKS, 4 DAYS (41W4D)

**DATE:** /

*I am too big to...*

grateful for...
- [ ] ...................................
- [ ] ...................................
- [ ] ...................................

### FETAL KICK COUNT TRACKER

- [ ] [ ] [ ] [ ] [ ] [ ] [ ] [ ] [ ] [ ]

Start time : | Stop time : | Time to 10 :

SLEEP:
APPETITE:
MOOD:

## 11 DAYS SINCE YOUR DUE DATE

 *The greatest thing
you'll ever learn
is just to love
and be loved in return.*
— Eden Ahbez

## DAY 292

### 41 WEEKS, 5 DAYS (41W5D)

**DATE:** /

*My revised birth prediction*

post-baby to-do list
- [ ] ...................................
- [ ] ...................................
- [ ] ...................................

### FETAL KICK COUNT TRACKER

- [ ] [ ] [ ] [ ] [ ] [ ] [ ] [ ] [ ] [ ]

Start time : | Stop time : | Time to 10 :

SLEEP:
APPETITE:
MOOD:

## 12 *days since your due date*

**ABOUT YOU**

Researchers from Tel Aviv University found that babies born after 42 weeks were more likely to be an unhealthy weight and have diabetes, — and their mothers had an increased risk of diabetes, too. The lead author of the study (reported in 2016) commented, "Our study implies that even in otherwise low-risk pregnancy, it is advisable not to postpone delivery beyond 42 weeks."

MONTH 6    MONTH 7    MONTH 8    MONTH 9    MONTH 10

WEEK 1
WEEK 2
WEEK 3
WEEK 4
WEEK 5
WEEK 6
WEEK 7
WEEK 8
WEEK 9
WEEK 10
WEEK 11
WEEK 12
WEEK 13
WEEK 14
WEEK 15
WEEK 16
WEEK 17
WEEK 18
WEEK 19
WEEK 20
WEEK 21
WEEK 22
WEEK 23
WEEK 24
WEEK 25
WEEK 26
WEEK 27
WEEK 28
WEEK 29
WEEK 30
WEEK 31
WEEK 32
WEEK 33
WEEK 34
WEEK 35
WEEK 36
WEEK 37
WEEK 38
WEEK 39
WEEK 40
WEEK 41
WEEK 42

## DAY  293

**41 WEEKS, 6 DAYS (41W6D)**

DATE:        /

### Recent revelations

must not forget
- ☐ .............................
- ☐ .............................
- ☐ .............................

### FETAL KICK COUNT TRACKER

☐ ☐ ☐ ☐ ☐ ☐ ☐ ☐ ☐ ☐

Start time   :   | Stop time   :   | Time to 10   :

SLEEP:      😴 ▭▭▭▭▭ 😵
APPETITE:  😋 ▭▭▭▭▭ 🤢
MOOD:       😊 ▭▭▭▭▭ 😠

## 13 days since your due date

BABY NAMES

### GIRLS IN BELGIUM

Emma, Louise, Elise, Léa,
Marie, Julie, Lina, Nina,
Olivia, Camille, Juliette

---

## DAY  294

**42 WEEKS, 0 DAYS (42W0D)**

DATE:        /

### I wish I'd known

stuff to research
- ☐ .............................
- ☐ .............................
- ☐ .............................

### FETAL KICK COUNT TRACKER

☐ ☐ ☐ ☐ ☐ ☐ ☐ ☐ ☐ ☐

Start time   :   | Stop time   :   | Time to 10   :

SLEEP:      😴 ▭▭▭▭▭ 😵
APPETITE:  😋 ▭▭▭▭▭ 🤢
MOOD:       😊 ▭▭▭▭▭ 😠

## 14 DAYS PAST YOUR OFFICIAL DUE DATE

~ A LITTLE NOTE TO THE FUTURE ~

☐ WISH  ☐ PREDICTION  ☐ PRAYER  ☐ HOPE  ☐ REMINDER

Date

Time

Place

Delivered by

# BABY IS HERE!

Time labor started

How I knew it was real labor

How active labor felt

Time delivery began

(Pushing phase start/C-section: OR arrival & incision time)

# Weight

# Length

# In attendance

# Earliest moments

Announced gender:

Cut the cord:

First to hold baby:

NAME:

# How early labor felt

# Admission time & stats

Hospital/center admission time:

Dilation/effacement/etc:

# How giving birth felt

# Feelings at the moment of birth

# LABOR & BIRTH

# THE BABY

# POSTPARTUM

# How are you?

Rate how you're feeling with a line, X or circle

(Date/time completed: _____)

  **IMMEDIATE POSTPARTUM MOOD MEASURE**

  **AFTER BIRTH ENERGY AMOUNT**

 **LABOR + BIRTH PAIN PROPORTION**

  **LABOR + BIRTH EMOTIONAL INTENSITY**

**"I HAVE A BABY NOW!" STRANGENESS SCOPE**

  **POSTPARTUM PAIN PROPORTION**

**HOSPITAL/BIRTH CENTER EXCELLENCE EXTENT**

**"I REALLY DID IT!" BELIEF BAROMETER**

---

## Possible warning signs

A few things to watch for and to report to your caregiver ASAP:

- Chest pain or trouble breathing
- Chills, dizziness, fainting, racing heart, clammy skin
- Fever above 100.4 F
- Bleeding heavier than a period or that gets worse
- Abdominal pain and/or vomiting
- Pain and swelling in lower legs
- Red streaks on/lumps in breasts
- Bad-smelling vaginal discharge
- Bleeding that you can't control
- Pain/burning when urinating

---

## ON THE DAY BABY WAS BORN

WEATHER:

HEADLINES:

VISITORS:

---

3 WORDS FOR WHAT'S ON YOUR MIND RIGHT NOW

---

## POSTPARTUM PARALLELS

My theme song:

Sitcom title:

Superhero identity:

Actress in my life story:

Product I could endorse:

The animal I would be:

---

~A LITTLE NOTE TO THE FUTURE~

☐ WISH  ☐ PREDICTION  ☐ PRAYER  ☐ HOPE  ☐ REMINDER

IN 2012, 3,952,181 BABIES WERE BORN IN THE U.S. AROUND THE SAME TIME, 386,044 BABIES WERE BORN IN CANADA, AND 698,512 IN ENGLAND & WALES.

# CHECKLISTS
# +
# PLANNERS
# +
# EXTRAS

- Emergency contacts & info
- Pregnancy tip sheet
- Calculate your due date
- Prenatal caregiver interview
- Birth plan ideas
- Baby gift record
- Menu ideas & meal plans
- Fun stuff: Astrology & more
- Nursery planning checklist
- Baby gear checklist
- Baby name worksheet
- Labor bag checklist
- Fertility chart
- About postpartum depression
- Prenatal appointments & tests
- Fetal kick count trackers
- Belly sticker designs
- Pregnancy firsts & dates

Cut out the bookmark to the right to keep track of your place in the calendar! (After you cut it out, it will also be easier to find this section with the bonus stuff.)

EVERY DAY
OF PREGNANCY
brings you
ONE STEP
CLOSER
to meeting
THE NEWEST
LOVE
of your
LIFE

REMEMBER TO *appreciate* THE BEAUTY AND WONDER *of these days* AS YOU CREATE *the heart* YOU WILL ADORE FOREVER

## EMERGENCY CONTACTS & INFORMATION

PRIMARY CAREGIVER NAME:

PRIMARY CAREGIVER CONTACT:

BACKUP CAREGIVER CONTACT:

HOSPITAL/BIRTH CENTER NAME:

HOSPITAL/BIRTH CENTER CONTACT:

SPOUSE/PARTNER PHONE:

SPOUSE/PARTNER BACKUP CONTACT:

OTHER FAMILY MEMBER NAME/CONTACT:

LABOR SUPPORT PERSON  NAME/CONTACT:

CHILDCARE PROVIDER NAME/CONTACT:

NEIGHBOR NAME/CONTACT:

TAXI COMPANY CONTACT*:

INSURANCE COMPANY:

INSURANCE GROUP/MEMBER ID:

*Tip: Consider installing + registering an app for a ride-sharing service*

## FUNDAL HEIGHT BY WEEK (APPROXIMATE)

Here's a look at how the height of your fundus (top of the uterus) may change over time. Note that late in pregnancy, fundal height may get lower after baby drops into the pelvis. *(Heights based on a single fetus.)*

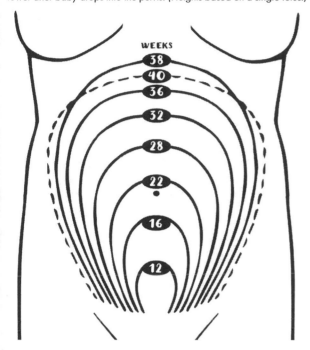

WEEKS
38
40
36
32
28
22
16
12

## TERMS ON YOUR MEDICAL CHART

Primigravida: First pregnancy
Multigravida: Second or subsequent pregnancy
Nullipara: Never before given birth
Primipara: Given birth once
Multipara: Given birth twice or more
Preterm: 20-37 weeks of pregnancy
Term: 37-42 weeks of pregnancy
Post term: More than 42 weeks

## BIRTH WEIGHT CONVERSIONS

(1 pound = 454 grams)

500 grams = 1 pound, 1 ounce
1000 grams = 2 pounds, 3 ounces
1500 grams = 3 pounds, 5 ounces
2000 grams = 4 pounds, 7 ounces
2500 grams = 5 pounds, 8 ounces
3000 grams = 6 pounds, 10 ounces
3500 grams = 7 pounds, 11 ounces
4000 grams = 8 pounds, 13 ounces
4500 grams = 9 pounds, 15 ounces
5000 grams = 11 pounds, 0 ounces

## PREGNANCY ABBREVIATIONS & ACRONYMS

ACOG: American Congress of Obstetricians & Gynecologists
AFP: Alpha Fetoprotein (subject of prenatal test)
AMA: Advanced Maternal Age (35+ years old)
AROM: Artificial Rupture of Membranes (amniotic sac)
BP: Blood Pressure
BPD: Biparietal Diameter (ultrasound measurement)
BPM: Beats Per Minute (heartrate)
BPP: Biophysical Profile (test of baby's health)
CNM: Certified Nurse Midwife
CPM: Certified Professional Midwife
CST: Contraction Stress Test (test of baby's health)
CVS: Chorionic Villus Sampling (prenatal test)
DPO: Days Post-Ovulation or Days Past Ovulation
EDD: Estimated Date of Delivery or Estimated Due Date
EFM: Electronic Fetal Monitoring
EFW: Estimated Fetal Weight
EGA: Estimated Gestational Age
FACOG: Fellow of the ACOG (professional designation)
FFN: Fetal Fibronectin
FH: Fundal Height
FHR: Fetal Heart Rate
FHT: Fetal Heart Tones
FSH: Follicle Stimulating Hormone
GBS: Group B Strep
GD: Gestational Diabetes
GP: General Practitioner
GTT: Glucose Tolerance Test (GD test)
ICU: Intensive Care Unit
IVF: In-Vitro Fertilization
LC: Lactation Consultant (for breastfeeding help)
LGA: Large for Gestational Age
LMP: Last Menstrual Period
NICU: Neonatal Intensive Care Unit
NP: Nurse Practitioner
NST: Non-Stress Test (test of baby's health)
OB: Obstetrician (OB/GYN: Obstetrician-Gynecologist)
PA: Physician Assistant
PCP: Primary Care Physician
PP: Postpartum
PROM: Premature Rupture Of Membranes (amniotic sac)
PTL: Preterm Labor
PUBS: Percutaneous Umbilical Blood Sampling
RN: Registered Nurse
ROM: Rupture of Membranes (amniotic sac)
SGA: Small for Gestational Age
SVE: Sterile Vaginal Exam
US: Ultrasound
VBAC: Vaginal Birth After Cesarean

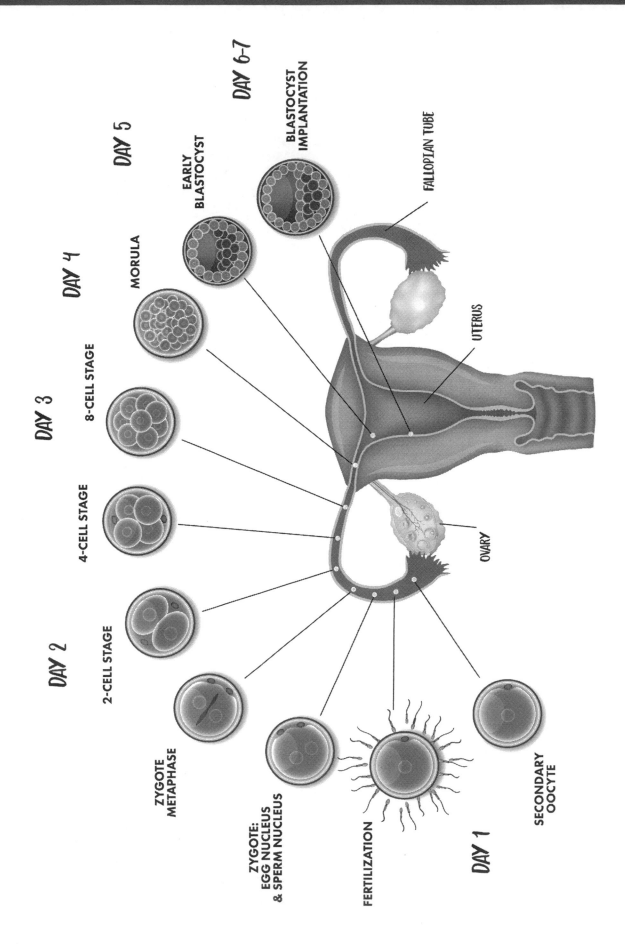

DAY 6-7

DAY 5

DAY 4

DAY 3

DAY 2

BLASTOCYST IMPLANTATION

FALLOPIAN TUBE

EARLY BLASTOCYST

MORULA

UTERUS

8-CELL STAGE

4-CELL STAGE

2-CELL STAGE

OVARY

ZYGOTE METAPHASE

ZYGOTE: EGG NUCLEUS & SPERM NUCLEUS

FERTILIZATION

SECONDARY OOCYTE

DAY 1

# IMPORTANT PERIODS IN FETAL DEVELOPMENT

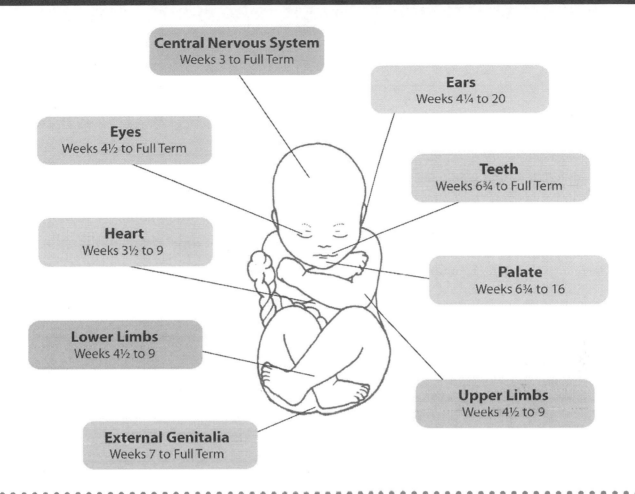

**Central Nervous System**
Weeks 3 to Full Term

**Ears**
Weeks 4¼ to 20

**Eyes**
Weeks 4½ to Full Term

**Teeth**
Weeks 6¾ to Full Term

**Heart**
Weeks 3½ to 9

**Palate**
Weeks 6¾ to 16

**Lower Limbs**
Weeks 4½ to 9

**Upper Limbs**
Weeks 4½ to 9

**External Genitalia**
Weeks 7 to Full Term

■ WHEN MAJOR DEFECTS IN BODY STRUCTURE CAN OCCUR
■ WHEN MAJOR FUNCTIONAL DEFECTS & MINOR STRUCTURAL DEFECTS CAN OCCUR

| PERIOD OF THE EMBRYO | | | | | | PERIOD OF THE FETUS | | | |
|---|---|---|---|---|---|---|---|---|---|
| Week 3 | Week 4 | Week 5 | Week 6 | Week 7 | Week 8 | Week 12 | Week 16 | Weeks 20–36 | Week 38 |

CNS
heart
eye
heart
eye
ear
palate
ear
brain
limbs
teeth
external genitals

Central Nervous System (CNS)–Brain and Spinal Cord

Heart

Arms/Legs

Eyes

Teeth

Palate

External Genitals

Ears

# CALCULATE YOUR ESTIMATED DUE DATE

**Calculate your due date!** Do you want to know when your baby will arrive? Find the date of your last period (LMP) in one of the darker rows, then look at the date below to get your due date. (Remember, though: Your due date is only an estimate, based upon a 28-day cycle — and only about 5% of babies actually arrive on the day they're technically "due.")

| | 1/1 | 1/2 | 1/3 | 1/4 | 1/5 | 1/6 | 1/7 | 1/8 | 1/9 | 1/10 | 1/11 | 1/12 | 1/13 | 1/14 | 1/15 | 1/16 | 1/17 | 1/18 | 1/19 | 1/20 | 1/21 | 1/22 | 1/23 | 1/24 | 1/25 | 1/26 | 1/27 | 1/28 | 1/29 | 1/30 | 1/31 |
|---|---|---|---|---|---|---|---|---|---|---|---|---|---|---|---|---|---|---|---|---|---|---|---|---|---|---|---|---|---|---|---|
| LMP DATE | 1/1 | 1/2 | 1/3 | 1/4 | 1/5 | 1/6 | 1/7 | 1/8 | 1/9 | 1/10 | 1/11 | 1/12 | 1/13 | 1/14 | 1/15 | 1/16 | 1/17 | 1/18 | 1/19 | 1/20 | 1/21 | 1/22 | 1/23 | 1/24 | 1/25 | 1/26 | 1/27 | 1/28 | 1/29 | 1/30 | 1/31 |
| DUE DATE | 10/8 | 10/9 | 10/10 | 10/11 | 10/12 | 10/13 | 10/14 | 10/15 | 10/16 | 10/17 | 10/18 | 10/19 | 10/20 | 10/21 | 10/22 | 10/23 | 10/24 | 10/25 | 10/26 | 10/27 | 10/28 | 10/29 | 10/30 | 10/31 | 11/1 | 11/2 | 11/3 | 11/4 | 11/5 | 11/6 | 11/7 |
| LMP DATE | 2/1 | 2/2 | 2/3 | 2/4 | 2/5 | 2/6 | 2/7 | 2/8 | 2/9 | 2/10 | 2/11 | 2/12 | 2/13 | 2/14 | 2/15 | 2/16 | 2/17 | 2/18 | 2/19 | 2/20 | 2/21 | 2/22 | 2/23 | 2/24 | 2/25 | 2/26 | 2/27 | 2/28 | | | |
| DUE DATE | 11/8 | 11/9 | 11/10 | 11/11 | 11/12 | 11/13 | 11/14 | 11/15 | 11/16 | 11/17 | 11/18 | 11/19 | 11/20 | 11/21 | 11/22 | 11/23 | 11/24 | 11/25 | 11/26 | 11/27 | 11/28 | 11/29 | 11/30 | 12/1 | 12/2 | 12/3 | 12/4 | 12/5 | 12/6 | 12/7 | 12/8 |
| LMP DATE | 3/1 | 3/2 | 3/3 | 3/4 | 3/5 | 3/6 | 3/7 | 3/8 | 3/9 | 3/10 | 3/11 | 3/12 | 3/13 | 3/14 | 3/15 | 3/16 | 3/17 | 3/18 | 3/19 | 3/20 | 3/21 | 3/22 | 3/23 | 3/24 | 3/25 | 3/26 | 3/27 | 3/28 | 3/29 | 3/30 | 3/31 |
| DUE DATE | 12/6 | 12/7 | 12/8 | 12/9 | 12/10 | 12/11 | 12/12 | 12/13 | 12/14 | 12/15 | 12/16 | 12/17 | 12/18 | 12/19 | 12/20 | 12/21 | 12/22 | 12/23 | 12/24 | 12/25 | 12/26 | 12/27 | 12/28 | 12/29 | 12/30 | 12/31 | 1/1 | 1/2 | 1/3 | 1/4 | 1/5 |
| LMP DATE | 4/1 | 4/2 | 4/3 | 4/4 | 4/5 | 4/6 | 4/7 | 4/8 | 4/9 | 4/10 | 4/11 | 4/12 | 4/13 | 4/14 | 4/15 | 4/16 | 4/17 | 4/18 | 4/19 | 4/20 | 4/21 | 4/22 | 4/23 | 4/24 | 4/25 | 4/26 | 4/27 | 4/28 | 4/29 | 4/30 | |
| DUE DATE | 1/6 | 1/7 | 1/8 | 1/9 | 1/10 | 1/11 | 1/12 | 1/13 | 1/14 | 1/15 | 1/16 | 1/17 | 1/18 | 1/19 | 1/20 | 1/21 | 1/22 | 1/23 | 1/24 | 1/25 | 1/26 | 1/27 | 1/28 | 1/29 | 1/30 | 1/31 | 2/1 | 2/2 | 2/3 | 2/4 | 2/5 |
| LMP DATE | 5/1 | 5/2 | 5/3 | 5/4 | 5/5 | 5/6 | 5/7 | 5/8 | 5/9 | 5/10 | 5/11 | 5/12 | 5/13 | 5/14 | 5/15 | 5/16 | 5/17 | 5/18 | 5/19 | 5/20 | 5/21 | 5/22 | 5/23 | 5/24 | 5/25 | 5/26 | 5/27 | 5/28 | 5/29 | 5/30 | 5/31 |
| DUE DATE | 2/5 | 2/6 | 2/7 | 2/8 | 2/9 | 2/10 | 2/11 | 2/12 | 2/13 | 2/14 | 2/15 | 2/16 | 2/17 | 2/18 | 2/19 | 2/20 | 2/21 | 2/22 | 2/23 | 2/24 | 2/25 | 2/26 | 2/27 | 2/28 | 3/1 | 3/2 | 3/3 | 3/4 | 3/5 | 3/6 | 3/7 |
| LMP DATE | 6/1 | 6/2 | 6/3 | 6/4 | 6/5 | 6/6 | 6/7 | 6/8 | 6/9 | 6/10 | 6/11 | 6/12 | 6/13 | 6/14 | 6/15 | 6/16 | 6/17 | 6/18 | 6/19 | 6/20 | 6/21 | 6/22 | 6/23 | 6/24 | 6/25 | 6/26 | 6/27 | 6/28 | 6/29 | 6/30 | |
| DUE DATE | 3/8 | 3/9 | 3/10 | 3/11 | 3/12 | 3/13 | 3/14 | 3/15 | 3/16 | 3/17 | 3/18 | 3/19 | 3/20 | 3/21 | 3/22 | 3/23 | 3/24 | 3/25 | 3/26 | 3/27 | 3/28 | 3/29 | 3/30 | 3/31 | 4/1 | 4/2 | 4/3 | 4/4 | 4/5 | 4/6 | 4/7 |
| LMP DATE | 7/1 | 7/2 | 7/3 | 7/4 | 7/5 | 7/6 | 7/7 | 7/8 | 7/9 | 7/10 | 7/11 | 7/12 | 7/13 | 7/14 | 7/15 | 7/16 | 7/17 | 7/18 | 7/19 | 7/20 | 7/21 | 7/22 | 7/23 | 7/24 | 7/25 | 7/26 | 7/27 | 7/28 | 7/29 | 7/30 | 7/31 |
| DUE DATE | 4/7 | 4/8 | 4/9 | 4/10 | 4/11 | 4/12 | 4/13 | 4/14 | 4/15 | 4/16 | 4/17 | 4/18 | 4/19 | 4/20 | 4/21 | 4/22 | 4/23 | 4/24 | 4/25 | 4/26 | 4/27 | 4/28 | 4/29 | 4/30 | 5/1 | 5/2 | 5/3 | 5/4 | 5/5 | 5/6 | 5/7 |
| LMP DATE | 8/1 | 8/2 | 8/3 | 8/4 | 8/5 | 8/6 | 8/7 | 8/8 | 8/9 | 8/10 | 8/11 | 8/12 | 8/13 | 8/14 | 8/15 | 8/16 | 8/17 | 8/18 | 8/19 | 8/20 | 8/21 | 8/22 | 8/23 | 8/24 | 8/25 | 8/26 | 8/27 | 8/28 | 8/29 | 8/30 | 8/31 |
| DUE DATE | 5/8 | 5/9 | 5/10 | 5/11 | 5/12 | 5/13 | 5/14 | 5/15 | 5/16 | 5/17 | 5/18 | 5/19 | 5/20 | 5/21 | 5/22 | 5/23 | 5/24 | 5/25 | 5/26 | 5/27 | 5/28 | 5/29 | 5/30 | 5/31 | 6/1 | 6/2 | 6/3 | 6/4 | 6/5 | 6/6 | 6/7 |
| LMP DATE | 9/1 | 9/2 | 9/3 | 9/4 | 9/5 | 9/6 | 9/7 | 9/8 | 9/9 | 9/10 | 9/11 | 9/12 | 9/13 | 9/14 | 9/15 | 9/16 | 9/17 | 9/18 | 9/19 | 9/20 | 9/21 | 9/22 | 9/23 | 9/24 | 9/25 | 9/26 | 9/27 | 9/28 | 9/29 | 9/30 | |
| DUE DATE | 6/8 | 6/9 | 6/10 | 6/11 | 6/12 | 6/13 | 6/14 | 6/15 | 6/16 | 6/17 | 6/18 | 6/19 | 6/20 | 6/21 | 6/22 | 6/23 | 6/24 | 6/25 | 6/26 | 6/27 | 6/28 | 6/29 | 6/30 | 7/1 | 7/2 | 7/3 | 7/4 | 7/5 | 7/6 | 7/7 | 7/8 |
| LMP DATE | 10/1 | 10/2 | 10/3 | 10/4 | 10/5 | 10/6 | 10/7 | 10/8 | 10/9 | 10/10 | 10/11 | 10/12 | 10/13 | 10/14 | 10/15 | 10/16 | 10/17 | 10/18 | 10/19 | 10/20 | 10/21 | 10/22 | 10/23 | 10/24 | 10/25 | 10/26 | 10/27 | 10/28 | 10/29 | 10/30 | 10/31 |
| DUE DATE | 7/8 | 7/9 | 7/10 | 7/11 | 7/12 | 7/13 | 7/14 | 7/15 | 7/16 | 7/17 | 7/18 | 7/19 | 7/20 | 7/21 | 7/22 | 7/23 | 7/24 | 7/25 | 7/26 | 7/27 | 7/28 | 7/29 | 7/30 | 7/31 | 8/1 | 8/2 | 8/3 | 8/4 | 8/5 | 8/6 | 8/7 |
| LMP DATE | 11/1 | 11/2 | 11/3 | 11/4 | 11/5 | 11/6 | 11/7 | 11/8 | 11/9 | 11/10 | 11/11 | 11/12 | 11/13 | 11/14 | 11/15 | 11/16 | 11/17 | 11/18 | 11/19 | 11/20 | 11/21 | 11/22 | 11/23 | 11/24 | 11/25 | 11/26 | 11/27 | 11/28 | 11/29 | 11/30 | |
| DUE DATE | 8/8 | 8/9 | 8/10 | 8/11 | 8/12 | 8/13 | 8/14 | 8/15 | 8/16 | 8/17 | 8/18 | 8/19 | 8/20 | 8/21 | 8/22 | 8/23 | 8/24 | 8/25 | 8/26 | 8/27 | 8/28 | 8/29 | 8/30 | 8/31 | 9/1 | 9/2 | 9/3 | 9/4 | 9/5 | 9/6 | |
| LMP DATE | 12/1 | 12/2 | 12/3 | 12/4 | 12/5 | 12/6 | 12/7 | 12/8 | 12/9 | 12/10 | 12/11 | 12/12 | 12/13 | 12/14 | 12/15 | 12/16 | 12/17 | 12/18 | 12/19 | 12/20 | 12/21 | 12/22 | 12/23 | 12/24 | 12/25 | 12/26 | 12/27 | 12/28 | 12/29 | 12/30 | 12/31 |
| DUE DATE | 9/7 | 9/8 | 9/9 | 9/10 | 9/11 | 9/12 | 9/13 | 9/14 | 9/15 | 9/16 | 9/17 | 9/18 | 9/19 | 9/20 | 9/21 | 9/22 | 9/23 | 9/24 | 9/25 | 9/26 | 9/27 | 9/28 | 9/29 | 9/30 | 10/1 | 10/2 | 10/3 | 10/4 | 10/5 | 10/6 | 10/7 |

# PRENATAL CAREGIVER INTERVIEW

## QUESTIONS FOR THE OFFICE

What are the office hours? (Evening/Saturday hours?)

Do you offer online appointment scheduling?

Do you have a web portal for lab results, etc?

How much time is allowed for a routine visit?

Do you have a lab (for blood draws) on-site?

Will I see the same primary caregiver at each appointment, or will I regularly see others in the practice?

What if I have an emergency outside of office hours?

At which hospitals/birth centers does the caregiver have privileges? (If needed: Does he/she attend home births?)

Are you a member of my health plan (insurance)?

What are terms for services/fees not covered?

## QUESTIONS FOR THE CAREGIVER

What is your basic philosophy of birth?

How many babies have you delivered?

What prenatal tests do you recommend, and why?

Do you manage high-risk pregnancies?

What is your cesarean section rate?

How often do you induce labor, why, and how?

How do you typically handle problems during labor?

Can we discuss health issues via phone or text?

What kind of medical training do you have?

Are you board-certified?

*Prenatal caregiver interview checklist: page 1 of 2*

## ANY OTHER QUESTIONS?

## WHAT DID YOU THINK?

- Do you and the candidate have compatible philosophies on medical care?
- How do your personalities and styles mesh?
- Would you feel good about this person making healthcare decisions for you?
- Will you feel comfortable asking questions and discussing all kinds of issues related to your body?
- What does your intuition tell you?
- Was the office staff friendly and helpful?
- Was the waiting room and office clean?
- How convenient was the location?
- Was parking or public transport available?

## NOTES AND FOLLOW UP

# BIRTH PLAN IDEAS

**The purpose of a birth plan is so that everyone involved understands your hopes and desires for labor and birth. On these two pages are some ideas for things that you may want to consider when creating your own plan! Check off the statements that align with your needs, write down any other ideas you would like to add, and combine them all in your own customized birth plan.**

Neither a contract nor a simple checklist, a birth plan should be considered as a clear, simplified statement of your preferences. It is also a great place to begin discussions with your caregiver(s) at a hospital or medical center. (Many of these points will automatically be addressed or not apply to a birth center or during a planned home birth.)

It is very important that you talk about the procedures and/or choices that appear your plan with your caregiver(s). Not only do obstetric practices often vary by caregiver, hospital, county and state, there are often many other important factors involved. It is your responsibility to evaluate and understand each request you make.

No matter your preferences, birth plans are best kept short and to the point — too many extra details may be lost on busy medical support staff. You may even wish to create two plans: one for yourself and your support team (coach, doula, etc.) and another, more concise document — no more than a page long — for your caregiver and the hospital staff.

## LABOR

___ I would like my partner/coach to be with me at all times.

___ I would like to be free to walk, change positions and use the bathroom as needed or desired.

___ Please do not administer an IV or heparin lock unless there is a clear medical indication that it is necessary.

___ I would like a quiet, soothing environment during labor, with dim lights and minimal interruptions.

___ I would like to have friends and family members with me during labor and delivery.

___ I have hired a doula to be with me during labor and birth.

___ I would like to play my own music.

___ Please limit the number of vaginal exams.

___ I wish to labor freely in the birthing tub or shower.

___ As long as the baby is doing well, I prefer that fetal heart tones be monitored intermittently.

___ Please allow me to vocalize as desired during labor and birth without comment or criticism.

___ Please do not allow observers such as interns, students or unnecessary staff into the room without my permission.

___ Please have everyone knock before entering my room.

## ANESTHESIA/PAIN MEDICATION

___ Please do not offer pain relief unless I ask for it.

___ If I ask for pain relief, please feel free to offer non-medical choices for coping and/or remind me how close I am to the birth.

___ I would like to avoid all narcotics, if possible.

___ I prefer an epidural to narcotic pain medication.

___ I prefer other pain medication to an epidural.

___ I would like to have an epidural as soon as possible.

___ I would like to have a light dose (walking) epidural.

___ I would like the epidural to wear off slightly as I approach full dilation and the pushing stage.

## LABOR INDUCTION/AUGMENTATION

___ I would like to avoid induction unless necessary.

___ As long as the baby and I are healthy, I do not want to discuss induction prior to 42 weeks.

___ If my pregnancy progresses past 40 weeks, I would prefer to base the decision to induce on the results of the baby's biophysical profiles, not on my discomfort or impatience.

___ I would like to try alternative means of labor augmentation, like walking or nipple stimulation, before pitocin or artificial rupture of membranes is attempted.

___ Please do not rupture my membranes artificially unless medically indicated, and only after informing me.

___ If induction is necessary, I would like to attempt it with prostaglandin gel or another means before pitocin.

___ If induction is attempted but fails, I would like to come back to the hospital at another time.

## CESAREAN SECTION DELIVERY

___ I feel very strongly about avoiding a cesarean delivery .

___ If a cesarean is necessary, I want to be fully informed of all procedures and participate in decision-making.

___ I would like (my coach/husband/partner/doula) to be present during the surgery.

___ Please explain the surgery to me as it happens.

___ I would prefer epidural anesthesia, if possible, in order to remain conscious through the delivery.

___ I would like to have a respectful atmosphere without chatter during any part of the surgical procedure.

___ Please lower the screen just before delivery so I may see the birth.

___ If conditions permit, I would like to be the first to hold the baby after the delivery.

___ If conditions permit, the baby should be given to (person) immediately after the birth.

## DELIVERY

___ Even if I am fully dilated, I would like to wait until I feel the urge to push before beginning the pushing phase.

___ I prefer to push (or not push) according to my instincts and would prefer not to have guidance or coaching.

___ I do not want to use stirrups while pushing.

___ I would like the freedom to push and deliver in any position I like.

___ I would appreciate help from (coach) and staff supporting my legs as I push.

___ I would like to deliver in a birthing pool and have made arrangements to rent one for the birth.

___ I would like to have a mirror available and adjusted so I can see the baby's head crowning.

___ I would like the opportunity to touch my baby's head as it crowns.

___ I would like a soothing environment during the actual birth, with dim lights and quiet voices.

___ I would like to ask that no one speak during the delivery.

___ I would like (coach) to help catch the baby.

___ I would like to help catch the baby.

___ I would like to have the pictures or video of the birth.

## AFTER BIRTH

___ Please place the baby on my stomach/chest immediately after delivery.

___ (Name) would like the option to cut the cord.

___ I would like the option to cut the cord.

___ Please allow the umbilical cord to stop pulsating before it is clamped/cut.

___ I have made arrangements for donation/banking of the umbilical cord blood.

___ Please show me the placenta after it is delivered.

___ I would like to take home the placenta.

___ Please remove my IV/Heparin lock/catheter as soon as possible after delivery.

## NEWBORN CARE

___ I would like to hold the baby skin-to-skin for the first hours.

___ I would like to hold the baby through the delivery of the placenta and any repair procedures.

___ If possible, please evaluate the baby at my bedside.

___ If possible, please perform routine newborn procedures at my bedside/in my room.

___ If the baby must leave for evaluation or medical treatment, (coach) will accompany the baby at all times.

___ I am not planning to have the baby circumcised.

___ I am planning for the baby to be circumcised before we check out of the hospital. (Anesthetic: yes/no)

___ Please delay eye medication for the baby until we are well past the initial bonding period.

___ I would like to waive the administration of eye antibiotics.

___ I would like to waive the administration of routine Vitamin K, unless medically indicated.

___ I would like to defer the PKU screening.

___ I would like to defer the following vaccinations...

___ If the baby has problems, please tell my coach first.

## FEEDING

___ I plan to breastfeed exclusively

___ I want to breastfeed immediately following the birth.

___ Please do not give the baby supplements (including formula, glucose, or plain water) without my consent, unless there is an urgent medical necessity.

___ Please do not give the baby a pacifier.

___ I would like to breastfeeding and formula feed.

___ I would like advice on formula versus breastfeeding.

___ I would like to know more about breastfeeding.

___ I would like to meet with a lactation consultant.

___ I do not plan to breastfeed.

## POSTPARTUM

___ I would like to have the baby room-in with me at all times.

___ Once I've had time to recover, I would like the baby to room-in with me.

___ I would like the baby to room-in with me during the day, but stay in the nursery at night.

___ I would like the baby in the nursery at night, but brought to me for breastfeeding on demand.

___ I would like the baby in the nursery and brought to me on request and for breastfeeding.

___ I would like my other children to visit as long as I wish.

___ I would like guests to stay as long as I wish.

___ I would prefer not to be catheterized until I've had some private time to attempt urination on my own.

___ I would like to stay in the hospital as long as possible.

___ I would like to leave the hospital as soon as possible.

## ALSO INCLUDE

Name/relationship of coach
Name/relationship of doula/others attending birth

## YOUR ADDITIONS

## ASTROLOGY/WESTERN ZODIAC

**Aries:** March 21 - April 19
**Taurus:** April 20 - May 20
**Gemini:** May 21 - June 20
**Cancer:** June 21 - July 22
**Leo:** July 23 - August 22
**Virgo:** August 23 - September 22
**Libra:** September 23 - October 22
**Scorpio:** October 23 - November 21
**Sagittarius:** November 22 - December 21
**Capricorn:** December 22 - January 19
**Aquarius:** January 20 - February 18
**Pisces:** February 19 - March 20

## CHINESE ZODIAC YEARS

Chinese New Year falls between January 21 and February 20 (depending on the year), so the Chinese zodiac years listed below begin after that date.

**Rat:** 2020, 2008, 1996, 1984, 1972, 1960, 1948
**Ox:** 2021, 2009, 1997, 1985, 1973, 1961, 1949
**Tiger:** 2022, 2010, 1998, 1986, 1974, 1962, 1950
**Rabbit:** 2023, 2011, 1999, 1987, 1975, 1963, 1951
**Dragon:** 2024, 2012, 2000, 1988, 1976, 1964, 1952
**Snake:** 2025, 2013, 2001, 1989, 1977, 1965, 1953
**Horse:** 2026, 2014, 2002, 1990, 1978, 1966, 1954
**Goat:** 2027, 2015, 2003, 1991, 1979, 1967, 1955
**Monkey:** 2028, 2016, 2004, 1992, 1980, 1968, 1956
**Rooster:** 2029, 2017, 2005, 1993, 1981, 1969, 1957
**Dog:** 2030, 2018, 2006, 1994, 1982, 1970, 1958
**Pig:** 2031, 2019, 2007, 1995, 1983, 1971, 1959

## BIRTH DAY OF WEEK RHYME

*Monday's child is fair of face.*
*Tuesday's child is full of grace.*
*Wednesday's child is full of woe.*
*Thursday's child has far to go.*
*Friday's child is loving and giving.*
*Saturday's child works hard for a living,*
*But the child who is born on the Sabbath Day*
*Is bonny and blithe and good and gay.*

## BIRTH STONES BY MONTH

**January**
Modern: Garnet
Traditional: Garnet

**February**
Modern: Amethyst
Traditional: Amethyst

**March**
Modern: Aquamarine
Traditional: Bloodstone

**April**
Modern: Diamond
Traditional: Diamond

**May**
Modern: Emerald
Traditional: Emerald

**June**
Modern: Pearl
Traditional: Alexandrite

**July**
Modern: Ruby
Traditional: Ruby

**August**
Modern: Peridot, Jade
Traditional: Sardonyx

**September**
Modern: Sapphire
Traditional: Sapphire

**October**
Modern: Opal
Traditional: Tourmaline

**November**
Modern: Yellow Topaz
Traditional: Citrine

**December**
Modern: Blue Topaz, Turquoise
Traditional: Zircon

## BIRTH FLOWERS BY MONTH

**January**
Carnation

**February**
Violet

**March**
Daffodil or Jonquil

**April**
Sweet Pea

**May**
Lily of the Valley

**June**
Rose

**July**
Larkspur or Delphinium

**August**
Gladiola or Poppy

**September**
Aster

**October**
Calendula or Marigold

**November**
Chrysanthemum

**December**
Narcissus or Holly

# DAILY MEAL PLAN SUGGESTIONS

**PREGNANCY NUTRITION SUGGESTIONS:** This daily meal plan from the USDA was made specifically for expectant moms, and offers a general suggestion of ways to meet your nutritional goals during pregnancy. As you will see, the plan shows slightly increased amounts of food recommended during trimesters two and three, due to changing nutritional needs.

**WEEKLY MEAL PLANNER & SHOPPING LIST** (on the opposite page): Copy this meal planner, or print off copies (including those in color) at myria.com/printables.

| Food Group | 1st Trimester | 2nd and 3rd Trimesters | What counts as 1 cup or 1 ounce? | Remember to... |
|---|---|---|---|---|
| | Eat this amount from each group daily.* | | | |
| Vegetables | 2½ cups | 3 cups | 1 cup raw or cooked vegetables or 100% juice / 2 cups raw leafy vegetables | Make half your plate fruits and vegetables. Choose a variety. Eat more dark-green and red and orange vegetables and beans and peas. |
| Fruits | 2 cups | 2 cups | 1 cup fruit or 100% juice / ½ cup dried fruit | |
| Grains | 6 ounces | 8 ounces | 1 slice bread / 1 ounce ready-to-eat cereal / ½ cup cooked pasta, rice, or cereal | Make at least half your grains whole. Choose whole instead of refined grains. |
| Dairy | 3 cups | 3 cups | 1 cup milk / 8 ounces yogurt / 1½ ounces natural cheese / 2 ounces processed cheese | Replace higher fat milk and milk products with fat-free or low-fat options. |
| Protein Foods | 5½ ounces | 6½ ounces | 1 ounce lean meat, poultry, or seafood / ¼ cup cooked beans / ½ ounce nuts or 1 egg / 1 tablespoon peanut butter | Vary your protein food choices. Include seafood, beans, peas, and unsalted nuts and seeds. |

* If you are not gaining weight or gaining too slowly, you may need to eat a little more from each food group. If you are gaining weight too fast, you may need to cut back by decreasing the amount of "empty calories" you are eating. Talk to your doctor about any concerns about your diet and the amount of weight gain during pregnancy.

230

# WEEKLY MEAL PLAN/SHOPPING LIST

## MEAL PLAN
FOR THE WEEK OF:

SUN

MON

TUES

WED

THURS

FRI

SAT

## SHOPPING LIST

# NURSERY CHECKLIST

**Things you might want to buy, borrow, fix, install or make for new your baby's bedroom**

## BEDDING

### Crib:

___ Crib
___ Crib bumpers
___ Crib mattress
___ Crib sheets
___ Crib toys and accessories
___ Mattress pads (waterproof)
___ Blankets

### Bassinet/Cradle:

___ Bassinet
___ Bassinet liners and quilts
___ Bassinet sheets
___ Cradle
___ Cradle sheet
___ Blankets

### Other:

___ Sidecar crib/co-sleeper
___ Portable crib/play yard

## FURNITURE

___ Dresser
___ Bookcase/s
___ Changing table
___ Glider/rocking chair (and ottoman)
___ Laundry hamper
___ Table
___ Nightstand
___ Small table and chairs
___ Easy chair
___ Loveseat
___ Guest bed/futon

## ACCESSORIES & DÉCOR

___ Diaper pail
___ Diaper holder
___ Waste basket
___ Clock

___ Wall hangings
___ Picture frames/photographs
___ Framed prints/posters
___ Hooks and hangers
___ Lamp
___ Night light
___ Mobile
___ Switch plate covers
___ Growth chart

### Extras:

___ Baby monitor/video surveillance
___ Music player & speakers
___ White noise generator
___ Air purifier/humidifier
___ Swing/jumper/bouncer

### Storage:

___ Open baskets
___ Toy boxes
___ Storage bins
___ Under bed storage bins
___ Closet storage

## ROOM IMPROVEMENTS

### Flooring:

___ Carpet
___ Rug/s
___ Sheepskin rug
___ Floor mats
___ Wood or laminate flooring
___ Vinyl flooring
___ Tile

### Window coverings:

___ Blinds/Mini-blinds
___ Accordion blinds
___ Rollerblinds
___ Curtains
___ Blackout curtains
___ Roman blind
___ Shutters

### Wall coverings:

___ Wallpaper - full-height
___ Wallpaper border
___ Wall stickers

### Paint:

___ Walls
___ Ceiling
___ Doors
___ Moldings

### Decorative paintwork:

___ Lettering
___ Characters
___ Sponging
___ Stencil
___ Faux finishing
___ Mural
___ Free-form

### Other considerations:

___ Lighting (dimmers, etc)
___ Heating/cooling
___ Fan/Ceiling fan
___ Closet shelving
___ Additional room shelving

### Repairs and safety:

___ Repair any cracked windows
___ Secure any loose cords
___ Trim cords from blinds and use a breakaway clip
___ Secure bookcases/dressers/tall furniture to wall
___ Window locks/safetys
___ Plug/outlet covers
___ Drawer/cabinet/door latches
___ Low-profile knobs/handles
___ Protect sharp corners/edges
___ Secure heater vent
___ Smoke/carbon monoxide detector

# BABY GEAR CHECKLIST

Layette & baby care items to buy, borrow or add to your baby gift registry

## NURSERY

___ Moses basket, bassinet or crib
___ Crib mattress
___ Crib bedding/mattress pad
___ Changing table
___ Dresser/chest of drawers
___ Glider or rocking chair
___ Hamper
___ Extra laundry basket
___ Night light
___ Baby monitor
___ White noise machine
___ Mobile

## CLOTHING

___ Coming-home outfit
___ Onesies (bodysuits) or rompers
___ T-shirts/side-snap tees
___ Pants
___ Kimonos/nightgowns
___ One-piece sleepers
___ Sleep sack/swaddle
___ Socks or booties
___ Sun hat/bonnet
___ No-scratch mittens

### Cold weather wear
___ Blanket sleeper
___ Bunting bag or snowsuit
___ Hat or cap
___ Shoes

## GENERAL BABY CARE

___ Receiving blankets
___ Cotton blankets
___ Gentle laundry detergent
___ Burp cloths (cloth diapers are great)
___ Pacifiers
___ Pacifier leashes/clips
___ Sling, baby wrap or carrier
___ Sidecar crib/co-sleeper

## HEALTHCARE/GROOMING

___ Baby bathtub or tub insert
___ Baby washcloths/soft washcloths
___ Hooded baby towels/soft towels
___ Baby shampoo & soap/body wash
___ Baby lotion
___ Baby nail clippers
___ Soft-bristled hair brush
___ Nasal aspirator/bulb syringe
___ Digital rectal thermometer
___ Infant pain relief drops
___ Infant gas relief drops
___ Vaporizer or humidifier

## DIAPERING

___ Diapers
___ Diaper rash ointment/cream
___ Changing table
___ Changing pad
___ Washable changing pad covers
      (king-size pillowcases may work)
___ Diaper pail
___ Diaper pail liners/bags
___ Baby wipes or washcloths
___ Tissues
___ Cotton swabs
___ Hand sanitizer

### Cloth diapering
___ Cloth diapers
___ Snaps/pins/other closures
___ Cloth diaper covers

## ENTERTAINMENT

___ Bouncy seat
___ Floor seat (Bumbo/Mega Seat)
___ Play mat/play gym
___ Swing
___ Infant toys & Books
___ Play yard
___ Baby gates

## FEEDING

### Feeding: Breastfeeding
___ Nursing pillow
___ Nursing bras
___ Breast pads (disposable/washable)
___ Nipple cream

### Feeding: Breastfeeding - Pumping
___ Breast pump
___ Breastmilk storage containers
___ Bottles and nipples
___ Bottle brush
___ Bottle drying rack
___ Insulated bottle carrier

### Feeding: Formula
___ Formula
___ Bottles and nipples
___ Bottle brush
___ Bottle drying rack
___ Insulated bottle carrier

### Feeding: Older babies
___ Bibs
___ High chair
___ Feeding seat/booster seat

## TRAVEL/OUT & ABOUT

___ Car seat
___ Head support (car seat or stroller)
___ Car seat strap covers
___ Stroller
___ Portable crib or travel bassinet
___ Diaper bag
___ Diapers & diapering accessories
___ Hand sanitizer
___ Diaper changing pad
___ Blankets & burp cloths
___ Sling, baby wrap or carrier
___ Shopping cart cover
___ Sun shade for car window
___ Rearview mirror for car

# BABY NAME PLANNING

**Not sure how to begin the search for a baby name?**
Here are ideas to consider (and some things not to forget)
when choosing a name for your new little one.

### NAMES THAT START WITH...

### NAMES THAT END WITH...

### NO MORE THAN # LETTERS

### NO FEWER THAN # LETTERS

### NO MORE THAN # SYLLABLES

### NO FEWER THAN # SYLLABLES

**NOTES:**

## NAME INFLUENCES

____ Ancestry/heritage
____ Celebrity-inspired
____ Close friend
____ Family member
____ Favorite artist or author
____ Cities/countries
____ Historical figure
____ Historical eras
____ Religion/spirituality
____ Specific meaning
____ TV book or movie character
____ ..........................................
____ ..........................................

## NAME STYLES

____ Classic/Old-fashioned
____ Combined name
____ Creative spelling
____ Exotic
____ Foreign
____ Hyphenated name
____ Last name as a first name
____ Popular/trendy
____ Simple
____ Traditional
____ Unique or one-of-a-kind
____ ..........................................
____ ..........................................

## DON'T FORGET TO CHECK...

____ Initials
____ Nicknames
____ Rhyming words?
____ Similar sounding words?
____ Foreign meanings?
____ Easy to pronounce?
____ Easy to spell?

# BABY NAME WORKSHEET

Throughout pregnancy, keep track of all of your baby name ideas right here.

### Name ideas: Parent 1

### Name ideas: Parent 2

### Suggestions from family

### Suggestions from friends

# BABY GIFT RECORD

| FROM | GIFT | THANK YOU NOTE |
|------|------|------|
|  |  |  |
|  |  |  |
|  |  |  |
|  |  |  |
|  |  |  |
|  |  |  |
|  |  |  |
|  |  |  |
|  |  |  |
|  |  |  |
|  |  |  |
|  |  |  |
|  |  |  |
|  |  |  |
|  |  |  |
|  |  |  |
|  |  |  |
|  |  |  |
|  |  |  |
|  |  |  |

# LABOR BAG CHECKLIST

**If you're planning a hospital or birth center birth, what should you bring with you?
Here's a handy checklist — just pick and choose what you want and need.**

## Most important
___ Hospital/birth center admission paperwork
___ Photo ID
___ Health insurance card
___ Cell phone
___ Camera
___ Chargers/Extra batteries
___ Car seat for baby

## Comforts of home
___ Books/magazines
___ Music and speakers or headphones/earbuds
___ Extra pillow/s
___ Tablet or laptop with downloaded movies

## For labor
___ Birth plan
___ Birth ball
___ Photo/focal point
___ Hot water bottle
___ Lollipops and hard candy (for dry mouth)
___ Lotion and/or powder (for massage)
___ Massage/aromatherapy oils
___ Tennis balls (for back massage)

## For your partner
___ Cell phone (add your important contacts)
___ Change of clothes
___ Basic toiletries
___ Slippers or flip-flops
___ Small cooler with drinks and snacks
___ Cash (for vending machines)
___ Reading material

## Clothing
___ Bathrobe
___ Loose, comfortable outfit for going home
___ Nursing bra / Nursing pads
___ Slippers / Thick socks
___ A few pairs of comfy underwear

## Personal care
___ Barrettes/hair clips/ponytail holders
___ Body soap
___ Brush/comb
___ Contact lens case/supplies
___ Dental floss
___ Deodorant
___ Earplugs
___ Eyeshade
___ Facial soap
___ Glasses
___ Lip balm
___ Lotion
___ Makeup/cosmetics
___ Mouthwash/breath mints
___ Nail clippers/nail file
___ Shampoo/conditioner
___ Toothbrush/toothpaste

## For baby
___ Going home outfit
___ No-scratch gloves
___ Receiving blankets

## Other ideas
___ Baby name book
___ Gift for a sibling
___ Gift for nurses/hospital staff

## You probably *will not* need
Maxipads*
Diapers for the trip home*
Baby hat*
Nightgown/nursing gown*
Medications*
Jewelry
Any other valuables

*Typically provided by the hospital/birth center

---

## Your additions:

# PRENATAL/POSTPARTUM DEPRESSION
## & THE POSTPARTUM PROMISE

*When it comes to prenatal or postpartum depression, most moms think, "Well, that won't be me." What many women don't realize is that it really __might__ happen to them — between one quarter and one-half of all women experience some form of a postpartum depressive illness. Here is one way to help you get treatment and support if you need it.*

## About prenatal & postpartum depressive illnesses

Depression during pregnancy and in the postpartum period is very real, and is also very treatable. Many women suffer unnecessarily, because their depression is undiagnosed or they are embarrassed or uncertain that something is wrong.

The Postpartum Promise (on the next page) was created for you to copy and share. Originally intended for the postpartum period, most of the points are also valid with relation to depression during pregnancy. The idea is to keep one copy for yourself, and give one to your partner, your mother, your father, your sister or your best friend. Help them to understand how they can help you — just in case you don't know how much you need it.

**Prenatal depression:** Of the nearly four million women who give birth each year in the United States, between 14 and 23% of pregnant women will experience a depressive disorder while pregnant, according to information published in the September 2009 issue of *Obstetrics & Gynecology*.

**Baby blues:** Between one quarter and one-half of women experience the baby blues after giving birth. The blues is a mild depression occurring in the first couple weeks after birth, usually disappearing within hours or days without the need for treatment. In the first weeks after birth, estrogen levels plunge by 90 percent or more — a wild hormonal fluctuation which, among other factors, can have a serious impact on a new mom's moods and emotions. Moms shouldn't feel guilty for not being as happy as they expected during this time.

**Postpartum depression:** During the first year after the birth of their babies, about 10% to 15% of mothers suffer from postpartum depression (PPD), a disorder that requires treatment because it can have serious consequences for not only the mother, but also the infant and the rest of the family. If caught before the depression is severe, PPD may be treated effectively with therapy. More advanced cases may require antidepressants, many of which are considered safe even while breastfeeding. Moms should not feel ashamed of being depressed because PPD is directly related to hormone imbalances and it is not something a woman can simply "snap out of." Some health care providers may dismiss a mom's concerns as the normal exhaustion experienced when taking care of a newborn. Women and their loved ones should seek support from a health care provider who will take their feelings seriously.

**Postpartum psychosis:** One or two of every thousand women suffer from postpartum psychosis (PPP). Unlike PPD, the risk for psychosis is much higher during the postpartum period than at other times of a woman's life — up to 20 times higher in the first month after the birth of her baby. PPP is considered a medical emergency and hospitalization is generally recommended because of the risk of suicide or infanticide. Medication is required for treatment, along with an intense amount of practical support to help moms recover while still bonding well with their babies.

# POSTPARTUM PROMISE

Postpartum blues, depression and psychosis are real illnesses that affect an estimated 20 to 30 percent of women following the birth of a child. If it happens to me, I probably won't just "snap out of it" — I may need help: from you, from my doctor or midwife, from a counselor or someone else.

I am giving you this contract because I may not recognize one or more of these symptoms I am experiencing, or may not want to recognize them.

After the birth, please read over the risk factors and symptoms listed below. Do they sound like what I am going through? If so, please make sure I get the help and support I need, especially if I cannot help myself.

## Risk Factors

I am more at risk for postpartum depression and psychosis...

- If I have suffered from depression before.
- If I have a family history of depression.
- If I have had other hormonal problems, such as PMS.
- If I'm taking certain medications.
- If I had a difficult pregnancy or birth.
- If my pregnancy was unplanned.
- If my partner is away from home a great deal.
- If I'm experiencing marital tension and/or feeling unsupported by my partner.
- If I am going through a separation or divorce.
- If someone close to me is ill or recently died.
- If either of my parents died during my childhood or adolescence.
- If I've just moved to a new home.
- If I recently changed jobs, quit or was fired.
- If I'm used to spending the majority of my time outside the home.
- If I have been under a lot of stress.

## Baby Blues
*Experienced by 25-50% of women*
**Severity level: Low**

- I may not be able to sleep well.
- I may cry a lot, even about little things.
- I might experience mood swings.
- I may seem irritable.
- I may express that I feel very vulnerable or inadequate.
- I may not feel like myself anymore.
- I may start showing signs of baby blues 3-5 days after our baby is born. I should not feel like this for more than a couple weeks, and if I do, it may be the sign of a bigger problem for which I need help.

## Postpartum Depression
*Experienced by 10-15% of women*
**Severity level: Medium to High** - seek treatment promptly

- I may seem to be tired all the time.
- I may not be able to sleep well.
- I may cry a lot, even about little things.
- I may have trouble remembering things.
- I may have a hard time concentrating or seem confused.
- I may express feelings of guilt or inadequacy.
- I may be very irritable or hostile.
- I may seem very anxious.
- I may say that I can't cope.
- I may not show much interest in the baby.
- I may be hyper-concerned for the baby.
- I may worry about harming myself - or the baby.
- I may have headaches or chest pains.
- I may not care about how I look.
- I may not want to leave the house.
- I may not feel like myself anymore.
- I may stop finding enjoyment in hobbies or activities I previously loved.
- I may not want to socialize and may withdraw from friends and loved ones.
- I may not be interested in sex/intimacy.
- I may be likely to start showing signs of depression anytime within six to twelve weeks after our baby is born, but these signs may also show up anytime in the first year.
- I may feel like this for more than a year if the depression is not treated.

## Postpartum Psychosis
*Experienced by 0.1 to 0.2% of women*
**Severity level: High** - seek immediate treatment! Possibly life-threatening to mother and/or child

- I may seem to be tired all the time.
- I may not want to eat.
- I may seem confused.
- I may have severe mood swings.
- I may feel hopeless or ashamed.
- I may talk about suicide, or hurting the baby.
- I may seem hyperactive or manic.
- I may talk very quickly or incoherently.
- I may act very suspicious of others.
- I may be having delusions and hallucinations, or might hear voices (such as that of the baby).

Thank you for your love and support!

# FERTILITY CHART

**CYCLE DATES:**

**CYCLE NUMBER:**

| Cycle day | 1 | 2 | 3 | 4 | 5 | 6 | 7 | 8 | 9 | 10 | 11 | 12 | 13 | 14 | 15 | 16 | 17 | 18 | 19 | 20 | 21 | 22 | 23 | 24 | 25 | 26 | 27 | 28 | 29 | 30 | 31 | 32 | 33 | 34 | 35 | 36 | 37 | 38 | 39 | 40 |
|---|---|---|---|---|---|---|---|---|---|---|---|---|---|---|---|---|---|---|---|---|---|---|---|---|---|---|---|---|---|---|---|---|---|---|---|---|---|---|---|---|
| Day of week | | | | | | | | | | | | | | | | | | | | | | | | | | | | | | | | | | | | | | | | |
| Date | | | | | | | | | | | | | | | | | | | | | | | | | | | | | | | | | | | | | | | | |
| Temp time | | | | | | | | | | | | | | | | | | | | | | | | | | | | | | | | | | | | | | | | |

**Basal body temperatures (degrees F)**

99.0
98.9
98.8
98.7
98.6
98.5
98.4
98.3
98.2
98.1
98.0
97.9
97.8
97.7
97.6
97.5
97.4
97.3
97.2
97.1
97.0

| CM type | | |
| OPK LH surge | | |
| Ovulation pain | | |
| Intercourse | | |

CM types: D=Dry | S=Sticky | C=Creamy | W=Watery | E=Egg white

Date: _____ S M T W Th F S  Time: _____

Provider: _____

Weight: _____ | Fundal height: _____ | BP: ___ /___

Notes:

Date: _____ S M T W Th F S  Time: _____

Provider: _____

Weight: _____ | Fundal height: _____ | BP: ___ /___

Notes:

Date: _____ S M T W Th F S  Time: _____

Provider: _____

Weight: _____ | Fundal height: _____ | BP: ___ /___

Notes:

Date: _____ S M T W Th F S  Time: _____

Provider: _____

Weight: _____ | Fundal height: _____ | BP: ___ /___

Notes:

Date: _____ S M T W Th F S  Time: _____

Provider: _____

Weight: _____ | Fundal height: _____ | BP: ___ /___

Notes:

Date: _____ S M T W Th F S  Time: _____

Provider: _____

Weight: _____ | Fundal height: _____ | BP: ___ /___

Notes:

Date: _____ S M T W Th F S  Time: _____

Provider: _____

Weight: _____ | Fundal height: _____ | BP: ___ /___

Notes:

Date: _____ S M T W Th F S  Time: _____

Provider: _____

Weight: _____ | Fundal height: _____ | BP: ___ /___

Notes:

Date: _____ S M T W Th F S  Time: _____

Provider: _____

Weight: _____ | Fundal height: _____ | BP: ___ /___

Notes:

Date: _____ S M T W Th F S  Time: _____

Provider: _____

Weight: _____ | Fundal height: _____ | BP: ___ /___

Notes:

Date: _____ S M T W Th F S  Time: _____

Provider: _____

Weight: _____ | Fundal height: _____ | BP: ___ /___

Notes:

Date: _____ S M T W Th F S  Time: _____

Provider: _____

Weight: _____ | Fundal height: _____ | BP: ___ /___

Notes:

Date: _____ S M T W Th F S  Time: _____

Provider: _____

Weight: _____ | Fundal height: _____ | BP: ___ /___

Notes:

Date: _____ S M T W Th F S  Time: _____

Provider: _____

Weight: _____ | Fundal height: _____ | BP: ___ /___

Notes:

Date: _____ S M T W Th F S  Time: _____

Provider: _____

Weight: _____ | Fundal height: _____ | BP: ___ /___

Notes:

Date: _____ S M T W Th F S  Time: _____

Provider: _____

Weight: _____ | Fundal height: _____ | BP: ___ /___

Notes:

Date: _____ S M T W Th F S  Time: _____

Provider: _____

Weight: _____ | Fundal height: _____ | BP: ___ /___

Notes:

Date: _____ S M T W Th F S  Time: _____

Provider: _____

Weight: _____ | Fundal height: _____ | BP: ___ /___

Notes:

Date: _____ S M T W Th F S  Time: _____

Provider: _____

Weight: _____ | Fundal height: _____ | BP: ___ /___

Notes:

Date: _____ S M T W Th F S  Time: _____

Provider: _____

Weight: _____ | Fundal height: _____ | BP: ___ /___

Notes:

Date:        S M T W Th F S   Time:

Provider:

Weight: _____ | Fundal height: ____ | BP: ___ /___

Notes:

Date:        S M T W Th F S   Time:

Provider:

Weight: _____ | Fundal height: ____ | BP: ___ /___

Notes:

Date:        S M T W Th F S   Time:

Provider:

Weight: _____ | Fundal height: ____ | BP: ___ /___

Notes:

Date:        S M T W Th F S   Time:

Provider:

Weight: _____ | Fundal height: ____ | BP: ___ /___

Notes:

Date:        S M T W Th F S   Time:

Provider:

Weight: _____ | Fundal height: ____ | BP: ___ /___

Notes:

Date:        S M T W Th F S   Time:

Provider:

Weight: _____ | Fundal height: ____ | BP: ___ /___

Notes:

Date:        S M T W Th F S   Time:

Provider:

Weight: _____ | Fundal height: ____ | BP: ___ /___

Notes:

Date:        S M T W Th F S   Time:

Provider:

Weight: _____ | Fundal height: ____ | BP: ___ /___

Notes:

Date:        S M T W Th F S   Time:

Provider:

Weight: _____ | Fundal height: ____ | BP: ___ /___

Notes:

Date:        S M T W Th F S   Time:

Provider:

Weight: _____ | Fundal height: ____ | BP: ___ /___

Notes:

# FETAL KICK COUNT TRACKERS

**Kick count tracking is an easy way you can keep track of your baby's well-being, with the goal of helping identify any potential problems early on.**

## HOW TO DO A KICK COUNT

Try to start around the same time each night or day, choosing a time when your baby is usually most active (often after you eat or drink, or do some light activity). Find someplace quiet, lie on your side or sit down with your feet up, and make sure the baby's awake. (Push on your belly, take a quick walk, or stay still for a moment and see if he or she starts wiggling.)

Write your starting time down, then pay close attention to your baby's movements, recording each separate movement — not counting hiccups — with a checkmark in a box. When you have filled in all 10 boxes, write down the time you stopped counting, and figure out how long it took to get to ten movements. (It often takes anywhere from 15 minutes to an hour and a half or so.) Even more important is getting to know your baby's patterns. For example, if you usually count after dinner, maybe she's usually awake and kicks ten times in 20 minutes. But if it starts to take much longer for her to reach 10 movements, contact your caregiver.

Track baby's movements here (women often start around week 28), and/or use the trackers on the starting on calendar day 274.

| Date: | S M T W Th F S |
|---|---|
| ☐ ☐ ☐ ☐ ☐ ☐ ☐ ☐ ☐ ☐ | |
| Start time : \| Stop time : \| Time to 10 : | |

| Date: | S M T W Th F S |
|---|---|
| ☐ ☐ ☐ ☐ ☐ ☐ ☐ ☐ ☐ ☐ | |
| Start time : \| Stop time : \| Time to 10 : | |

| Date: | S M T W Th F S |
|---|---|
| ☐ ☐ ☐ ☐ ☐ ☐ ☐ ☐ ☐ ☐ | |
| Start time : \| Stop time : \| Time to 10 : | |

| Date: | S M T W Th F S |
|---|---|
| ☐ ☐ ☐ ☐ ☐ ☐ ☐ ☐ ☐ ☐ | |
| Start time : \| Stop time : \| Time to 10 : | |

| Date: | S M T W Th F S |
|---|---|
| ☐ ☐ ☐ ☐ ☐ ☐ ☐ ☐ ☐ ☐ | |
| Start time : \| Stop time : \| Time to 10 : | |

| Date: | S M T W Th F S |
|---|---|
| ☐ ☐ ☐ ☐ ☐ ☐ ☐ ☐ ☐ ☐ | |
| Start time : \| Stop time : \| Time to 10 : | |

| Date: | S M T W Th F S |
|---|---|
| ☐ ☐ ☐ ☐ ☐ ☐ ☐ ☐ ☐ ☐ | |
| Start time : \| Stop time : \| Time to 10 : | |

| Date: | S M T W Th F S |
|---|---|
| ☐ ☐ ☐ ☐ ☐ ☐ ☐ ☐ ☐ ☐ | |
| Start time : \| Stop time : \| Time to 10 : | |

| Date: | S M T W Th F S |
|---|---|
| ☐ ☐ ☐ ☐ ☐ ☐ ☐ ☐ ☐ ☐ | |
| Start time : \| Stop time : \| Time to 10 : | |

| Date: | S M T W Th F S |
|---|---|
| ☐ ☐ ☐ ☐ ☐ ☐ ☐ ☐ ☐ ☐ | |
| Start time : \| Stop time : \| Time to 10 : | |

| Date: | S M T W Th F S |
|---|---|
| ☐ ☐ ☐ ☐ ☐ ☐ ☐ ☐ ☐ ☐ | |
| Start time : \| Stop time : \| Time to 10 : | |

| Date: | S M T W Th F S |
|---|---|
| ☐ ☐ ☐ ☐ ☐ ☐ ☐ ☐ ☐ ☐ | |
| Start time : \| Stop time : \| Time to 10 : | |

| Date: | S M T W Th F S |
|---|---|
| ☐ ☐ ☐ ☐ ☐ ☐ ☐ ☐ ☐ ☐ | |
| Start time : \| Stop time : \| Time to 10 : | |

| Date: | S M T W Th F S |
|---|---|
| ☐ ☐ ☐ ☐ ☐ ☐ ☐ ☐ ☐ ☐ | |
| Start time : \| Stop time : \| Time to 10 : | |

Date: _____  S M T W Th F S

☐ ☐ ☐ ☐ ☐ ☐ ☐ ☐ ☐ ☐

Start time ___ : ___ | Stop time ___ : ___ | Time to 10 ___ : ___

Date: _____  S M T W Th F S

☐ ☐ ☐ ☐ ☐ ☐ ☐ ☐ ☐ ☐

Start time ___ : ___ | Stop time ___ : ___ | Time to 10 ___ : ___

Date: _____  S M T W Th F S

☐ ☐ ☐ ☐ ☐ ☐ ☐ ☐ ☐ ☐

Start time ___ : ___ | Stop time ___ : ___ | Time to 10 ___ : ___

Date: _____  S M T W Th F S

☐ ☐ ☐ ☐ ☐ ☐ ☐ ☐ ☐ ☐

Start time ___ : ___ | Stop time ___ : ___ | Time to 10 ___ : ___

Date: _____  S M T W Th F S

☐ ☐ ☐ ☐ ☐ ☐ ☐ ☐ ☐ ☐

Start time ___ : ___ | Stop time ___ : ___ | Time to 10 ___ : ___

Date: _____  S M T W Th F S

☐ ☐ ☐ ☐ ☐ ☐ ☐ ☐ ☐ ☐

Start time ___ : ___ | Stop time ___ : ___ | Time to 10 ___ : ___

Date: _____  S M T W Th F S

☐ ☐ ☐ ☐ ☐ ☐ ☐ ☐ ☐ ☐

Start time ___ : ___ | Stop time ___ : ___ | Time to 10 ___ : ___

Date: _____  S M T W Th F S

☐ ☐ ☐ ☐ ☐ ☐ ☐ ☐ ☐ ☐

Start time ___ : ___ | Stop time ___ : ___ | Time to 10 ___ : ___

Date: _____  S M T W Th F S

☐ ☐ ☐ ☐ ☐ ☐ ☐ ☐ ☐ ☐

Start time ___ : ___ | Stop time ___ : ___ | Time to 10 ___ : ___

Date: _____  S M T W Th F S

☐ ☐ ☐ ☐ ☐ ☐ ☐ ☐ ☐ ☐

Start time ___ : ___ | Stop time ___ : ___ | Time to 10 ___ : ___

Date: _____  S M T W Th F S

☐ ☐ ☐ ☐ ☐ ☐ ☐ ☐ ☐ ☐

Start time ___ : ___ | Stop time ___ : ___ | Time to 10 ___ : ___

Date: _____  S M T W Th F S

☐ ☐ ☐ ☐ ☐ ☐ ☐ ☐ ☐ ☐

Start time ___ : ___ | Stop time ___ : ___ | Time to 10 ___ : ___

Date: _____  S M T W Th F S

☐ ☐ ☐ ☐ ☐ ☐ ☐ ☐ ☐ ☐

Start time ___ : ___ | Stop time ___ : ___ | Time to 10 ___ : ___

Date: _____  S M T W Th F S

☐ ☐ ☐ ☐ ☐ ☐ ☐ ☐ ☐ ☐

Start time ___ : ___ | Stop time ___ : ___ | Time to 10 ___ : ___

Date: _____  S M T W Th F S

☐ ☐ ☐ ☐ ☐ ☐ ☐ ☐ ☐ ☐

Start time ___ : ___ | Stop time ___ : ___ | Time to 10 ___ : ___

Date: _____  S M T W Th F S

☐ ☐ ☐ ☐ ☐ ☐ ☐ ☐ ☐ ☐

Start time ___ : ___ | Stop time ___ : ___ | Time to 10 ___ : ___

Date: _____  S M T W Th F S

☐ ☐ ☐ ☐ ☐ ☐ ☐ ☐ ☐ ☐

Start time ___ : ___ | Stop time ___ : ___ | Time to 10 ___ : ___

Date: _____  S M T W Th F S

☐ ☐ ☐ ☐ ☐ ☐ ☐ ☐ ☐ ☐

Start time ___ : ___ | Stop time ___ : ___ | Time to 10 ___ : ___

Date: _____  S M T W Th F S

☐ ☐ ☐ ☐ ☐ ☐ ☐ ☐ ☐ ☐

Start time ___ : ___ | Stop time ___ : ___ | Time to 10 ___ : ___

Date: _____  S M T W Th F S

☐ ☐ ☐ ☐ ☐ ☐ ☐ ☐ ☐ ☐

Start time ___ : ___ | Stop time ___ : ___ | Time to 10 ___ : ___

# FETAL KICK COUNT TRACKERS (PAGE 3)

Date: _____ S M T W Th F S

☐ ☐ ☐ ☐ ☐ ☐ ☐ ☐ ☐ ☐

Start time : | Stop time : | Time to 10 :

Date: _____ S M T W Th F S

☐ ☐ ☐ ☐ ☐ ☐ ☐ ☐ ☐ ☐

Start time : | Stop time : | Time to 10 :

---

Date: _____ S M T W Th F S

☐ ☐ ☐ ☐ ☐ ☐ ☐ ☐ ☐ ☐

Start time : | Stop time : | Time to 10 :

Date: _____ S M T W Th F S

☐ ☐ ☐ ☐ ☐ ☐ ☐ ☐ ☐ ☐

Start time : | Stop time : | Time to 10 :

---

Date: _____ S M T W Th F S

☐ ☐ ☐ ☐ ☐ ☐ ☐ ☐ ☐ ☐

Start time : | Stop time : | Time to 10 :

Date: _____ S M T W Th F S

☐ ☐ ☐ ☐ ☐ ☐ ☐ ☐ ☐ ☐

Start time : | Stop time : | Time to 10 :

---

Date: _____ S M T W Th F S

☐ ☐ ☐ ☐ ☐ ☐ ☐ ☐ ☐ ☐

Start time : | Stop time : | Time to 10 :

Date: _____ S M T W Th F S

☐ ☐ ☐ ☐ ☐ ☐ ☐ ☐ ☐ ☐

Start time : | Stop time : | Time to 10 :

---

Date: _____ S M T W Th F S

☐ ☐ ☐ ☐ ☐ ☐ ☐ ☐ ☐ ☐

Start time : | Stop time : | Time to 10 :

Date: _____ S M T W Th F S

☐ ☐ ☐ ☐ ☐ ☐ ☐ ☐ ☐ ☐

Start time : | Stop time : | Time to 10 :

---

Date: _____ S M T W Th F S

☐ ☐ ☐ ☐ ☐ ☐ ☐ ☐ ☐ ☐

Start time : | Stop time : | Time to 10 :

Date: _____ S M T W Th F S

☐ ☐ ☐ ☐ ☐ ☐ ☐ ☐ ☐ ☐

Start time : | Stop time : | Time to 10 :

---

Date: _____ S M T W Th F S

☐ ☐ ☐ ☐ ☐ ☐ ☐ ☐ ☐ ☐

Start time : | Stop time : | Time to 10 :

Date: _____ S M T W Th F S

☐ ☐ ☐ ☐ ☐ ☐ ☐ ☐ ☐ ☐

Start time : | Stop time : | Time to 10 :

---

Date: _____ S M T W Th F S

☐ ☐ ☐ ☐ ☐ ☐ ☐ ☐ ☐ ☐

Start time : | Stop time : | Time to 10 :

Date: _____ S M T W Th F S

☐ ☐ ☐ ☐ ☐ ☐ ☐ ☐ ☐ ☐

Start time : | Stop time : | Time to 10 :

---

Date: _____ S M T W Th F S

☐ ☐ ☐ ☐ ☐ ☐ ☐ ☐ ☐ ☐

Start time : | Stop time : | Time to 10 :

Date: _____ S M T W Th F S

☐ ☐ ☐ ☐ ☐ ☐ ☐ ☐ ☐ ☐

Start time : | Stop time : | Time to 10 :

# FETAL KICK COUNT TRACKERS (PAGE 4)

Date: _____ S M T W Th F S

☐ ☐ ☐ ☐ ☐ ☐ ☐ ☐ ☐ ☐

Start time ___:___ | Stop time ___:___ | Time to 10 ___:___

Date: _____ S M T W Th F S

☐ ☐ ☐ ☐ ☐ ☐ ☐ ☐ ☐ ☐

Start time ___:___ | Stop time ___:___ | Time to 10 ___:___

---

Date: _____ S M T W Th F S

☐ ☐ ☐ ☐ ☐ ☐ ☐ ☐ ☐ ☐

Start time ___:___ | Stop time ___:___ | Time to 10 ___:___

Date: _____ S M T W Th F S

☐ ☐ ☐ ☐ ☐ ☐ ☐ ☐ ☐ ☐

Start time ___:___ | Stop time ___:___ | Time to 10 ___:___

---

Date: _____ S M T W Th F S

☐ ☐ ☐ ☐ ☐ ☐ ☐ ☐ ☐ ☐

Start time ___:___ | Stop time ___:___ | Time to 10 ___:___

Date: _____ S M T W Th F S

☐ ☐ ☐ ☐ ☐ ☐ ☐ ☐ ☐ ☐

Start time ___:___ | Stop time ___:___ | Time to 10 ___:___

---

Date: _____ S M T W Th F S

☐ ☐ ☐ ☐ ☐ ☐ ☐ ☐ ☐ ☐

Start time ___:___ | Stop time ___:___ | Time to 10 ___:___

Date: _____ S M T W Th F S

☐ ☐ ☐ ☐ ☐ ☐ ☐ ☐ ☐ ☐

Start time ___:___ | Stop time ___:___ | Time to 10 ___:___

---

Date: _____ S M T W Th F S

☐ ☐ ☐ ☐ ☐ ☐ ☐ ☐ ☐ ☐

Start time ___:___ | Stop time ___:___ | Time to 10 ___:___

Date: _____ S M T W Th F S

☐ ☐ ☐ ☐ ☐ ☐ ☐ ☐ ☐ ☐

Start time ___:___ | Stop time ___:___ | Time to 10 ___:___

---

Date: _____ S M T W Th F S

☐ ☐ ☐ ☐ ☐ ☐ ☐ ☐ ☐ ☐

Start time ___:___ | Stop time ___:___ | Time to 10 ___:___

Date: _____ S M T W Th F S

☐ ☐ ☐ ☐ ☐ ☐ ☐ ☐ ☐ ☐

Start time ___:___ | Stop time ___:___ | Time to 10 ___:___

---

Date: _____ S M T W Th F S

☐ ☐ ☐ ☐ ☐ ☐ ☐ ☐ ☐ ☐

Start time ___:___ | Stop time ___:___ | Time to 10 ___:___

Date: _____ S M T W Th F S

☐ ☐ ☐ ☐ ☐ ☐ ☐ ☐ ☐ ☐

Start time ___:___ | Stop time ___:___ | Time to 10 ___:___

---

Date: _____ S M T W Th F S

☐ ☐ ☐ ☐ ☐ ☐ ☐ ☐ ☐ ☐

Start time ___:___ | Stop time ___:___ | Time to 10 ___:___

Date: _____ S M T W Th F S

☐ ☐ ☐ ☐ ☐ ☐ ☐ ☐ ☐ ☐

Start time ___:___ | Stop time ___:___ | Time to 10 ___:___

---

Date: _____ S M T W Th F S

☐ ☐ ☐ ☐ ☐ ☐ ☐ ☐ ☐ ☐

Start time ___:___ | Stop time ___:___ | Time to 10 ___:___

Date: _____ S M T W Th F S

☐ ☐ ☐ ☐ ☐ ☐ ☐ ☐ ☐ ☐

Start time ___:___ | Stop time ___:___ | Time to 10 ___:___

# PREGNANCY BELLY STICKER DESIGNS

**These sticker designs can make capturing your growing baby bump in pictures a little more fun!**

Pregnancy belly stickers like these are popular because they're a fun and cute way to show your progress in photos. Here are two ways you can use them:

- Photocopy the images on to sticker paper, then color them in before cutting them out.
- Color the images below. Cut them out and put tape loops on the back to attach them to your shirt.

*To download a full set of these sticker designs, along with several sets of other free printable colored sticker designs, please visit myria.com/pregnancy-printables .*

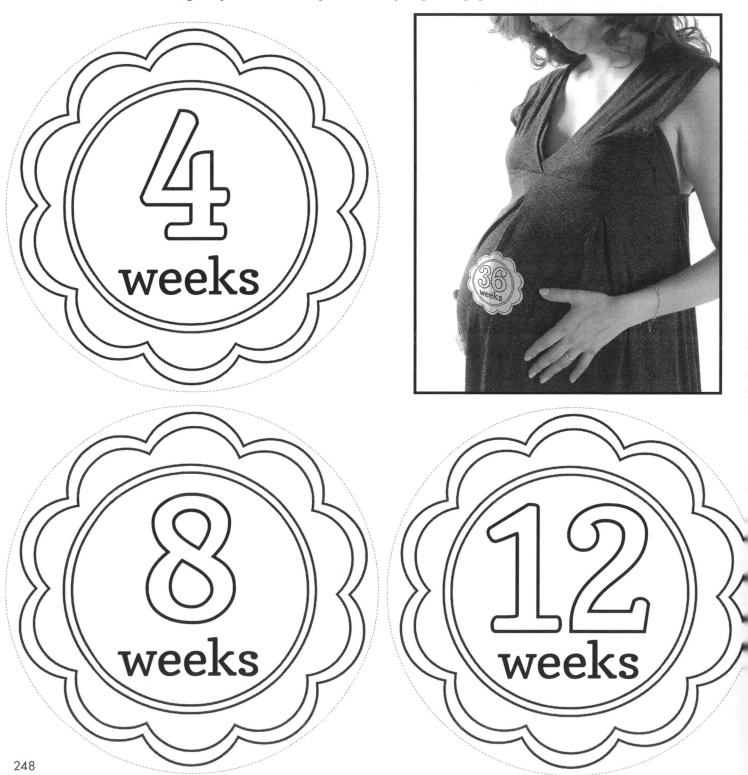

# dear me, one year from now

date:

# CREDITS & REFERENCES

## SOURCES AND REFERENCES

Sources for this book include the American Congress of Obstetricians and Gynecologists (ACOG), American Society for Reproductive Medicine (ASRM), Society for Maternal-Fetal Medicine (SMFM), American College of Nurse-Midwives (ACNM), US National Library of Medicine (NLM), US Centers for Disease Control (CDC), US Food and Drug Administration (FDA), the US Department of Health and Human Services, and the March of Dimes.

## CREDITS

### Images:

- Cover woman: © Pimonova
- Watercolor frame on cover: © Fajar Budiman
- Menstrual cycle wheel: © Csuzda
- Ovum: © Database Center for Life Science
- Trimester silhouettes: © Alla Shost
- Month silhouettes: © Burlesck
- Early embryonic development: © Csuzda
- Trimester stages of pregnancy: © Oguzaral
- 12 week fetal ultrasound © Wolfgang Moroder
- Intro stages of pregnancy: © Aksiporn Ryan
- Miscellaneous pregnancy icons © Juliarstudio

### Other:

- Birth Plan Ideas & Postpartum Promise co-written by Nancy J. Price and Betsy Bailey

## DISCLAIMERS/NOTICES

The information presented in this book is for educational purposes only, and provides information of a general nature. If you have any concerns about your health or your child's health, please consult your family's health care provider immediately. None of the information or other material presented herein should be considered a substitute for personal medical attention, diagnosis or treatment. This information is provided as is, and you, its user, assume all risks when using it.

All brand names, product names or names of organizations are the trademarks or trade names of their respective holders.

## TECHNICAL REFERENCES

### Regarding embryonic/fetal development

Details about baby's size early in pregnancy were based on the findings in the journal article "New crown–rump length curve based on over 3500 pregnancies," by A. Pexsters et al, published in *Ultrasound in Obstetrics & Gynecology*; June 2010.

### Regarding due date estimation

In October 2014, the American College of Obstetricians and Gynecologists, the American Institute of Ultrasound in Medicine and the Society for Maternal-Fetal Medicine made the following recommendations regarding the method for estimating gestational age and due date:

*Ultrasound measurement of the embryo or fetus in the first trimester (up to and including 13 6/7 weeks of gestation) is the most accurate method to establish or confirm gestational age.*

*If pregnancy resulted from assisted reproductive technology (ART), the ART-derived gestational age should be used to assign the estimated due date (EDD). For instance, the EDD for a pregnancy resulting from in vitro fertilization should be established using the age of the embryo and the date of transfer.*

### Regarding the length of pregnancy

In a joint Committee Opinion released in October 2013, The American College of Obstetricians and Gynecologists and the Society for Maternal-Fetal Medicine (SMFM) discouraged use of the general label 'term pregnancy' and replaced it with a series of more specific labels. The following represent the four current definitions of 'term' deliveries:

| Early Term | Between 37 weeks 0 days and 38 weeks 6 days |
|---|---|
| Full Term | Between 39 weeks 0 days and 40 weeks 6 days |
| Late Term | Between 41 weeks 0 days and 41 weeks 6 days |
| Postterm | Between 42 weeks 0 days and beyond |

### Fertility/infertility

RESOLVE: The National Infertility Association: resolve.org
Infertility at about.com: infertility.about.com
Society for Reproductive Endocrinology and Infertility: socrei.org

### Pregnancy and birth

American Association of Birth Centers: birthcenters.org
Doulas of North America (DONA): dona.org
American College of Nurse-Midwives (ACNM): acnm.org
Midwives Alliance of North America (MANA): mana.org
National Association of Certified Professional Midwives (NACPM) nacpm.org
American Congress of Obstetricians and Gynecologists: acog.org
International Cesarean Awareness Network: ican-online.org

### Childbirth preparation

International Childbirth Educators Association (ICEA): icea.org
Lamaze International: lamaze.org
Birthing From Within: BirthingFromWithin.com
The Bradley Method: BradleyBirth.com
Hypnobirthing: HypnoBirthing.com
Coastal Hypnobabies (San Diego): CoastalHypnobabies.com
Birth Prep Childbirth Classes (San Francisco): BirthPrep.com

### Breastfeeding

La Leche League International: llli.org

### More

Pregnancy & parenting articles & more at Myria: myria.com/pregnancy
Pregnancy & parenting book author Ann Douglas: having-a-baby.com
Parenting book author Elizabeth Pantley: ElizabethPantley.com
Mr Dad, Armin Brott: MrDad.com
Myria - Smart stuff for real life: Myria.com
Click Baby Names: Search 28,000+ names: ClickBabyNames.com

*If you liked this book, please leave a review online — and tell a friend!*

# about the author

Nancy J. Price started self-publishing music fanzines at age 14, and graduated to interviewing major-label rock bands at 16. Not quite a decade later, during a three-year-stint in the music industry, she moonlighted as a freelance writer, earning bylines in *Parents* and the *San Francisco Chronicle*, among others.

Together with her best friend, Betsy Bailey, Nancy co-founded Myria.com, ePregnancy.com and SheKnows.com in the late 1990s. Their experience with the ePregnancy site led to the two becoming the founding editors-in-chief of two national print magazines: *Pregnancy*, then a few years later, *ePregnancy*.

in 2003, Nancy helped turn SheKnows.com into a top lifestyle website for women, reaching more than 30 million readers per month. In addition to serving as the site's Executive Editor until 2011, Nancy was heavily involved in the launch of three more national newsstand magazines, including *Diet & Fitness* and *Cooking Smart*.

A fourth-generation San Francisco Bay Area native, Nancy now lives in Arizona with her four kids and her partner, novelist Daniel Price. When she's not spending time with her family, Nancy is always creating — words, websites (actively working on Myria.com and ClickAmericana.com) and various projects for print.

In addition to her web work, she wrote a time travel novel, *Dream of Time*, and created the *Vintage Women: Adult Coloring Book* series, which features authentic antique fashion images.

Otherwise, and although she can't draw anything more than a (mostly) straight line, she adds to the world's image stores by scanning and restoring vintage pictures and magazine pages, as well as creating new works of digital photography. Other interests include autism advocacy, travel, and a daily appreciation of books, movies, TV and music. See more from her online at nancyjprice.com, or on Twitter (@andwhatsnext).

# about the publisher

Synchronista LLC is a boutique creative company, with a passion for website development, web design, print design and publishing, photography, writing & editing, brand creation and other media pursuits. Published books include the *Vintage Women Adult Coloring Book* series and *Dream of Time* (a novel), while current websites include ClickAmericana.com, PrintColorFun.com and ClickBabyNames.com.

Visit Synchronista.com to find out more.

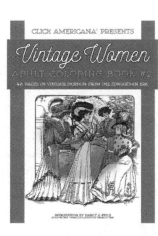

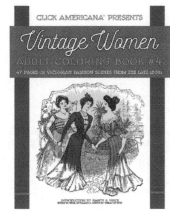
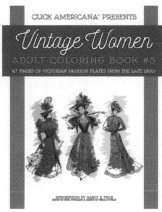
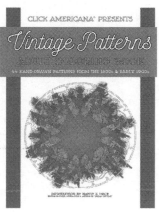

## First + pregnancy test

Date:

Brand:

How many tests?

## First pregnancy symptoms
Symptoms/dates

## How I announced the news

## First time someone noticed
When/who/reaction

# MY PREGNANCY

## First time I felt baby move

Date/time:

What it felt like:

## Boy or girl?

Date found out (or decided not to):

First reaction:

## Childbirth education classes

Dates/time:

Instructor:

Location:

## Work & maternity leave
When I told work/Maternity leave schedule

254

## First prenatal caregiver visit

Date:

Caregiver name:

Location:

## How I told the family

When/who/reaction

## First thing I bought for baby

Date:                    Store:

Item:

Why this?

## My maternity clothes

Date:

Clothes:

First wore on:

# FIRSTS+DATES

## First baby gift

Date:

Given by:

Item:

## Baby shower

Date:

Given by:

Attendees:

## Ready for baby: Dates

Carseat bought:

Baby's layette ready:

Nursery/sleeping area ready:

Hospital bag packed:

## Baby's name will be...

Name:

Date decided:                    Suggested by:

Meaning:

notes

Made in the USA
Lexington, KY
01 November 2018